Mud On Your OWN Boots

The Story of Health Talents International

Marie Bryant Agee

Mud On Your Own Boots
The Story of Health Talents International
Copyright 2013 by Marie Bryant Agee
All rights reserved
www.healthtalents.org

No part of this publication may be used or reproduced in any manner without written permission except in case of brief quotations embodied in articles and reviews.

ISBN-13: 978-1492773276
ISBN-10: 1492773271
Also available in eBook

Cover Design: Jessy Mayfield
Interior Book Design: Ellen C. Sallas, The Author's Mentor,
   www.theauthorsmentor.com

PUBLISHED IN THE UNITED STATES OF AMERICA

Dedicated to

Dr. Robert Clark and Charles Bates,
who conceived the vision and built the dream.

And to Carl, my husband,
who loved and supported me every step of this journey.

Contents

Acknowledgments 1
Preface 3
Chapter 1: Last Days in Las Cruces 9
Chapter 2: The Founding Years 15
Chapter 3: Las Cruces Rising 24
Chapter 4: "We are going…we *will* get there." 37
Chapter 5: The Belize Years 83
Chapter 6: Back to Guatemala…from Rural to Urban 121
Chapter 7: Surgical Ministry Arises 145
Chapter 8: Chocolá Surgery Clinic in Action 153
Chapter 9: Dr. Mike Kelly and Clinica Cristiana 165
Chapter 10: Call to Nicaragua 170
Chapter 11: Chocolá Clinic Continues 176
Chapter 12: Road to Clinica Ezell 187
Chapter 13: Dedication of Clinica Ezell 209
Chapter 14: The Highlands Ministry 223
Chapter 15: Looking to the Future 231
In Conclusion 233
HTI Board of Directors 235
MET Alumni 237

Acknowledgments

This is the story of Health Talents International (HTI). It is not *my* story, but it is very personal to me and I have written it from that perspective. I have been too involved to write it any other way. During the past 40 years, however, there is much that I experienced only vicariously, and I want to give credit where credit is due.

My gratitude begins with acknowledging the efforts of the many missionaries who labored in Guatemala years before HTI arrived. Their dedicated labor produced fertile ground on which we were able to build.

Personal diaries from former HTI missionaries helped me reconstruct daily events at mission sites. Kathy Bates Burch, Alice Sorrells Bush, Joe Crisp, Lisa Cantrell and Glenda Corley-Topham provided great detail through their personal journals. Roger McCown and Bill Searcy filed extensive reports that had lain dormant for years in my filing cabinet. Jim Miller took time to reflect and record his remembrances of the Las Cruces construction period. Doris Clark, Melissa Redding Myrick, Donna Finto-Burks and Steve and Magda Sherman graciously spent hours with me as I picked their brains for distant memories. Ellie Evans provided both memories and many photographs of Las Cruces that I had never seen. I am deeply grateful that the late Dr. Robert Clark took time to write his *Tales from the Boonie Stomper*, the legendary newsletter he published during the Petén years. They provided a wealth of stories about life in Las Cruces, all with a humorous bent.

I especially want to thank all those men and women who either served in the field at one time or on the HTI Board of Directors. (I served on the Board myself in the 1980s.) I witnessed their dedication, courage and total belief in this ministry that Dr. Robert Clark envisioned so long ago. Without their wisdom, insight and tenacity, Health Talents would have wilted to a whimper. Without their faith in God, they wouldn't have even bothered to try. The odds against succeeding were just too great.

Because of the dedicated assistance of both my avid reader sister, Jimmie Rosati, and my editor, Sandy Kilgo, the book is in a format that is easy to read and comprehend, plus free from glaring misspellings and grammatical errors. They both diligently plowed through early drafts, providing helpful suggestions each time they read it. I am deeply grateful to them.

I am thrilled that Jessy Mayfield, the young artist/graphic designer daughter of my long-time HTI bookkeeper Vanessa Mayfield, designed the maps and the book cover. She did a magnificent job on the cover of reflecting both the faith and work aspects that I tried to convey throughout the telling of the tale.

There is no way I can name everyone individually who had a part in building this ministry, so I offer this book as a thank you to all who took part along the way...for this is your story, too. Thousands of you have gone to Guatemala to personally use your talents be they medical or non-medical, while others participated by providing needed funds, medical supplies and equipment. Still others took part by stuffing fundraising envelopes (including my own children), designing promotional material, contributing money or on occasion even providing a bed for me to sleep in as I traveled around the country. Most importantly, many of you offered prayers on HTI's behalf. You may have never stepped foot in Guatemala, but your participation was vital to the effort of bringing people to the Lord by offering compassionate medical care in Jesus' name.

I hope all who have had a part in creating Health Talents realize the value of what, by God's grace, we have been able to do. We've created something that will live on long after we are gone and will continue to impact lives for the better. The HTI ministry is a living tribute to the power of God, as well as a beautiful representation of the ministry of Jesus. HTI's aim is and always has been to bring people to Him. It is very humbling to witness firsthand how God has taken our meager efforts and built them into something that so richly benefits mankind. Blessings to all.

Preface

Have you ever considered being a missionary? Most people have not. The idea of leaving family and friends to travel halfway around the globe only to perhaps share a grass hut with snakes and tarantulas sounds bleak. After spending more than half my life recruiting for, participating in and promoting missions through Health Talents, I have seen it up close. I know how wonderful it can be and how deeply mission efforts affect lives. This is equally true of both the lives of the missionaries and those they serve.

The added component of "medical" in missions provides an even greater impact. The correct term for what Health Talents does is *"medical evangelism"* because it more fully expresses HTI's concern for both the physical and spiritual needs of mankind. The HTI logo represents this concept well. Go back to the title page and look at the logo again. What it the first thing you see? The cross is bigger than the world. Inside the cross is a globe overlaid by a stick figure of a man with his extremities outstretched, representing the various needs of mankind: physical, spiritual, mental and social. Herein is our mission.

Medical evangelists offer help for today with the promise of hope for the future. Adding medical to missions is often an asset when requesting permission to enter a new country. Foreign governments sometimes feel overrun with missionaries but are open to medical evangelists who will address the physical needs of their people. Such was the case in Belize.

Charles Bates introduced me to missions. One Sunday morning in 1975 I was coming out of church with my young daughter in tow when he stopped me and told me he needed help with Health Talents. He knew I typed dissertations to earn a little extra money, so he asked me if I would be willing to *type a letter for him once in a while.* Little did I know where that conversation would lead. I certainly had no idea it would pull me into a lifetime of service in medical evangelism and consume much of my life for the next 38 years.

The workload escalated quickly as the dream to establish the Center for Medical Missions Training began to turn into reality. During the first five years of groundwork, medical evangelism was just a philosophical idea to me. That all changed in July 1980 when I visited the HTI clinic in Las Cruces, Guatemala. That trip changed my life.

A couple of months earlier Charles had told me that he thought I should attend the upcoming dedication ceremony for the new clinic. I protested, citing reasons why I couldn't go…children, husband and expense. Charles responded each time with continued pressure. Finally, he said something that stopped me in my tracks. He said, "Marie, you have been working in this ministry for a long while now, but you will never, ever be able to understand what it is all about until you get *"mud on your own boots."* I remember not saying anything for a moment. I just sat there thinking, *"You know, he is absolutely right."* So I went. The Lord even provided the money for my husband and children to go.

When I arrived in Las Cruces, a jungle area in the northern lowlands of Guatemala, I saw our mission team in action. I witnessed the press of people who showed up at the clinic each morning and heard them as they expressed appreciation when they were treated. I could literally *feel* their gratitude. That's when the "scales of my eyes" fell away and I began to realize the importance of what we were doing. I began to sense that this thing we were doing was pretty incredible. It could dramatically change lives both here on earth and in the afterlife. By bringing the people of Las Cruces a medical clinic, we were bringing them healing. By bringing them healing, we were helping them *feel* the love of God. And once they felt that love, they were deeply grateful and often wanted to know more about our Savior.

That's when I began to get it...and became a true believer in our mission. That's when I understood that by serving them, we were serving God. By offering love and care in the name of Jesus, we were practicing Christianity at its best. Using this medical facility to train future missionaries would multiply its impact beyond measure. That was the day I got mud on my OWN boots...and I haven't been able to shake it loose since.

The rationale for medical evangelism comes from Jesus Himself. Traveling around during His three years of ministry, Jesus met multitudes of people in need of both physical and spiritual healing. Two things were constant as He met people in need: He was filled with compassion...and that compassion compelled Him to respond. He preached to the masses, but He healed them...one by one.

HTI's mission statement says it all: *The mission of Health Talents International is to proclaim the Gospel of Jesus Christ through teaching and healing ministries.* By following Jesus' pattern, Health Talents both presents and validates the Gospel. This method is especially effective in cultures where there is a basic belief that sickness and sin are connected. Such is the case among the Mayan Indians in Guatemala.

Dr. Richard Rheinbolt discussed this in his review of the Clinica Cristiana work in Quetzaltenango, Guatemala, entitled "Looking Back: The First Two Years (September 1970-December 1972)." He quoted Professor Allen Tippett as saying that "unless a presentation of the Gospel is made, the hospital (or medical program) will more than likely not be accepted as an institution for the pagan community to go to when the traditional curers and healers have failed."[1]

HTI's initial target population in the Petén Department (state) was primarily ladino, a mixture of Spanish/Indian blood. They spoke Spanish, wore western clothing and were more educated than the indigenous people (the Maya). The Mayan Indians, some of the most disadvantaged people on earth, would later become our focus as our awareness of their plight grew. Though comprising nearly half of the Guatemalan population, they have been looked down

---

[1] Alan Tippett. Unpublished article, www.faqs.org/minorities/South-and-Central-America/Maya-of-Guatemala.html.Fuller Theological Seminary. Pasadena, California.

upon and discriminated against since the Spanish Conquest in the 1500s. They are accustomed to being abused, not served. Their cultural beliefs about health and God are so intermingled, however, that we soon realized they were ideal targets for medical evangelism.

Though the form of the Health Talents ministry has changed somewhat through the years, from the very beginning HTI has focused on these four things:

- Preaching the gospel in word and deed
- Training local Christians in medical evangelism
- Providing opportunities for North American Christians to use their talents in medical evangelism.
- Providing North American university students with a real-life medical evangelism experience.

Training future missionaries is still a primary focus, though it is now called MET (Medical Evangelism Training). Each year 12 junior and senior mission-minded, medically oriented university students travel to Guatemala for six weeks to experience medical evangelism at its best. They work within the confines of a real-life medical evangelism ministry where they witness both the challenges and rewards of such a mission. They continue to follow the basic curriculum created in Las Cruces and they still live with local Christian families.

Clinically speaking, the work has decentralized. Rather than having one primary clinic, we now conduct mobile medical clinics in 30 different villages. These are staffed by a full time HTI ministry team that is primarily Guatemalan. The annual schedule provides opportunities for visiting medical teams to give of their time and talents as well. We began hosting mobile medical teams in 1990 to assist the resident team with the overwhelming numbers of patients showing up at clinic. When the need for surgical care became apparent, HTI began hosting surgical teams. We held our first surgery clinic in December 1993. We now conduct 10 week-long surgical clinics a year manned by volunteers, both medical professionals and non-medical personnel from the U.S.

Volunteers also conduct five mobile medical clinics a year: two in Guatemala, two in El Salvador and one in Nicaragua.

During the course of a year approximately 750 volunteers participate in these trips. This number includes many who come with a strong faith in God, some who are nominal Christians, and still others who have never given much thought to God. Undoubtedly, the vast majority of volunteers have been impacted by their experience of helping people in such a personal way. How do we know? They keep coming back!

This has convinced me of the enduring value of the short-term mission trip experience for the "givers" as well as for the recipients. The experience of being in a new place that is totally outside your comfort zone and coming face to face with people whose pain and suffering are an everyday occurrence touches something deep inside you. You cannot look into a patient's face and not feel their deep gratitude for the compassionate pain-relieving and life-changing help they are receiving. Doing so compels you to take stock of your own blessings. The residual impact of a medical evangelism experience can be dramatic. In real life terms, I've seen team members be baptized, recommit their lives to God, and marriages strengthened.

In one specific case a couple was on the verge of divorce when the husband went on one of HTI's early surgical trips. He returned home recommitted to his marriage. Every now and then the couple sends me a "thank you" note or a little gift for helping to save their marriage, though at the time of the trip I was not aware they were having problems. But God was.

I sincerely hope you are encouraged by this tale of faith and dedication. And if you are reading this but have never participated in any sort of mission work yourself, I challenge and heartily encourage you to do so. Opportunities abound with Health Talents and around the world. The needs are great; the mud is plentiful…and just waiting to stick onto YOUR boots!

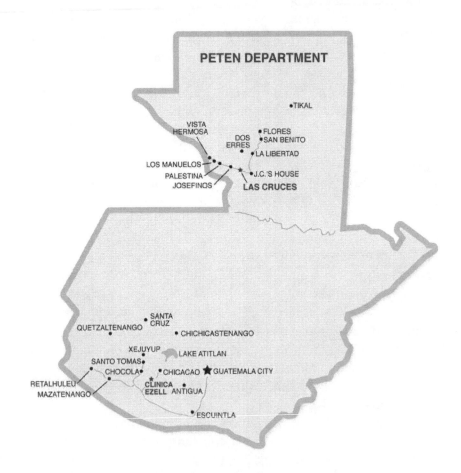
GUATEMALA

Chapter 1:
Last Days in Las Cruces

1981

"I am fighting fear," wrote nurse Alice Sorrells in her journal the night of November 13, 1981. *"When will this all stop?"*

Alice had just returned to Las Cruces, Guatemala. She was looking forward to being home after attending the Pan American Lectureship in Merida, Mexico. She and most of her 19 teammates had spent a week there with missionaries from all over Latin America. That had been followed by a relaxing three-day Health Talents' team retreat at Gringo Perdido, a tourist spot not far from Las Cruces. New Testament scholar Dr. Carroll Osburn from Abilene Christian University was with them, and he presented lessons each morning. Each afternoon the team enjoyed the cool waters of the lake. As soon as Alice arrived home, however, she learned that her good friend, Don Rosario, had been murdered.

Don Rosario had been an upstanding leader of the Las Cruces community, but Alice remembers him more as a kind and caring family man. She remembers how he had made their medical team feel very welcome in Las Cruces. The shock of learning he had been dragged from his house in the middle of the night and murdered in the street was beyond comprehension to her.

Likewise, MaryBeth McCown, wife of clinic director Roger McCown, came face to face with the intensifying civil war. She and her two young sons, Paco and Roger Lee, were headed home to

Las Cruces after the retreat. As their bus neared the community of La Libertad, it was stopped by a group of five or six masked men armed with machine guns. Two of the masked men boarded the bus with their guns and stormed up and down the aisle.

Their eyes glared threateningly over their masks at the frightened riders. One of them kept pointing his gun at passengers. *"Agacharse,"* he shouted tersely. *"Bajen la vista. No miren arriba."* In English it meant, *"Bend over! Look down! Don't look up!"*

The younger of MaryBeth's two boys, 9-year-old Paco McCown was wearing shorts, and MaryBeth noticed he was leaning as far forward as he could while trying to cover his thighs with his hands. She asked him later what he had been doing. He said, *"I was trying to keep them from seeing that I'm white!"*

Fortunately, the guerrillas weren't looking for white people that day—likely only for a woman who could cook for them at their camp. They found such a suitable woman, stopped at her seat and ordered her to come with them. She had a child with her who appeared to be about five. She asked, *"What about him?"* The guerrilla shrugged and said, *"Bring him with you if you want."* Instead, she whispered to her child to go to his aunt's house when he got to his village, then she left the bus with the guerrillas. Despite having spent more than 10 years in the mission field, MaryBeth was shaken.

Fellow team members Joe and Linda Crisp and Steve and Magda Sherman were also on that bus. They had been to the bank earlier that day to get cash for daily living expenses. As the guerillas marched up and down the aisle, they were hurriedly stuffing that cash into their boots.

Clinic Director Roger McCown and nurse Donna Finto had gone to Guatemala City to visit the American Embassy. They went seeking advice on what to do about the increasing violence in the area. When Dr. Robert Clark learned of the bus incident, he called them and asked them to come back immediately. Two other team members, Jon Jernigan and Wanda Miles, were on vacation in the States, and Barbara Thompson was on her way to a conference in Europe. All the remaining 15 team members were in Las Cruces.

The team knew there was a civil war going on in Guatemala. They had known for a good while but until recently had felt immune to it. They were in the Petén, after all, the most remote section of the country—far away from any reports of guerilla violence. But tension had been building for some time. Although the team did not feel targeted in any way, they were keenly aware that the political situation was deteriorating.

On September 3, 1981, two-and-a-half months earlier, Alice recorded in her diary that she had been awakened at 2:25 a.m. by a grenade blast. It was followed by the rat-a-tat sound that usually signaled another murder in the middle of the night. That night went on and on. Alice said she wanted to run out her back door, but the shots seemed to be coming from all directions! Amid the gunfire, she could hear babies crying. The shooting finally stopped at 3:45 a.m. She learned the next morning what had caused team members to scramble under their beds for safety. A band of guerrillas had entered their village and attacked the local military garrison, killing a commander and another soldier. She watched that morning as military helicopters arrived to collect the dead and wounded and deliver more troops.

In the days that followed, the team determined to continue focusing on its mission, but it was becoming harder and harder to ignore the events going on around them. Joe Crisp remembers that during that time Las Cruces affected an air of peace and tranquility during the day…and suspicion and stress at night. He said he and Linda consciously prayed each night for a peaceful rest, then thanked God every morning for their night of safety.

On September 20 the team met to discuss long-term planning. During that meeting, Roger sensed that everyone was feeling anxious, so he gave them an opportunity to share. All had heard the frequent midnight gunfire, and one had seen a body lying in a rain puddle on the way to work one morning. Dr. Brian and Ruth Smith told of hearing from their neighbors that the guerrillas were camped at the spring in the jungle, about a mile from their house. Everyone confessed to feeling more uneasiness when traveling around and when they were on call at the clinic at night.

They all agreed that the situation was bad…and getting worse. It was clear to all that Guatemala's civil war had come to them.

At that meeting, they devised codes to protect their goings and comings and to alert each other if things were to get really bad. They were simple codes. One referred to "good weather" and "bad weather." The other used the names of baseball teams. Clinic team members were to be called by one team name, the military by another. The guerillas were to be known as the Yankees. Most importantly, all agreed that if the majority of team members felt it was time to leave, everyone had to leave. No one was to be left behind.

It all came to a head on the bus that day...Friday the 13th in November 1981.

When Robert learned of the bus incident, he visited the Mary Knoll Order of Catholic nuns as well as some leading community leaders for counsel. They told Robert that they felt it was no longer safe for the medical team to be there. They had all heard rumors that the medical team was in danger of being kidnapped by the guerrillas.

On Saturday morning, November 14, the team met in the Clarks' home for breakfast. The "godparents" of the team, J.C. and Mim Reed, were there as well. They discussed recent violence, shootings and murders. Steve and Magda added that they had seen three decapitated heads that very morning as they were on their way to the meeting. This led to the clear and unmistakable conclusion that it was time to go. They knew they had not started the conflict and that was there nothing they could do to stop it. They knew that as a medical team they could be used as pawns by either side, increasing the risks to their personal safety. They also knew that the seven children on the team were relying on their parents to keep them safe. Thus, making the decision to leave was easy, yet emotionally challenging.

Remember the agreement made at the meeting in September? Well, that agreement held this day. All were committed to leaving. The next question was *"When?"* With the most difficult decision made, the need to leave *immediately* seemed clear. The question of *"How to evacuate?"* followed.

J.C. Reed told me years later that at this point in the discussion he said, *"Well, I've got my pickup truck outside. I could take a load right now."* He chuckled slightly then continued, *"With that, whoosh, the entire room emptied as people ran home to pack."*

A short time later J.C. and Mim left with a truck load of people and suitcases. Alice Sorrells, Joe and Linda Crisp, and Dr. Brian Smith with his pregnant wife, Ruth, rode out with him. Steve and

Magda left with them on Steve's motorcycle. When they reached a military guard shack, the soldiers asked to inspect their bags. When Ruth Smith opened her bags, empty tuna fish cans fell out and rolled across the pickup truck bed. She had packed in such a hurry that she had grabbed the garbage, too! Everyone had a good laugh, even the guards. It provided a needed break in the tension they were all feeling.

Later that day Robert drove his pickup out of town, loaded with the remaining team members and children. They were stopped by the same military guards. The guy in charge asked where they were going. Robert, in his forthright manner, said, *"Man, we're getting out of here! It's too hot for us!"*

The guards burst into laughter, so Robert asked them what was so funny. They told him that when J.C. had come through earlier, they had asked him the same question. J.C.'s response had been quite different. Despite his people- and suitcase-laden pickup, J.C. had simply said, *"Oh, we're just going out for a drive."*

By 6:00 that evening the team was gathered in Robert and Doris' house in Santa Elena, Guatemala, near Flores. The house was filled with people, but everyone somehow found a place to sleep that night, even in tents out on the patio. A few went to nearby hotels.

They awoke to a beautiful Sunday morning, which also happened to be Robert's birthday. Craving normality in the midst of chaos and uncertainty, some of the women began planning a birthday party for Robert.

After breakfast, however, the evangelists announced that they needed to go back to Las Cruces. Amid much protest, they explained they felt a moral obligation to say goodbye to the churches they had started. Thus, Joe Crisp, Steve Sherman and Billy Copeland piled into Robert's pickup and, with Robert at the wheel, started back down the road to Las Cruces.

Needless to say, their wives were filled with fear all day. The situation was so tenuous in Las Cruces that they knew there was a real likelihood their husbands would not return. They worried and prayed throughout the day until they saw that pickup return that afternoon.

Despite their worry, everyone felt better knowing that the toughest decisions were behind them. They spent the day in leisure, some swimming, some getting and giving pedicures, others simply trying to relax as they worked to make sense of it all. That evening they gathered for a period of worship and their last Lord's Supper together as a team. Roger encouraged them with these words:

"We have done something we have no reason to be ashamed of. The Lord chose us to go to that place, Las Cruces, at that time, and it was an honor. We are going home to well-meaning people who will not really understand what we've been through. They will for a while show interest in what has happened to us, but very quickly we will be absorbed into the church scene and our culture. We must gracefully allow this experience to become a part of our life and our personality. Do not forget the lessons learned here or the cost."

Such was the end of a perfectly good beginning. With heavy hearts and great sadness, everyone turned their backs on Las Cruces and the effort that had been started there with such enthusiasm…and went home.

Though that marked the end of Health Talents' first mission effort, it proved to be only the beginning. The experiences there set the stage for what was to come. The vision that began with Dr. Robert Clark still shone brightly, only now it was clutched tightly in the hearts of a far greater number of people.

Chapter 2:
The Founding Years

1969-78

In 1969, the year after their marriage and immediately after his third year of medical school at the University of Arkansas, Robert and Doris Clark spent part of their summer in Guatemala. They traveled to the northwestern mountain area seeking medical evangelism experience. They were both excited about this opportunity because one of the things that attracted them to each other originally was their shared interest in missions.

Robert was looking especially for experience that would prepare him for a future as a medical missionary. He was disappointed. He came away from his time in Guatemala unimpressed with the doctor with whom he had worked. He felt the doctor had not been prepared to practice medicine in a Third World setting, nor did the doctor understand how to combine Christian evangelism with his medical practice.

This experience, however, birthed a deep vision in Robert. Because of his personal desire for training, he resolved to establish a field training center to prepare U.S. medical personnel to work as medical missionaries. The training would focus on the treatment of health problems common to Third World nations as well as provide an understanding of cultural context in both the delivery of health care and the Gospel of Jesus.

While in Guatemala that summer Robert visited J.C. Reed, a pioneering Church of Christ missionary working in the Petén. Robert had never met J.C., but he had heard about him and his move to Guatemala through his father, who had been one of J.C.'s professors at Harding College. Robert sensed that the Petén would be a perfect setting in which to develop a medical mission training program someday.

El Petén is located in the north of Guatemala. It is hot, dry and sparsely populated. At that time it was the site of a land distribution program by the government. The government's intent was to populate its northernmost region while establishing a borderline with Belize. There had been much dispute for many years over whether Belize was a part of Guatemala or a separate country. Guatemala, of course, declared ownership, and for years every map sold in Guatemala showed no border between the two countries. In the 1960s the government began offering land grants to anyone willing to homestead in the Peten. J.C. took them up on it and moved there in 1964.

J.C. and Mim Reed had been schoolteachers in Alice, Texas, before they followed their hearts to the mission field. J.C. was intent from the beginning on being a self-supporting missionary. Their four children were grown and on their own, giving J.C. and Mim the freedom to serve God in a whole new way.

They established a life there in Guatemala. Legend has it that J.C. literally hacked his way through the jungle to claim his 200 hectares of land in La Libertad, El Petén. They farmed and J.C. preached.

Eventually J.C. began a weekly radio program where he preached in Spanish, sharing the Gospel of Jesus Christ with a growing population. He began dreaming of having some missionaries join him to help with the ever-expanding population. He dreamed of attracting a

J.C. and Mim Reed in front of their house in 1978

community of missionaries to come help establish the church in the Petén. Some people came, but none stayed longer than six hours. So, in the end, J.C. worked alone, with Mim sometimes back in the States working to support him.

He stayed on, struggling against the jungle to build his ranch while teaching the Gospel to his neighbors. It was a difficult job, he soon learned, because people were both spiritually ill *and* physically ill. Many people came to him for help, and he so wanted to help them that he would guess at diagnoses and give injections. He treated malaria, both his own and others. Quite often he was on the road taking emergency cases to the hospital in his pickup. He imagined what it would be like to have both a church *and* a clinic to provide the care that was so desperately needed.

This was what Robert found when he arrived in the Petén. When he and J.C. stood side by side on the banks of the Rio de Pasión, they shared their dreams with each other…and decided to merge them into one. Thus began the first glimpse of what would become the first Church of Christ "Center for Medical Mission Training." J. C. proved to be a valuable mentor and guide through the often murky waters of establishing this new mission.

Robert returned home that summer and spent the first two weeks of August visiting Churches of Christ in Texas and other southern states to share his vision. All he was asking was that they send someone with him to visit the Petén area of Guatemala. As he went from church to church, he became discouraged. Not a single church expressed any interest in sending anyone to investigate mission opportunities in Guatemala.

Disheartened upon his return to Little Rock, Robert went to see his friend and fellow Harding College graduate, Jim Miller. He shared his vision with Jim then expressed his disappointment at the lack of interest in churches he had visited. As Jim listened he began to get interested and agreed to make a trip to Guatemala with Robert. On that trip Jim truly *caught* Robert's vision for a medical evangelism training center. He signed on to help make it happen.

As they considered ways to provide the financial support needed for such an extraordinary project, Jim suggested creating a non-profit organization. He assumed at that time that his contribution would be limited to helping establish the organization and raise funds.

Soon afterward Robert went on active duty with the U.S. Navy at the Naval Medical Research Unit 2 (NMRU-2) based out of Taipei, Taiwan, spending the next three years doing tropical disease research in several remote areas in the Pacific Theater with a NARU-2 mobile research team. He returned to the U.S. in the summer of 1974 and that fall began a U.S. Navy-sponsored residency in pediatrics in Philadelphia.

Jim and his wife Emilie began to feel God was leading them into a deeper commitment to the Robert's vision. Jim knew that if a hospital was to be a part of the dream, someone was going to have to run it. So, in May 1972, Jim, Emilie and their two children, Karen and Patrick, moved to Birmingham, Alabama, where Jim entered the Masters Program in Hospital and Health Administration at the University of Alabama at Birmingham School of Allied Health.

Shortly afterward Jim attended a Tuesday night Bible study where Charles Bates was present. He shared his plan to partner with Dr. Robert Clark to start a medical evangelism ministry somewhere in the developing world. Charles listened intently and began to see the possibilities. By the evening's end, Charles was onboard.

Charles agreed to spearhead the organizational and financial groundwork so all would be in place when Robert finished his training and was free to move to Guatemala.

There was a period of gathering interested people to form the first Board of Directors, half of whom were from the newly formed Cahaba Valley Church of Christ in Birmingham. Charles' wife Lois suggested the name "Health Talents International." "Health" reflected the medical aspect of the mission. The "Talents" was based on Matthew 25 and conveyed the idea that everyone has talents that could and should be used to advance the Kingdom of God. The Board wrote the Articles of Incorporation and bylaws that allowed Health Talents International to become a non-profit organization and licensed in the State of Alabama. The incorporation was granted on December 16, 1973. Sometime later we received the coveted 501(c)3 certification from the IRS.

The first HTI Board of Directors is listed below—a group of remarkably forward-thinking men. I say that because it takes a special kind of imagination to create something like Health Talents completely out of nothing. I daresay that these men did not imagine at the time that their modest efforts would grow into the expansive ministry it is today.

> Charles E. Bates, President
> Robert T. Clark III, MD, Vice-President and Medical Director
> David E. Young Jr., Secretary/Treasurer
> J. Claude Bennett, MD
> Jimmie D. Lawson
> James Miller

Charles labored several years to help lay the groundwork before he and Robert actually met. That happened in 1975, I believe. I remember well when I first met Robert. It was a couple of years later on a bright, sunny summer day. Charles brought him to my house, and I remember opening my front door to find Robert standing there wearing a cowboy hat, his "Bwana Jim" clothing, and cowboy boots. After I got to know him, I often reflected on how well Robert's appearance that day exhibited both his personality and adventurous spirit. And anyone who knew Dr. Robert Clark knew that he had plenty of both.

Things began to move at this point. There was so much that needed doing: deciding specifically upon a mission site, developing concrete mission goals and philosophy, recruiting missionaries and, of great importance, raising the capital to make it happen.

But Why Guatemala?

"Why Guatemala" is easy to answer. Aside from the established relationship with J.C., there were four strong reasons why HTI went to Guatemala. Because of the resettlement efforts in the Petén mentioned earlier, there was considerable population growth there. This created social and economic factors that favored "change" in the lives of the newcomers, providing great potential for rich evangelistic opportunities.

The second factor for considering Guatemala was the receptiveness of the Guatemalan government. After the earthquake in 1976 the government was short on money. What funds it had were being directed toward the areas that had sustained the heaviest earthquake damage, principally in the highlands in western Guatemala. They were quite willing to facilitate someone else's providing medical services to the Petén.

The third factor was the environment itself in the Petén. The tropical climate of northern Guatemala produces diseases that are much the same as in many developing countries. Diseases like dysentery, amoebiasis, enteritis, pneumonia and malaria flourish there. Additionally, because of the developing nature of the community and lack of medical care, many other diseases and conditions are abundant, i.e., malnutrition, measles, whooping cough and obstetrical complications. All of this was important in providing field training for future medical missionaries.

The fourth consideration: Guatemala is easily accessible from the United States, making travel costs manageable and procurement of medical supplies easier. These are major considerations when the two main goals are to educate students for missions and to provide medical care for Guatemalans. During the late 1970s the price of a roundtrip airplane ticket was only $300.

Why the Mayan Indians?

Guatemala was once the seat of the great Mayan Indian Empire, generally accepted as perhaps the most advanced civilization in the world for over 1,000 years before the Spanish Conquest. The Mayan Indians are a strong, proud and resilient people. With their troubled history, they had to be. Beginning with the arrival of the Spanish, as an ethnic group they were exploited for more than 500 years.

Two major classes of people make up Guatemala today: the indigenous, commonly known as the Maya, and Ladinos. The indigenous are direct descendants of the Mayan Indians who built the "lost" jungle cities of Central America. They speak 22 different Mayan dialects and are universally quiet, gentle and reserved. It is estimated that the Maya officially comprise around 40% of the population of Guatemala, although it is uncertain how accurate that number is.[2] For 800 years they flourished as builders, astronomers and philosophers. They are given credit for creating the astounding concept of zero. During the 200 years before the Spanish arrived, however, they had degenerated into several small, fortified kingdoms, with the strongest being the Quiche and Kaqchiquel in Guatemala.[3]

The ladinos, on the other hand, are people of mixed Indian and Spanish descent. It is common knowledge that they are the ruling class in Guatemala today and have a distinct economic advantage. Any Indian may become a ladino if he wishes by simply moving away from his home village, adopting the customs and dress of the ladino, and becoming a part of the larger world. This freedom to move from indigenous to ladino is one reason why it is difficult to determine the precise number of Mayans living in Guatemala.[4]

The first known European to have come anywhere near Guatemala was Christopher Columbus in 1502. On his fourth voyage to the New World, he cruised off the eastern coast of Guatemala and Honduras where he came upon a large seagoing canoe filled with Mayan Indians with goods for trading.[5] The Spaniards arrived just a few years later in 1523.

The life of the Mayan Indians changed dramatically with the arrival of Spanish Captain Henán Cortéz. With a force of only 500 Spanish soldiers, Pedro de Alvarado, one of Cortéz' top lieutenants, proceeded to conquer the Mayans.[6] This conquest was successful in large part by pitting one group of Mayans against another. The Kaqchikels, who had initially allied with the Spanish, were the last to surrender…in 1530. An interesting side note concerns the site of the battle where the Quiche, the largest sub-group of Mayans, were finally defeated by the Spanish in March 1524. It took place in Retalhuleu, Suchitepéquez, only about an hour away from where Clinica Ezell is located.[7]

The defeat of the Mayans by the Spaniards was followed by

---

[2] www.faqs.org/minorities/South-and-Central-America/Maya-of-Guatemala.html.
[3] http://latinamericanhistory.about.com/od/coloniallatinamerica/p/guatecolon.html, Christopher Minster, "The Colonization of Guatemala."
[4] www.faqs.org/minorities/South-and-Central-America/Maya-of-Guatemala.html
[5] http://www.athenapub.com/coluvoy4.html.
[6] http://latinamericanhistory.about.com./od/coloniallatinamerica/p/guatecolon.html, Christopher Minster, "The Colonization of Guatemala."
[7] http://en.Wikipedia.org/wiki/Spanish_conquest_of_Guatemala.

decades of heavy exploitation of the indigenous people. Because Alvarado's conquistadors were all volunteers and most did not receive a fixed salary, they shared in the spoils of victory. After the war the conquistadors and other faithful supporters were awarded large tracts of land, and the Indians were *herded* into settlements to become virtual slaves. They were uprooted from their rural homes, forced to give up many of their customs, religious ceremonies, and sometimes their names on drastic penalty, even death.[8] The new owners, in return for the Mayans working the land, were theoretically responsible for their religious education. In reality, the system created a form of legalized slavery as the Mayans were expected to work with very little reward. Though this system was gone by the seventeenth century, the damage had been done to the Mayan psyche.[9]

Catholicism was introduced as the main vehicle for cultural change.[10] Interestingly enough, because some symbols of Catholicism had parallels with Mayan beliefs, the Indians were able to adopt them and still maintain their Mayan way of life. The resulting beliefs and practices are commonly referred to today as "folk Catholicism."

I learned about the stigma against being Mayan on my first trip to Guatemala in July 1980 when I shared a bus seat with a ladino woman who hitched a ride with us at Lake Atitlan. She explained to me how the system worked. She said that anyone could become a ladino…but no one would ever **want** to become a Mayan Indian. In fact, she said in whispered tones that the worst insult one could inflict upon a ladino would be to tell him that he looked Mayan.

History of the Civil War in Guatemala

In 1944 a progressive-minded college professor, Juan José Arévalo was elected president of Guatemala, in its first relatively free and fair election. President Arévalo brought great reform,

---

[8] Richard Mahler, *Guatemala, A Natural Destination*,8-9, Santa Fe, New Mexico; John Muir Publications, 1993.
[9] http://latinamericanhistory.about.com./od/coloniallatinamerica/p/guatecolon.html Christopher Minster, "The Colonization of Guatemala."
[10] Michael D. Coe. *The Maya*. 231-232. Ancient peoples and places series (6th ed.). London, UK and New York, USA: Thames & Hudson, 1999.

called "spiritual socialism," to Guatemala. He started a national welfare program, built new schools, rewrote the labor code, unharnessed the news media and sent power back to the local governments.

When Arévalo's six-year term was completed in 1950, Jacobo Arbenz was elected to replace him. His *plan to bring equity to the Indians through land distribution* was the root of the civil war that lasted from 1960 until the Peace Accords were signed in 1996. President Arbenz' plan allowed small farmers to take over any unused public land and cultivate new private parcels from idle tracts held by large private corporations. As one can imagine, this was met with great resistance from wealthy landowners and corporations, the United Fruit Company being one of those. The United States' CIA soon got involved and actively participated in the successful takeover of the government of Guatemala in 1954. Violence continued to escalate, and in 1968 the U.S. Ambassador to Guatemala, John Gordon Mein, was assassinated.

By the 1970s and well into the 1980s the country was torn apart by violence. An aggressive, reform-minded guerrilla movement on the left and government death squads on the right operated against each other in full force. During that time 150,000-200,000 people were killed or simply disappeared.[11] The Guatemalan military's "scorched earth" campaign was so violent that approximately 440 villages were completely destroyed. More than a million people were refugees in their own land, while yet another 200,000 escaped to other countries.[12] This was a time of tremendous unrest as great fear and uncertainty filled the land.

The Catholic Church initiated peace negotiations in 1991 that were later brokered by the United Nations. Finally, after 36 years of civil war, all sides signed the Peace Accords on December 28, 1996.

---

[11] *The Guatemalan Peace Accords*, NACLA Report on the Americas, May/June 1997.
[12] Richard Mahler. *Guatemala: A Natural Destination*, 11-13. Santa Fe, New Mexico: John Muir Publications, 1993.

Chapter 3:
Las Cruces Rising

1978-79

"Pioneers Wanted," HTI's earliest brochure declared. Unlike our pioneering ancestors who settled and tamed the country that would ultimately become known as the United States of America, HTI was looking for members of the Church of Christ with evangelistic hearts and medical skills. HTI was searching for those Christians who could embrace the biblical charge that was part of its mission statement:

"He sent them out to preach the kingdom of God and to heal the sick" (Luke 9:2). "So they set out and went from village to village preaching the gospel and healing people everywhere" (Luke 9:6).

By 1978 Robert had identified the village of Las Cruces, El Petén, as the most advantageous place for HTI's mission. Las Cruces was a relatively new community that had only been established in 1972 with a mere 24 people. It had grown quickly and in 1978 had a population base of nearly 13,000.

The Petén is the largest department (state) in Guatemala—at 12,960 square miles—and accounts for about one third of Guatemala's area. Its picturesque capital, Flores, is located in the middle of Lake Petén Itza, only 45 minutes from Tikal. Tikal is one of the largest archaeological sites and urban centers of the pre-Columbian Maya civilization. The island of Flores is named after Cirilo Flores, who was one of the first Guatemalans to call for independence from the Colonial powers. The Petén remained lightly populated because of its remoteness and the difficulty of living in the jungle.

The Guatemalan government was intent upon integrating the Petén more fully with the rest of the country. It was offering land in the Petén to any citizen willing to settle on it for a fee of only $25. They even opened up a land bridge to Flores, although it was unpaved. The bus trip from Guatemala City to Flores was notorious for taking up to 24 hours to travel the 300 miles. In the early 1970s they opened a road from Tikal to Belize. There were no paved roads in all of the Petén until 1982. The government built a small airport in Santa Elena to increase tourism to Tikal, but it was chilling to fly into that airport. At the end of the runway lay the remains of a DC-3...still lying where it had crash-landed years earlier.

Las Cruces was wilderness territory...and it would be where the HTI pioneers would go. Its reputation reflected this characterization. It was known throughout the Petén as the *"Wild West"* for its violence and lawlessness—fertile ground for a missionary team offering both physical and spiritual care.

Despite its reputation, an early survey showed that Las Cruces already had an evangelical community of about 25-30%. The people who comprised the remaining 70-75% were largely unbelievers. Aside from a small pharmacy, Las Cruces had no modern medical care.

The people in El Petén were of mixed Spanish and Indian blood; their primary language was Spanish. The high rate of migration into the area because of the land grant offer seemed to indicate an acceptance of change. A survey done of Las Cruces by Pat Hile, Gene Luna and Jim Miller in March 1978 indicated the people were predisposed to hearing the Gospel. They learned that the prevailing cultural view of illness in the area was that it was the result of sin in one's life. A Wycliffe Bible translator in Guatemala said that 80% of Christians in that country had become Christians to be healed of some disease.[13] Overall, the culture of the area made it seem tailor-made for medical evangelism.

This was the backdrop when Jim and Emilie Miller and their children moved to Guatemala in mid-1978 to begin language school. Their plan was to study Spanish in Huehuetenango for a year then move to Las Cruces to begin building the clinic.

The Miller Family Journey

Jim Miller continued his efforts to get a master's degree in Hospital and Health Care Administration through the University of Alabama in Birmingham, Alabama. Upon completion of his studies, he and his family moved to Nashville, Tennessee, where Jim underwent a year of residency at Vanderbilt Medical Center and the VA hospital. The internship lasted from August 1973 through July 1974. As members of the Belmont Church of Christ, they were offered an opportunity to share the vision of Health Talents and the Center for Medical Mission Training with the Belmont Missions Committee. Afterward, the committee expressed interest in supporting them.

Upon completion of his internship, Jim felt he needed some hands-on experience in health care administration. The ideal situation would be one that replicated the Third World experience as much as possible, he thought. So, in September 1974 Jim and his family moved again, this time to rural Mississippi where he worked in three of the most poverty-stricken counties in the United States.

Two years later (August 1976) it was time to make another move in preparation for their big move to Guatemala. They returned to Nashville for a few months to spend time with the Belmont Church of Christ, which had by this time committed to be their sponsoring congregation. A few days before Christmas in 1976, they were Guatemala-bound! Jim, Emilie, Karen (age 8) and Patrick (age 6) spent Christmas Day that year in a little motel just beyond Veracruz on the gulf side of Mexico. They arrived in Huehuetenango, Guatemala, three days later. Their "job one" was to learn the language.

---

[13] Jim Miller, Master's Thesis, 5, University of Alabama in Birmingham, 1974.

During Jim's time in Huehuetenango he was also making trips around Guatemala, identifying and establishing relationships with various organizations that were already working in the Petén. He knew that two things would be necessary before moving forward with obtaining land for the project. The first was to secure legal status for HTI with the Guatemalan government. It wasn't long before Roger McCown began working on that. The second was to develop a relationship with the mayor of La Libertad. Fortunately, J.C. Reed already had a good relationship with him, so Jim felt we could build on that. That relationship proved to be quite helpful during the land purchase.

The Millers remained in Huehuetenango until August of 1978, when they made a move to Guatemala City to facilitate Jim's more frequent trips to the Petén. The land was now in HTI's possession, so construction planning could begin.

The Roger Factor

A long, tall Texan, Roger McCown, his wife MaryBeth and their two young sons, Roger Lee and Paco, had been living among the Indians in the Sacapulas in the western highlands of Guatemala. By 1977 they had been there about eight years, working with Dr. Richard Rheinbolt, Pat and Carol Hile, and Ralph and Susie McCluggage. Then Dr. Robert Clark visited. He shared with them his vision to provide both medical and spiritual care and to train North Americans for service in missions. There were varying degrees of interest/support expressed among the group, but Roger seemed interested from the start.

Roger and Robert had known each other since fourth grade when Roger's father preached for a church in New Braunfels, Texas, where Robert and his family attended. Robert's father was at the time a civilian employee working at Lackland AFB as a medical research scientist. (This was the predecessor for NASA's astronaut-training program.) But as young boys, Robert and Roger just played, like young boys do. Roger admits that he is responsible for Robert's chipped front tooth. They had had a rock fight...and Roger "won."

Sometime after Robert's visit with the Rheinbolt team, Robert asked Roger to act as a consultant for this new work. Knowing

Roger's depth of experience in tilling the earth of the Indian culture, Robert felt that Roger could provide them with good solid advice on how to evangelize in the Petén. Roger readily agreed but reiterated that his first commitment was to the Rheinbolt team.

From that point on, Roger became the axis for organizing the project. He became involved in many aspects of the process, including developing a practical approach for evangelizing the area, pushing for a demographic survey of Las Cruces, aiding in the land acquisition, helping establish staff recruitment guidelines, and initiating the legalization process for Health Talents in Guatemala. By September 1978 he had cobbled together the first Talentos de Salud Board of Directors in Guatemala. This step was essential for obtaining legal permission from the Guatemalan government for Health Talents to operate freely in Guatemala. The following were members of that first Board:

> Roger McCown, President
> Rene de Leon, Vice President
> Ruth Morales, Secretary
> Humberto Castillo Garcia, Treasurer

It was becoming clear to both Robert and Charles that Roger was just the man they needed to be director of the new Center for Medical Missions Training. Robert approached him about it in early 1978, but Roger was non-committal at the time although he continued to take the lead in Guatemala to develop the Center. This did not go unnoticed, so a few months later Charles Bates wrote and made the offer of director to Roger once again. In late 1978 Roger finally agreed to accept the role of Director of the Center for Medical Mission Training in Las Cruces, El Petén.

Philosophical Considerations

The most consistent objection Robert and Charles heard as they went about publicizing their vision was that Health Talents would be seen as a "missionary society." There had been long-standing resistance in the Churches of Christ against such institutions based on the belief that all church work should be overseen by autonomous church elderships.

What made Health Talents different, Robert and Charles argued, were two primary things. The first was the fact that since it was to be a medical evangelism organization, it would require specific medical knowledge and talents that most typical elderships did not possess. It would be impossible to oversee and conduct medical clinics without understanding diseases likely to be present and the subsequent treatment of those diseases. Without a thorough knowledge of the medical industry, it would be a challenge to know what supplies and equipment a medical evangelism clinic would require. Robert and Charles stressed, therefore, that an organization like Health Talents was needed to handle the logistical arrangements of such a ministry.

Secondly, there was the issue of missionary financial support. The HTI Board required that each team member have a local supporting congregation to directly oversee his work. The leadership of this local congregation would provide both financial and spiritual care. This policy alone would keep HTI from meeting the definition of a missionary society. Because it would not be directly employing missionaries, but rather working in cooperation with sponsoring congregations, its role would be that of facilitator whose mission was to set policy, raise money and oversee the medical work.

In the very beginning, the elders of the newly formed Cahaba Valley Church of Christ in Birmingham, Alabama, agreed to oversee the evangelism efforts since half of the Board members of HTI were members of that local church. Elders Homer Dobbs and Charles Wilson agreed to make periodic site visits to Guatemala as well as provide consultation on evangelism efforts.

As time went by, the issue of whether or not HTI was a missionary society began to wane. As HTI consistently followed its carefully considered policies, its mission became more and more accepted across the country. Because HTI was the first Church of Christ organization to operate in this distinct fashion, its presence literally influenced attitudes about how medical evangelism should be conducted.

Land Acquisition and Clinic Construction

The actual community of Las Cruces was selected as the clinic site for one primary reason: The Health Minister of the Petén recommended it. It was a bonus that the community was excited about it as well. The governing body of Las Cruces immediately offered to donate land necessary to build the clinic. They offered HTI a choice between two different sites, each measuring approximately 11 acres. The site ultimately selected was only a quarter of a mile from the center of town, had already been cleared somewhat, and was accessible to the community by an already existing road. In early April 1978 the community leaders drew up an agreement giving HTI "right of possession" to the land. There was one big glitch, however.

Left to Right in back row: Billy Copeland, Dr. Robert Clark, Charles Bates and Roger McCown

At this time, Las Cruces was still under the municipal jurisdiction of La Libertad. On April 3 Roger learned that the document he possessed would not be valid *unless* it was issued by the mayor of La Libertad. As soon as the mayor of La Libertad reissued the document, he wrote a letter to the mayor of Las Cruces instructing him to go with Roger and other HTI personnel to stake out the land. The very next morning, April 4, they returned to Las Cruces with the document in hand, signed by the Municipal Mayor of La Libertad. It gave them a right to own the land in question. The Vice-Mayor of Las Cruces issued a similar document giving Health Talents right of possession to the land. Everything now seemed in place to make Dr. Robert Clark's dream a reality.

The property was located on a highway heading west toward Mexico. The east side of the property fronted the road and was 480 feet. The north side was bounded by municipal property and measured 1,080 feet. The western side measured 480 feet and was also bounded by municipal property. The remaining south side bordered privately owned property that was planted in corn, and measured 1,080 feet. The piece of land covered 11.9 acres...or 6 manzanas. The value of the land was 2 cents a square meter. The property measured 49,079.28 square meters, which made its stated value $981.58.

From this point the path to ownership involved buying it symbolically for a stated price. Someone suggested to Roger that since the clinic was for the common good, HTI shouldn't have to pay taxes on it. Roger felt that since HTI was there precisely to benefit the community it was essential that they pay the property tax. Besides, a mere $200-300 would pay the taxes for the next 20-25 years.

After the site was selected, transferred to HTI and surveyed, the city fathers went even further. They volunteered to fence the land before construction began. They did the calculations needed to determine how many fence posts they would need then asked each family in town to donate one fence post each. When they had accumulated what was needed, 80 men dug the post holes with their machetes and set the posts. The final step was to string the wire to secure the property. Without such demonstrable support, the whole process would have been more difficult and the likelihood of success not as great. The interest and support of various levels of government and the community provided just the stimulus needed to get the project off the ground. We were now ready to build.

From Vision to Reality...Witnessing the Hand of God

After all the years of dreaming and preparing, the time had come to build. Jim Miller, with his health administration training, was designated the supervisor of the project. His admitted total lack of actual construction experience made his selection as leader an act of faith by the Board. Blinded by their vision of what was to be, however, they forged ahead.

Jim, I'm sure, was feeling more than a few pangs of anxiety about this responsibility. One morning shortly after he had moved his family to Guatemala City he attended an inter-denominational prayer breakfast at the Pan American Hotel. This was a gathering of U.S. missionaries from various organizations and religious denominations, all of whom were volunteering their time in Guatemala for various reasons. Some were there as missionaries, others to aid in the reconstruction efforts after the February 1976 earthquake, and yet others were leaders of international organizations. All were united in the desire to serve humanity in the name of our Lord and Savior, Jesus Christ.

The leaders of the prayer breakfast asked Jim to share the vision for the "Center for Medical Mission Training," as it was commonly called at the time. Jim shared that morning, and what happened next was truly amazing. He said there was a tremendous outpouring of support for the project, with many offers of specific help. Some of these later proved to be exceedingly useful.

Russell Fox was an engineer and former commercial building contractor. He was sponsored by the Indian Hills Baptist Church in North Little Rock, Arkansas, and the University Baptist Church in Fayetteville, Arkansas. He offered to design and oversee the building construction, all for only the cost of transportation, food, and a place to sleep. It was he who turned out to be the master at keeping the construction moving forward.

Mark Geppert, sponsored by the Dayspring Christian Center in Oakmont, Pennsylvania, had come to Guatemala to help with disaster relief right after the earthquake. He proved to be invaluable as he walked alongside Jim, providing him with advice and counsel. He also volunteered use of his truck to transport supplies between Guatemala City and Las Cruces, a very long and arduous stretch of road that took days of travel each way. Mark also spent many, many hours working with the construction crew in the heat of the Guatemalan jungle.

Hector Zetino, an 18-year-old Guatemalan who had worked on some of Mark's teams during the earthquake reconstruction effort, became an integral part of the team. It was he who stayed in Las Cruces during those times that Jim, Mark and Russell made trips back to Guatemala City to be with their wives and children. On average, these three men were spending two weeks in Las Cruces for every one they had with their families. Bear in mind that there were no cell phones back then, so any sort of communication between Las Cruces and Guatemala City was extremely limited. The nearest telephone was an hour and a half away. What a challenging time it must have been for all of them.

During this time there were two special instances where God's hand of guidance seemed clear. The first involved the pouring of the concrete columns in Las Cruces. Andy Petersheim just showed up that day. He and his wife Betty were then and are still living in Guatemala as missionaries sponsored by The Worship Center in Lancaster, Pennsylvania. Andy was from an Amish background with experience as a ...concrete contractor! Andy immediately became a valued consultant. Not only was he uniquely trained in concrete construction but also in creating building forms out of whatever material was available. Each time the team removed the forms from the newly created columns, the columns were amazingly straight! Jim said that each revelation was a reminder to him of God's provision to HTI through Andy.

The second instance involved concrete blocks...or lack thereof. Clinic construction was movingly along well. But when the walls on the ground floor for building #2 were only half finished, the crew ran out of concrete blocks. There was not a concrete block for sale in all of the Petén. Not only was there a shortage of supply due to the continuing need in post-earthquake reconstruction, but the cost of what few blocks could be found in Guatemala City was *way beyond* what the project could afford. The cost of transporting them from Guatemala to Las Cruces was just too much.

The Guatemala director of the Salvation Army, who *just happened* to attend the breakfast where Jim had shared the vision, heard about Jim's plight and responded immediately. He was in a unique position to help. As a part of their alcohol and drug rehab ministry in Guatemala City, the Salvation Army owned a plant that made concrete blocks. It provided work for the rehab patients. The director immediately donated a truck load of these blocks to Jim's construction efforts, along with several bags of cement. Finally, as significant as this donation was, it was made even better by the director's donation of the cost of transportation of these supplies to Las Cruces!

Jim daily felt the continual time pressure of having the clinic buildings ready when Dr. Robert Clark and other staff would begin arriving in mid- to late-1979. He remains convinced that without God's touching hearts in the missionary community in Guatemala, there would have been no buildings in place when the team arrived and the mission outcome might have been very different.

Furthermore, Jim insisted that God's favor did not stop with the missionary community. God even worked on the hearts of the Guatemalan military. One day early on when the work crew was busily engaged in the final clearing of the property, they looked up and saw the Guatemalan Army unloading bulldozers and other heavy equipment. They were able to do in only a couple of days what would have taken weeks to do by hand.

Life of the Construction Crew

Jim Miller, Russell Fox, Mark Geppert, Hector Zetino, Andy Petersheim, and a mere six men hired from the community comprised the construction crew. Tim and Bev Maddux and Dale Martin arrived from the States later and also became regular crew members. Additionally, from time to time volunteers came from the States to help for a week or two at a time.

Las Cruces was remote and isolated, so conditions were difficult. One of the biggest problems was that there was no electricity except what could be had from small gasoline-powered generators. Because heavy rains had washed out several bridges earlier in the year, the Guatemalan army built temporary bridges, which were not able to withstand the weight of the tanker trucks. Thus, during most of the eleven months of construction time, gasoline needed to operate both the generators and vehicles had to be transported in 55-gallon drums all the way from Guatemala City.

Because of the tropical heat and humidity, the crew would typically arrive at the clinic site about 7:00 each morning. They would work until about noon then take a break until 3:00 in the afternoon. They would then take up where they had left off and work until 7:00 in the evening. Dripping wet with sweat and tired to the bone, they would stop on their way home each evening at a small *tienda* (store). This little tienda boasted a kerosene refrigerator and served what Jim and the others knew without a doubt had to be the "coldest Cokes on earth!"

After that refreshing stop, they would hurry on up to J.C. Reed's house about 15 minutes away. In the waning light, they would grab their soap and towels and walk down the dirt road to bathe in the clear, cool water of the Subin River. J.C. would have supper ready when they returned, and they ate by kerosene lamp.

With supper and visiting over, they would wearily find their way to the cots on the screened-in porch of J.C.'s house and settle down for a night of welcome rest.

In the morning when they awoke, J.C. would have breakfast ready. It was usually just oatmeal, but J.C. did a remarkable job hosting this work crew in light of the fact that his wife Mim wasn't there during any of this time. Jim affectionately characterized this time in his life as the "perfect male bonding experience!"

J.C. Reed and Jim at the job site

Construction Specifics

Ventilation is an important consideration in any new construction, but it is particularly important in a sub-tropical climate. Russell Fox, therefore, gave considerable attention to this issue. He designed and installed vents in each building that ran the full length of the roof. Hot air would find its way to these vents and make its way outside, thus providing temperature relief below. The vents themselves could be closed on the outside chance that it ever got too cold. Russell made sure that all the windows were louvered to aid in cooling as well. Russell further designed the septic system for the two buildings, ensuring that there would be indoor plumbing.

All the wood used in the construction was mahogany, including the wood for framing. Jim bought mahogany directly from the lumber yard at 23 cents per board foot. There was no soft wood available in the Petén. He could have bought pine in Guatemala City, but the cost of transporting it to the Petén would have resulted in it costing more than the mahogany. The crew learned early on to buy the wood a little at a time, though. They found out the hard way that as mahogany dries, it gets harder and harder, making it more and more difficult to drive nails into.

Water was provided by surface wells. This was decided after a consultant working with a Canadian governmental agency evaluated the site for options. He concluded that even though the spring that was only five kilometers away could provide an ample supply of water, there was not a sufficient drop from the spring to the clinic site to provide for a gravity flow system. The cost of a more sophisticated system to provide water with adequate pressure was prohibitive, so they settled on surface wells. This consultant provided his services and a written copy of his findings free of charge. This was yet another example of God providing who we needed at just the right time.

By the time Dr. Robert Clark arrived with his family in Guatemala in late summer of 1979, guest house #1 was completed, and the exterior of guest house #2 was completed but work was still needed on the inside. Jim learned from Robert that because funds had been slow in coming in, the HTI Board had decided to pursue a different path for the completion of the facility. What was to have been two guest houses with a third building (yet to be built) as a clinic was now to be, at least for awhile, two buildings with exam rooms and lab on the first floors. The second floors would contain offices and limited guest housing. This dramatic shift in direction would mean significantly more construction time in order to meet the opening day deadline. Exhausted from his year of hard work, Jim became discouraged.

Thus, in November of 1979, after much prayer and careful consideration, Jim and Emilie decided to return to the States. But he had left his mark on Las Cruces. The magnitude of his effort and contribution to the Center for Medical Mission Training is evident in the photograph above. Without the pivotal role Jim played in catching the vision early on, Health Talents might never have happened. His work to get these buildings in place before the team arrived facilitated the timely beginning of providing holistic medical care, in the name of Jesus, to a population so in need and so ready for it.

Chapter 4:
"We are going...we *will* get there."

1979-81

Las Cruces Comes to Life

The opening lyrics of the Simon and Garfunkel song that speaks of g*oing but not knowing exactly how you will get there* became the theme song of the Las Cruces clinic. That song filled the background of the video that Carol and Tom Taylor of the Decatur Church of Christ in Atlanta created to recruit staff for Health Talents. It affirmed that we knew we were going, but heaven only knew how we would get there! The moving words of this song reflected well the uncertainty and the faith needed to embark on this new mission. The video inspired many people to grasp the vision. Some were so moved they made the decision to go to Guatemala after watching it.

Doris Clark remembers well her family's journey to Las Cruces in the fall of 1979, especially the road...the one from the airport in Santa Elena. She described it in one word: *torturous*. It was a dirt road filled with rocks...*HUGE* rocks...the kind that made you yell out as you bumped over them in a pickup. Twenty miles of this would dampen one's enthusiasm for sure. It seemed to Doris that the trip would *never* end and that they would *never* arrive in Las Cruces.

Las Cruces...the town

But they did finally arrive, and Doris was pleased with what she saw. Las Cruces was an actual little town, one with thatch-roofed houses clustered in neatly squared-off blocks, complete with a cantina called Rosie's, a couple of bars, a store and even a pharmacy. The closest she had been to Las Cruces before was to J.C. and Mim's house, which was a 30- to 45-minute drive depending upon how muddy the road was. She remembered how lonely J.C.'s house had looked as it sat all by itself on the side of a main road. Living in a community would make life infinitely easier, Doris thought.

Robert and Doris had already been in Guatemala City for the past year hosting visiting North Americans. Their children, Kendra and Robert Jr., were 8 and 7 at the time. Along with veteran Guatemala missionary Dianne Martin, Doris spent much of her time that year feeding the non-stop stream of visitors who came in and out of Guatemala to see the manifestation of Robert's dream. Robert spent most of his time ferrying these visitors back and forth to Las Cruces. The time had finally come for them to move there.

Robert had previously arranged for the Las Cruces rental house, and Doris saw that it was made of concrete block with a tin roof. As she entered the front door, she thankfully noted that it had a concrete floor. Farther inside, she spied a kerosene refrigerator. What luxury! These benefits counterbalanced the inconvenience of the outhouse and well that were in the backyard.

By the time the Clark family arrived in Las Cruces, Jim Miller along with Billy and Terri Copeland were already in the country but not living in Las Cruces. Billy had been interning under missionary Jerry Hill, one of the first U.S. missionaries to evangelize Guatemala. Nurses Ellie Evans and Diane Nelson were still in language school.

Donna Finto was the first of the nurses to arrive. She and Tim and Bev Maddux had arrived in March 1979. Tim and Bev traveled to Las Cruces to help with construction for a time, while Donna went on to language school. Later that summer she stayed a few weeks in Las Cruces by herself, but by fall she was spending most of her time in the city arranging supply lines and applying for her Guatemalan nursing license. This process took several months and included spending a clinical day at the Roosevelt Hospital where she experienced Guatemalan health care firsthand. In the end she was the only nurse on the team to receive certification in Guatemala.

Donna's roommate, Wanda Miles, arrived in the spring of 1980. Wanda was also a nurse. Their first residence together in Las Cruces was a room above the movie theater, but that did not last long. Trying to sleep with a movie playing below was nearly impossible.

The immediate task in Las Cruces after Jim Miller left was to finish the two clinic buildings so they would be ready for the opening in May. That task fell to Steve Sherman, who arrived in January 1980. A recent graduate of the Harding University Graduate School of Religion in Memphis, he was recruited as an evangelist and was eager to put his "book-learning" into practice. Fortunately, Steve was a flexible man, because the reality of what he was asked to do upon his arrival didn't fit at all with how he had anticipated his missionary experience to begin.

Steve moved into one of the not-quite-ready buildings and went to work converting them into clinic buildings rather than guest quarters. He did a good bit of manual labor himself. In addition to supervising the Guatemalan workers, he built much of the furniture.

Magda Luna was a native Guatemalan who had been hired by HTI as a bi-lingual administrative assistant in December. She arrived in Las Cruces about the same time Steve did. (*Steve remembers this as his big lucky break in life!*) Her job was to set up the office and take care of hiring the workers needed to finish the clinic buildings. She found a bed to rent in a corn crib in the home of one of the town leaders. She remembers with horror the rats constantly running over her bed at night to get to the corn!

Every day Steve and Magda took a break from work and walked into town for lunch…just the two of them. Not surprisingly, their relationship began to grow. To quote Steve:

"No electricity, having to walk most places, tropical jungle, and full moons (not to mention a very beautiful young woman) encouraged a romantic relationship from the very beginning of our working together. As we worked on the clinic and as we grew closer, we started studying the Bible together. Magda came from a Christian family but had never confessed Christ as Lord of her life. That moment came on May 5, 1980. This was the same day we opened the clinic."

As team members made their way to Las Cruces, Doris observed that not all houses were created equal. When Ellie and Diane moved in, their house was only about 8' x 15' and was made from wooden slats that you could see between, a thatch roof and a dirt floor. Diane had rented it then excitedly told Ellie that in anticipation of their arrival, the owner was *putting fresh new dirt on the floor!* Except for the fact that they were living directly across the road from the Monte Rico bar, they lived there fairly peacefully…until June when the rains came. That was when they discovered that the roof leaked like a sieve.

Diane Nelson and Ellie Evans in front of their new home

Because of the tropical climate, they routinely slept under mosquito netting to keep from being feasted upon by mosquitoes as they slept. One morning in the midst of the rainy season Ellie discovered mosquito larvae growing on the outside of her net! Shortly afterward, they began building their own house.

Joe Crisp arrived in Las Cruces the first of June 1980. He initially shared Jon Jernigan's rented room then later rented his own from a local family. It was a typical dwelling with a thatch roof and dirt floor. Joe's room was separated from the rest of the house by a wall made of sticks or boards. His bed was a hard, wooden one overlaid with a one-inch foam pad, covered by his sleeping bag. He got all this for only $10 a month. A year later, Joe went back to Texas to marry his fiancée, Linda. He brought her to Las Cruces immediately after their honeymoon.

When Joe and his new bride arrived in Las Cruces, Roger and MaryBeth McCown asked them to house sit because they needed to be in Guatemala City for a few weeks. It was quite a treat for the Crisps because, as Joe put it, "The McCowns had the best house, even beautiful by Las Cruces standards." Off the beaten path, it consisted of a thatch roof house with a couple of rooms and a kitchen, separated by a veranda where they could sit and enjoy the cool morning air. Eventually, it even had an indoor bathroom. Now that alone would make it a prize winner!

Roger's challenge to have a good water supply, indoor plumbing and a septic tank is worth hearing:

> "**Septic tank** is a bit of a stretch. It was an 8' hole in the ground where 'dark water' ended up—as far away from my well as I could get it and not put it on my neighbor's property. The little piece of ground I 'bought' (we couldn't really 'own' land in El Petén) already had a well on it with a good water supply, but it was uncovered and had no lip above ground level.
>
> "The owner sold me the parcel of land and then did not visit it any more. In the intervening weeks before I started construction, a little choate (small pig) wandered onto the property and fell into the well and drowned. When we were finally ready to build the house, the well was full of rotting pig and maggots. The little man who sold me the property said, 'No problem, amigo. We just bail out the water, pour lime into the well, let it fill up again—that kills the maggots and 'purifies' the well. We do that a couple of times and you are good as new.' Sorry, I had seen too much. So, on the back of the property I hand dug another well down to about 9'. The water table was so high that we could not go any deeper because we could not keep it pumped out enough to work. And with a water table that shallow, the trick was to get the well as far as possible away from the neighbor's outhouse."

The *comforts of home* were clearly hard to come by in a place like Las Cruces.

Like many other team members, Joe decided to build his own house, one his new bride would be proud of. He said it was made to typical specs of a Mayan home, with cane poles and a thatch roof, much like many other houses in Las Cruces, but it would have that coveted concrete floor that was such a blessing during the rainy season.

After the floor was poured, the walls went up. They were made of logs cut from guano palm. They were straight and strong, eight feet in length, and anywhere from four to eight inches in diameter. They were cut in the jungle and delivered to Joe's door, at a cost of only 50 cents per log.

The roof was thatch with the long, fan-shaped leaves of the guano palm tree. They were placed on the roof while still green, and in just a few days they turned a lovely dry brown color. Joe said that it took about 2,300 of them to make a roof. The leaves were cut green in the jungle and transported by oxcart to the construction site at a cost of only 8 cents apiece.

Gamaliel, the contractor, was a jack-of-all-trades but master of none, Joe remembers. He said the framework of 2" x 4"s wasn't level, and the flimsy doors and windows hung at odd angles, but the roof was good, the floor level, and the house basically solid. Best of all, he said, it belonged to him and Linda. All told, it cost about $1,400 to build.

Alice Sorrells arrived in August 1980 and rented a room from Angel, the bus driver, and his wife Tamasa. When Alice moved in, Ellie brought over two armoires for her to use until she and Diane could get their house built. Alice proceeded to make it look "homey" by setting out her dishes on it. She said that by Las Cruces standards, her little room was "Fifth Avenue, New York!" LaVonne Taylor, the school teacher, arrived in September and shared Alice's room for a time before moving into her own place.

The Las Cruces Clinic Family

By mid-1980 most of the staff had arrived, each bringing their own combination of hopes, dreams and expectations. They were young, eager and excited to bring health and wholeness to a broken world, in the name of Jesus.

With Dr. Robert Clark serving as medical director, his wife Doris acting as unofficial hostess and counselor for the team, and J.C. and Mim Reed available for advice and guidance, they amassed quite a little family of missionaries. Some were medically trained, others had evangelistic skills, and still others had skills in various areas essential to the success of the mission. Each person came with strengths to share. All were committed to working together as a medical evangelism team...and all were cross-trained on site in both medical and evangelistic basics to ensure that the ultimate goal of the mission would be accomplished: to bring people to Christ.

The nursing staff included the original three (Donna Finto, Diane Nelson and Ellie Evans) plus Terri Copeland, Wanda Miles and Alice Sorrells. Dr. Brian Smith and his nurse wife Ruth arrived in December 1980.

The evangelists included Joe Crisp, Billy Copeland, Steve Sherman, and, of course, Roger McCown, who also served as clinic director. Their non-medical wives (Linda Crisp, Magda Sherman and MaryBeth McCown) served as effective team members as well, making home visits with the evangelists and medical staff. The Clarks had two children, the McCowns two and the Copelands had three very young children (Jessica, Christopher and Katherine Ann).

There were three team members in a class by themselves. Barbara Thompson was a public health researcher. Her primary task was to conduct an extensive survey of the people of Las Cruces. This survey helped the team understand the people of Las Cruces. LaVonne Taylor joined the team to serve as schoolteacher for the Clark and McCown youngsters. Jon Jernigan was a medical technologist extraordinaire.

Left to right: Diane Nelson, Mim Reed, Doris Clark, Dr. Robert Clark, Billy Copeland, Terry Copeland, Linda Crisp, Alice Sorrells, Steve Sherman, Donna Finto, Wanda Miles, Jon Jernigan, Barbara Thompson, Joe Crisp, Ellie Evans, MaryBeth and Roger McCown

Robert Clark used to say that what separated their clinic from the witch doctors was the lab. There is a lot of truth in that. Without lab tech Jon Jernigan's professional skills and service, there would have been no way to know if a patient with chills and fever had the flu or malaria. Jon held the highest training and certification a lab tech could hold, had worked at one of the finest labs not only in Memphis but in the South, and had also already done mission work at the Nigerian Christian Hospital.

Yes, Jon was one valuable team member…with no counterpart on the team. If there was lab work to be done, Jon did it. The other team members knew that Jon would work twenty-four hours a day seven days a week to get the job done, if necessary. Everything he did, he did cheerfully and enthusiastically. His skills as a lab tech were made ever so much more effective because of his servant heart. The team knew they could count on Jon.

Days started early in Las Cruces. With no electricity, most people followed the "early to bed…early to rise" philosophy. Each morning there would be a line already formed at the clinic by the time the team arrived at 7:00. And every morning Jon was there to start the generator.

Dr. Clark's Guatemala Internship in San Benito

On March 1, 1980, Robert began his government-required internship that would allow him to obtain a Guatemala license to practice medicine. He rented a little house in San Benito and moved his family there to be near him. The children studied every day during that time under the tutelage of Mim Reed.

The most effective means we had at the time of publicizing this new medical evangelism effort was Dr. Clark's creation: *The Boonie Stomper*. In these periodic newsletters Robert chronicled daily life in Las Cruces. His reports were so colorfully written that they took on a life of their own! Most people looked forward with great anticipation to the next edition; some thought they were irreverent. In either case, they made an impact on the reader.

According to Robert in his first *Boonie Stomper*, dated March 15, 1980, the hospital where he was fortunate to have been assigned to work was the National Hospital at San Benito, El Petén. It was near enough to Las Cruces to be as convenient as an internship could possibly be. He described the hospital but first explained his need to share these stories. He said:

"This newsletter not only helps me to get some of my frustrations out but also to share with you conditions prevalent outside the U.S. Guatemala has a few first-class clinics and hospitals, but these are only available to a select few.

The National Hospital was built sometime before 1950 when the only way to it was by horseback. The money to build the operating room was donated by the chicleros, those folks who go into the jungle to get the gum from the trees to make chiclets (chewing gum). Nothing has been done to the hospital since except to add lights and sometimes running water. We even have this roach that has lived in this one bed for 31 years. We call him Sam after another old timer here. The hospital is designed for 100 beds—50 on the male ward, and 50 on the female ward. The beds are so close together that the other day a patient rolled over the wrong way and was stuck for three hours. There is no place to wash hands on the ward and no sinks in the hospital with soap. One keeps his hands in his pockets a lot."

During the first month of his internship, Robert had the company of Donna Finto and Diane Nelson. Both nurses had been granted a one-month rotation at the hospital. Their being there was of great advantage to the hospital. Incredibly, there were only two RNs on the entire regular staff...so Donna and Diane's presence doubled the nursing staff. Donna was over 6' tall, so she created a lot of attention as she worked with Guatemalan doctors who averaged about 5'2" in height.

Robert had to be on call at the hospital every third night. He complained that he was definitely "too old" for this rigorous schedule. He also found it frustrating to work with physicians who had very little training in diagnoses and treatment, citing one doctor in particular. Robert said he worked with him on the female medicine unit for a time, and this doctor worked an entire week without bringing or using a stethoscope or any other diagnostic equipment...even once. In the same *Boonie Stomper* cited above, Robert related the story about one of this doctor's patients:

"We had this one lady on the ward, age 27 with four kids, who had a severe cough. I looked her over and thought she was probably dying of TB. I asked my doctor about her, and he said she did have TB but wouldn't take her medicine. The diagnosis of TB was made by hearing the cough. No smear, no skin test, no X-ray was ever done in the two months she had been in the hospital. Her treatment consisted only of PAS, which she vomited. No blood counts were ever done, but according to the doctor she was doing better. She died two days ago. She was from Las Cruces."

In a *Boonie Stomper* dated a month later, Robert acknowledged that one of his most frustrating experiences in the hospital was in trying to suture wounds:

"One of the most frustrating minor experiences is sewing people up. We do that a lot down here. Last Sunday morning I was greeted by one lady with a severed hand, 16" laceration of her shoulder and back, exposed humerus, and her head essentially scalped. Another lady had her ear cut off and other lacerations. There were three kids, one with all fingers of the right hand gone, another with no thumb, and another with a gunshot wound to the

arm and hand. From there my day went downhill. I'm going to write up the tropical disease, 'machete.'

Almost all the suture material here is old cotton and we use stone-age needles. (I've broken two needle holders trying to get through skin.) In the suture pack are a couple of very large or very small dull needles, two small spools of cotton which we have to thread ourselves. Now the ER has virtually no ventilation and gets very hot and humid with all the sangre (blood) flowing around."

It was that smell of hot blood as well as the putrid odor of infection they often experienced that caused Robert to call me before my first trip to Guatemala in July 1980. He asked that I bring him three large cans of aromatic Captain Jack tobacco. I said, "Whatever for, Robert? You don't smoke."

He replied, "I need it to put in the room when we do surgery. Putting a little in a bowl in the corners of the room then lighting it makes the surgical procedures a bit more tolerable."

One more story from the hospital, then we'll move on. This one involves children. Robert said that although rural hospitals like this one did a decent job of surgery, they were generally quite lacking in the quality of medical care. As a result of this, people were resistant to going to the hospital, thinking that they would only die there. Robert said that in his first month alone at the San Benito hospital, 31 children had died; all from medical problems. Fifteen died from complications of malnutrition, others from fluid and electrolyte imbalance due to excessive vomiting and diarrhea, and two succumbed from malaria.

Robert took away from his internship experience two things. The first was a deeper understanding of the Guatemala health care system. This enhanced his awareness of just how scarce good medical care was in the outlying areas of Guatemala. Secondly, it impressed upon him how vital decent lab capabilities were. He would use this knowledge to create a quality clinic that without a doubt served the people of Las Cruces well.

Final Clinic Planning

The mission of Talentos de Salud (Health Talents in Spanish) in Guatemala was like a three-legged stool. The medical clinic, Clinica Protalsa, was one facet of the Center for Medical Missions Training. Evangelism was another, and the program to train future missionaries was the third. The different aspects were interrelated and interdependent. The establishment of the medical clinic would be the first big step.

A major consideration in carrying out such an ambitious program was the team members' personal spiritual health. Missionary burnout is a major risk factor in medical evangelism missions. Because medical emergencies are unpredictable and unending, missionary teams often find themselves succumbing to the "tyranny of the urgent" and neglecting the overall spiritual vision of the mission. They devised several different things to help prevent it.

The first challenge was to create a manageable schedule. Because Ellie had previously worked with Dr. Bob Whitaker at the Nigerian Christian Hospital in Onicha Ngwa, a small community in the bush country of Southern Nigeria, she was the only nurse who had significant across-the-board primary care experience. Her time in Africa proved to be quite an asset.

Ellie had witnessed firsthand the potential for burnout in such a setting. The hours were long, the work grueling, and the patient load never ending. When Robert and Charles first contacted her about working with the Center for Medical Missions Training, it struck her that this more comprehensive approach, using Jesus as their role model and based on the commitment to care for the *whole* person, offered a wonderful way to provide such care. She knew it would also be important to find realistic ways to meet the needs of those serving. Making sure to do so would increase the odds for greater longevity in the field as committed missionaries.

They achieved this after much discussion between Robert and Ellie. Robert advocated 24 hours a day/7 days a week, seeing patients during the day and providing emergency service during nights and weekends. Ellie kept remembering how exhausted she had become in all areas in Nigeria: mentally, physically and spiritually. The schedule they finally agreed upon had the clinic open every day from 8 AM until 12 noon only, with emergency staff scheduled for all other times. Each weekday afternoon would be devoted to home visits. Medical and evangelistic team members alike would be scheduled for both clinic and home visits. This was essential to provide the physical/spiritual focus they were aiming for.

Underpinning this was their decision to begin each clinic day with a team devotional. They met at the clinic each morning at 7:00 Monday through Friday. They sang hymns of praise together, and the evangelists took turns offering devotionals. It was generally felt that this was one of the most valuable decisions they ever made. Not only did the team receive the spiritual food they needed to sustain them, but the group bonded ever more tightly in the common goal to serve the Lord in this place.

As time went by, they were able to establish a little church in Las Cruces that met on Sunday morning. The service was held in Spanish, of course, and led as much as possible by Guatemalans. Doris Clark remembered that it had no walls—only a thatch roof held up by cane poles. On Sunday evening they gathered for gringo church, a time of worshipping together in their heart language. The morning service was important to the mission; the second was vital for themselves.

The Center for Medical Missions Training Opens

The day finally arrived…May 5, 1980…opening day for the Protalsa clinic. Robert stated in his *Boonie Stomper* later that month that "open" was a relative term since the clinic buildings still had no doors or windows. The clinic building did have exam rooms and a laboratory. They had decided to call the clinic "Clinica Protalsa," a Spanish acronym for "Project of Health Talents." In Spanish that would read "**Pro**jecto de **Tal**entos de **Sal**ud."

The plan was to open the clinic without a lot of fanfare in order to refine their systems before any public announcement was made. They succeeded…in part. On Day 1 no one came. On Day 2 three patients showed up. Day 3? Fifty people lined up outside for care! It wasn't long before they would consider having *only* 50 patients a "light" day.

With Robert still in San Benito, the three registered nurses in place in Las Cruces ran the clinic. Donna Finto served as Clinic Coordinator; Diane Nelson was the "mainstay" nurse; and Ellie Evans, a masters-prepared Certified Nurse Midwife with years of experience in both primary care and education, served as Director of Clinical Services.

Donna and Diane rotated taking night call every other night, with Ellie serving as backup. Because neither Donna nor Diane had much experience in primary care, Ellie took the lead in the beginning, then worked with each nurse who came later to help them learn to take histories and do clinical assessments in this challenging setting. Ellie said they were all quick studies…and the magnitude of what they were able to do within a very short period of time could only be explained by God's powerful working in their willing hearts, minds and spirits.

Donna, Ellie and Diane were capable, self-confident registered nurses, so Robert felt comfortable having to be away. He was on duty every third night at the hospital, at home the second night, and at the clinic every third night. None of them, except perhaps Ellie, had any idea how unpredictable clinic life could be. They were about to find out.

One morning shortly after they opened, one of their first patients was an elderly, weathered-looking Mayan Indian woman they found stretched out on the concrete floor of the outside waiting area. She was taking what appeared to be her last breaths. Suspecting she had pneumonia and more, the nurses gently picked her up, carried her into the "intensive care room" and began filling her full of antibiotics, aminophylline, and other similar meds. In a matter of a few hours, she was remarkably better.

Meanwhile, the patients were piling up outside and they were all quite sick. It wasn't long before the intensive care room became a "ward." Robert said that the nurses saw more critically ill patients in that half day alone than a typical U.S. practice sees all year. He recalled that they treated everything from malnutrition to anemia, pneumonia, UTI, malaria, leishmaniasis, syphilis, tuberculosis, and GYN problems.

Robert arrived at the clinic from San Benito about 4:00 that same afternoon after he had finished his shift at the hospital. There were 15 patients yet to be seen, so he jumped in to help. When they finally finished seeing the last patient about 6:30, their first OB patient walked in. She was in labor with her first baby and had dilated to 5 cm. Exhausted as everyone was, they all wanted to stay and help.

Things were going along fairly well until about 11 PM when they lost the baby's heart tones. The mother was fully dilated and just beginning to crown a little. Everything had been going so well that they hadn't expected something like this. Robert said that at first they thought that they just couldn't hear the tones, but rapidly realized that something was seriously wrong.

The clinic wasn't set up to perform C-sections, but it did have forceps, so they quickly retrieved them. Robert set to work to bring the baby out. While Diane assisted him, Donna was desperately trying to get heart tones and Ellie was trying to talk to the mother to let her know what was going on. As Robert frantically tried to fit the forceps around the baby's head, he spotted on the wall behind Donna an 8" tarantula crawling toward Donna. It was red with big velvety hairy legs that made it seem as big as a dinner plate! Robert said to Donna quietly, "Donna, just keep still, but the biggest tarantula in the world is going to crawl up your leg in about two seconds."

The tarantula, however, crawled *over* Donna's feet and headed *straight toward* Ellie. Without batting an eye or stepping away from the mother's side, Ellie removed one of her sandals, pulled her arm back, and tossed the sandal at the spider. Both went sailing across the room! They never did find that dead spider.

But the challenge of working in such a primitive place had raised its ugly head. The baby girl was stillborn. She was small for her gestational age and had an abnormal ear and hand. Everyone was heartbroken, not only for the mother to lose her first child, but for their first delivery to end that way. They knew, however, that this could likely have been prevented had the mother received good prenatal care.

Their night finally ended about 3 AM when they all settled down for a quick nap on any exam table they could find. At 5 AM they were up and ready for another day. For Robert, that meant getting back on his "moto" and riding back to San Benito to resume his internship.

But How Do You "Do" Medical Evangelism?

"Medical" evangelism is one of the most misunderstood forms of mission work. One of the first questions the team had to answer was, "Exactly how do you do it?" To some degree missionaries have always practiced medical evangelism. Wherever North Americans minister in the world, they seem to always be besieged with requests for medical help. J.C. and Mim Reed had been no exception. But medical evangelism is so much more than a Band-Aid and a prayer. Getting the best results from it requires intentionality. It also requires an understanding of the surrounding culture. The Las Cruces team developed a plan that was both.

"To preach and heal" is the core of medical evangelism. People have four broad needs: physical, spiritual, mental and social. Effective medical evangelism recognizes this and seeks to address all these needs in an interrelated way. People need God. However, it is difficult to think about the hereafter in the midst of hunger, pain or trouble. HTI's model for ministry is Jesus, who understood this, making Him the first medical evangelist of wide renown. The Gospels record how He went about the countryside teaching and healing. Hordes of people were drawn to Jesus for the healing He offered, and many believed He was the Son of God because of it.

I once did a Bible search to find all the verses that contained the words "Jesus" and "compassion" in the same sentence. I was surprised to find there were only seven in my New International Version of the Bible.[14] In each of these verses, one thing was constant. When Jesus met someone in need and was filled with compassion, He *did* something about it. In those seven verses, Jesus dealt compassionately with various needs. In those seven examples, He showed us how to deal compassionately with the needs of mankind. His goal in all cases was to reflect the love of His Father in heaven and to bring people to know Him.

This proven method of reaching out to people is the one they followed in Las Cruces. Clinica Protalsa was the only 24-hour emergency care available for miles around. When patients visited the clinic for whatever reason, they would likely receive a home

---

[14] Matthew 9:36; Matthew 14:14; Matthew 15:32; Matthew 20:34; Mark 6:34; Luke 7:13; 2 Corinthians 1:3.

visit by a team of both medical and evangelistic personnel. These home visits were as important—perhaps more so—than the clinic visits because they allowed for more personal interaction. There were more detailed discussions about God and prayer times in home visits than clinic structure would allow.

It was precisely through these personal visits that the team built trust. As the team treated the people of Las Cruces respectfully, tenderly, and with honest concern about their physical problems, they were able to lead them toward a closer relationship with God. To quote Roger McCown, "*Speaking the Word while ministering to the body gently bridges the gap between life and death.*"

Such was the mission of Clinica Protalsa.

The Yolanda Story

With a solid medical evangelism philosophy to guide them, the team developed a plan to live it out. Yolanda is a perfect example. Robert recounted her story in *Boonie Stomper* #14.

Robert first met her while he was still working at the San Benito hospital. Gravely ill, little eight-year-old Yolanda showed up at the Las Cruces clinic. She was not a pretty child. Her normally black hair was thin and short with a reddish hue. Her skin was pale, her eyes puffy, and her legs and feet were swollen. Her little chest was as skinny as her abdomen was swollen. Even her fingers were puffy and ended in clubbed white fingernails. Her pale eyes had an apathetic look. She also had a bad cough. Her condition was so fragile that the Las Cruces clinic nurses sent her on to the hospital where Robert was.

Upon examining her, Robert diagnosed Yolanda with a classic case of kwashiorkor (an acute form of childhood malnutrition) with anemia, pellagra, pneumonia, and probably tuberculosis.

She didn't do well in the hospital, but with some special attention, she was coaxed to eat enough to correct the edema and some of the anemia. The pneumonia cleared some, but later chest x-rays showed what was likely TB, although no definite diagnosis could be made.

After three weeks in the hospital, she was discharged on an anti-TB medicine in an inadequate dose. She returned home to her remote village, Los Manueles, and was then lost from any care until about six months later when she showed up at the Las Cruces clinic once more.

Her return visit in the spring of 1981 was providential because it happened about the same time that evangelist Steve Sherman had identified Los Manueles as a new area to begin evangelizing. He was already pondering the first challenge that comes with any new effort: making good contacts and being accepted by the people. Then, in walks Yolanda.

She did not actually "walk" in. She was just too weak. Her condition had deteriorated markedly since Robert had seen her last. After examining her again, he wrote a protocol that included proper nutrition and tripled her meds for the tuberculosis. The problem was follow-up.

She couldn't stay at the clinic because it had no inpatient facilities, and she lived too far away to come in often. Because they were a medical evangelism "team," the evangelists had received some basic medical training, so Robert turned her case over to Steve and Magda Sherman. They taught Yolanda's father how to give her the streptomycin shots, and Steve and Magda followed up twice a week. Soon several families looked forward to their weekly visits, and before long the Shermans had begun a Tuesday night *culto* (Spanish for church service).

As Los Manueles began looking more productive evangelistically, they pulled all the charts for that area. The charts contained both medical and evangelistic information. They flagged the charts of those who appeared to be promising candidates for evangelism and targeted them for home visits by the medical evangelism team.

It turned out that nearly all of the folks living in Los Manueles had visited the clinic at one time or another, so Steve and Magda decided to step up their efforts. In the summer of 1981 they began offering small, low-key mobile medical clinics each Tuesday and Thursday afternoon in the village. Through that clinic, Steve and Magda were eventually able to get into just about every house in Los Manueles. This was the first instance of HTI sending mobile medical clinic teams to remote villages.

The sad part was that they still had no success with Yolanda's case. Though her TB was under control, she continued to do poorly. Even though they could hear no heart murmur, Robert felt she probably had a heart condition with severe pulmonary hypertension. Her resting heart rate was over 140 and her respirations were over 60. She was always too sick to come to *culto*.

Sometime later during one of the *cultos* in Los Manueles, Jose, a local *campesino* (farmer), stood before his friends and neighbors and confessed Christ. As Robert watched Jose confess, he was convinced even more of the value of medical evangelism. Despite their not being able to heal Yolanda, the spiritual message was impacting lives. It was too late in the day to go to the river to baptize him, so they scheduled it for Sunday. Robert recounted the story of the baptism at the conclusion of *Boonie Stomper* #14:

"That Sunday we put about 25 people in my pickup and headed out to the jungle. Once we arrived in Los Manueles, we got Jose, Zonia, and the town and walked four kilometers in the blazing sun to the Los Chorros River, which is at the end of the world. We were all so hot and thirsty we almost decided to get rebaptized. Steve conducted a very meaningful service and Jose was baptized into the Lord's church in the rapids. Back home when someone is baptized, we are usually pretty sedate, sing a song, hug them after church and go home. Could you imagine what it would be like if everyone ran down the aisle and jumped into the baptistry, too, and had a good time? Well, that's just what we did. We all jumped in and rejoiced!"

He ended his recollection with this thoughtful summary:

"Thus, through the tragedy and sadness of Yolanda and the hard work of the Shermans, the church is now established and bringing joy to the people of Los Manueles."

Alice Sorrells "Baptized" with Fire

Robert told this story as "Alice in Jungleland."

Some days at the clinic offered more drama than others. Alice Sorrells' first scheduled day of clinic work was in late August 1980. She was nervous, but she plowed ahead. Robert recounted Alice's first day at the clinic in his August 1980 *Boonie Stomper*.

Her third patient of the morning was a pregnant 17-year-old girl who forced her way in, insisting to be seen for a headache. As Alice was preparing to examine her, the young woman began having acute abdominal pains. When Alice checked her temperature, she found it to be nearing 105 degrees. A little lab work confirmed that she was 32 weeks pregnant and that she also had malaria. This was not good. The medicine used to treat malaria is not good for either the mother or the child. After a while, the young woman settled down, and Alice volunteered to "run the store" while the other team members left for lunch at Rosie's.

As Alice looked after her pregnant patient, she was also monitoring the "pit drip" IV for a 40-something year old woman in exam room #1 who had just miscarried. She suddenly heard a desperate call from her younger patient: "*Seño! Seño! Yo tengo ir al bano ahora!"* (I have to go to the bathroom NOW!) Alice proceeded to help her to the bathroom, hung the IV on the nail above the commode and walked out, telling the young girl to call if she needed help.

Alice had barely gotten out of the room when the patient screamed! Alice ran back in to see the girl trying to get off the seat...and there was blood everywhere!

"Oh, no!" Alice thought, "She's had that baby in the john!" She looked down into the commode and, sure enough, the 32-week-old baby was face down in the toilet bowl.

Except for her clinic helper and Pedro the guard, Alice was alone. She was now faced with several logistical problems: (1) Clearly the baby floating in the john couldn't stay there. (2) The hysterical mother was tangled in the IV tubing. (3) The cord was still attached to the unpassed placenta. (4) There was no emergency kit in the bathroom.

Practical-minded Alice proceeded with first things first. She reached through the tangled mess of mother, tubing and cord to get the baby out of the toilet. It was a baby girl! Since she had no tools with which to cut the cord, Alice had the mother lie down on the bathroom floor and placed the newborn baby on her stomach to keep it warm. She then began to resuscitate the infant, clearing the airway with a bulb syringe while simultaneously using cardiac massage with her right hand.

Having gotten things somewhat under control, Alice called out urgently for help! Pedro, the clinic's faithful watchman, responded. One look at the bloody scene sent him into momentary shock as he cried out repeatedly, *"Dios mio! Dios mio! O, es un bebe!"* With a stern look from Alice, he quickly recovered and took off running to Rosie's for help!

While waiting for that help to arrive, Alice was able to stabilize the baby. When the baby was crying well, Alice used the emergency kit that the clinic helper brought her to cut the cord. With that accomplished, she proceeded with the appropriate maneuvers to deliver the placenta.

Finally, the others showed up, congratulated Alice on her good work, and began cleaning up the mess. Despite Alice's best efforts, however, the baby continued to have a number of problems as the day wore on. Her main problem was that as evening fell she was cold in the night air. Ellie solved that problem by putting a blanket on the floor under the table so she could be near the mother in case she needed anything. Ellie then spent the night lying on that blanket cradling the baby under her shirt next to her skin. By morning the baby was just fine.

Pregnancy problems occupied much of the clinic staff's time. A woman in the Petén was likely to become pregnant ten times before the age of thirty, compared to two or three times in the U.S., according to Robert. The clinic began advertising a comprehensive prenatal program that they hoped would help prevent problems at birth. They further began to dream about establishing a maternal/child health center that would provide them an even greater likelihood of success in alleviating some of the more common problems among the women and children of Las Cruces.

Cultural Cues

The clinic staff learned early on that picking up on cultural cues in Las Cruces allowed them to better understand the significant traditional beliefs of the culture and helped them develop a deeper connection with the people they had come to serve.

Living next door to her landlady provided MaryBeth McCown one of those special moments. Her landlady had a pink flowering confetti vine that wound up a trellis in the backyard of her profuse garden. After praising the flowers, MaryBeth learned that this was also her neighbor's "pharmacy." The landlady taught MaryBeth how to relieve headaches by making lemon grass tea. This simple act opened MaryBeth's eyes to the wonder of natural healing.

MaryBeth later used this experience as a springboard to research the hot/cold theory so prevalent in the Mayan culture. She compiled her findings into an in-depth manual that the team found very helpful. The hot/cold theory generally ascribes to the belief that all of life is in balance. It derives historically from the Hippocratic humeral theories where diseases were classified as hot, cold, wet or dry. The underlying belief is that effective treatment must "balance" the disease. If a disease is considered "hot," the treatment must be "cold." I explain this further in the Medical Evangelism Training section.

Another time MaryBeth was visiting a different neighbor when she noticed a bright red beaded bracelet on the baby's little plump wrist. Following is the exchange they had:

"*'I'm sorry little Juanito is sick,'* MaryBeth said to his mother, Marta.
'Yes, he has diarrhea and a little fever,' she responded then added, *'Oh, children just keep you constantly worried!'*
'Do you think it could be evil eye?' MaryBeth asked.
"*'Yes. Yes, I do, and he's not getting better even though we've given him our treatments,'* she confided.
"*'We know about evil eye at the clinic. Why not take him over there today?'* MaryBeth suggested."

What had cued her to suggest that the ailment was evil eye? She noticed the bracelet on the baby and knew that in Marta's world the risk of evil eye is very real. The gaze of a "strong-blooded" person, such as a drunk or a pregnant woman, is enough to weaken and sicken an unprotected infant. The red bracelet protects the child by directing the attention of the gazer to the bright red rather than to the baby.

It was generally believed that there are three periods in a person's life when he is particularly susceptible to evil eye: during infancy, old age and illness. To protect their babies outdoors they wrapped them up tightly. Indoors they depended on the protective red bracelets.

Dr. Brian Smith tells of a developing concern the Protalsa staff had about several babies born at the clinic that later became very lethargic and refused to nurse. There had been three in a short amount of time, and the doctors were beginning to worry about a possible infection epidemic. One of Ruth Smith's (Dr. Brian Smith's wife) duties as a nurse was to visit the new moms in their homes to provide post-natal checkups for the babies and mothers.

As was all the staff, Ruth was interested in cultural differences, especially the hot/cold theory of disease. Most everyone in Las Cruces was a relatively new arrival from somewhere else in Guatemala, and each little locale had a difference of opinion about what foods were 'hot" and which were "cold." All of them agreed that newborns could not stand to be physically cold. Since most had come from the mountains, they were prepared with knitted caps and receiving blankets as well as "over blankets" to swaddle the newborns to prevent them from getting cold.

Las Cruces is a jungle climate, not high in the mountains, and before the rainy season begins it can be stifling hot. Further complicating the issue was that as a mark of "moving up in the world" everyone who had the money changed their thatch roofs for tin roofs just as soon as they could. There are definite advantages to tin over thatch, but one disadvantage is that tin roofs don't "breathe" like thatch roofs do. They really heat up a house.

One day Ruth was making her visits and found a mother and newborn baby girl preparing to go to the clinic because the baby was lethargic. Ruth took the baby out of the house, carefully removed the coverings from her and put her in the hammock by the *pila* (the outside sink). In less than twenty minutes the baby was moving all around and demanding her mother. She nursed like a pro. Ruth went back to the clinic and told them that the problem was the combination of incredibly hot houses and over-wrapped babies! Thereafter, Brian dubbed the epidemic the "tin roof disease."

Evangelizing the Frontier

Las Cruces Church of Christ was located a bit out of town, out near Roger and MaryBeth's house. Doris remembers meeting under the thatch roof and looking at the surrounding countryside as they worshipped. Not through windows, mind you, as there were no walls…just a roof and a floor.

Much of the evangelistic work was done toward the west of Las Cruces. Joe Crisp remembers that a single road passed through Las Cruces and continued on toward the west for 50 km or so before coming to a dead end in the jungle. If you kept going through that jungle you would end up in Mexico. Along the way you would pass tiny villages nestled in the jungle with charming names like Rancho Alegre, Josefinos, Palestino, Vista Hermosa (Beautiful View), Los Manueles and Las Dos Erres. People from these jungle villages would come to the clinic for treatment, walk back down the same road they had walked in on, and disappear into the jungle. It was the evangelists' job to find them.

Joe Crisp heading into the jungle

One of the first evangelistic efforts was also one of the most immediately successful ones. It took place in Rancho Alegre, which means Happy Ranch, and was located westward from the clinic about 16 km down the road. Billy Copeland recounted their first visit there in a report he filed back in 1980.

"With our packs full of medicines and supplies, we entered the village and headed for the mayor's hut. This visit is expected, and it is considered a form of courtesy. We had a letter of introduction that the mayor read...upside down, but he was polite. He had heard of the clinic, and he gave us permission to visit the people and to hold a culto. There is already a small church in Rancho Alegre made up of three members. Celso Gonzales Riviera is the leader. He has been a Christian for about fifteen years. Celso was in prison after killing his two-year-old daughter in a drunken rage. He prayed that the Lord would send someone to show him the Truth. God, being true to His word, did just that. Jerry Hill visited the prison and studied with Celso and baptized him into Christ. Since that time Celso has worked hard for the Lord."

Billy knew Celso because Celso had worked closely with J.C. to evangelize the area before the HTI team arrived. Billy described how he and Joe first visited each of the three church members and asked them to go with him and Joe as they visited the families who had come to the clinic. Their purpose was to check on their progress plus invite them to the *culto* on Sunday. He describes their time there:

"For the next two days we visited the people, ate with them, lived with them, and shared the message of Jesus. After two days, all our medicines were given out. One woman complained of a tingling in her left side. After taking her blood pressure and seeing that it was 215/100, we were able to get her on some medication and to bed. Many invited us in, more for prayers for the sick than the medicines we were carrying. These people associate sickness with sin. They strongly believe that the medicine will not work unless you pray over it. We told them of Jesus' love and concern for them and of His compassion for their illnesses. There were infected ears, throats, abscesses, worms, amoebas, and cancer. Joe and I both saw the fear that appeared in their eyes. They seemed to have no hope and were bound by superstitions, fearful of the religion of the 'Gringos.'

"They listened and begged us to pray for them, but they seemed reluctant to go to the service on the following day. By this time, Joe and I were tired out, sick from drinking the contaminated water, and a bit discouraged with the results of our work. We hadn't come to give out medicine but to give Life. It seemed that no one was interested, or each was fearful of breaking with the superstitions. By candlelight I prepared my message for the next day, taking the text of the fifth chapter of James, verses 13-16. I tried to center the theme on the topic of forgiveness. Joe and I had observed their belief that associated sickness with sin. This passage seemed to offer hope that God was interested in their health, that He could and did forgive, and it called for them to confess their sins.

"Early Sunday morning we visited again with the people, reminding them of culto, and again there was a lack of response. About this time we were wishing we hadn't passed out all the medicine, as we were feeling quite sick and were often running out behind the banana trees. Our arms were eaten up with mosquitoes,

and we had become afraid to ask 'what' they were serving us to eat.

"Time came for us to open the hut used for culto. All the members were there, and Joe and I made a total of five. But in about five minutes people started showing up, and after about 30 minutes the building was wall to wall with people. We were so excited! We taught them several songs...and they all joined in the singing. We delivered the message and observed the Lord's Supper, sang some more, and prayed for the sick. Many came forward to ask for special prayers. Celso will study with several families, and we will go back again next weekend.

"This visit has greatly encouraged us. I have never seen a response like this. Our prayer now is that the Lord of Harvest will send forth reapers. We have so many invitations to study...in Josefinos, Nueva Caanan, Rancho Alegre, Palestino, La Gloria, Nueva Libertad, and, of course, in Las Cruces. We know that God's word will not come back void. We know that in Rancho Alegre there is no exception to that promise...."

Village of Josefinos and Rosauro

Josefinos was the village nearest to Las Cruces. In mid-1980 Joe Crisp began making home visits to some of the many residents from there that had frequented the clinic. Joe found himself traveling regularly to Josefinos on his bicycle two or three nights a week. He began holding *cultos* on Friday nights. He and Rosauro, a leader in the community, had become friends, so after *culto* each week, he would spend the night at Rosauro's house. The evangelists were a hardy lot and endured much. Joe remembers his nights in Josefinos well:

"Nights in Rosauro's house were long and uncomfortable. The house was only half walled in, and I slept on a hammock in the open part. Hammocks are wonderful for short naps, but they can become torturous over the course of the whole night. Only with great difficulty can one shift position. And, since the sleeper is surrounded by air both above and below, it can feel quite chilly even on warm tropical nights. Rosauro always gave me a folded sheet to put under me and a blanket to go over me. These also afforded some measure of protection against the mosquitoes. I

spent many a fitful night in Rosauro's hammock, longing for the first light of dawn."

Rosauro was rotund and impressive, and Joe recalled that Rosauro's vivid imagination matched his wide experience and learning. He enjoyed reading and would often ask Joe's opinion about life on Mars or some other such subject. He continually badgered Joe to teach him English.

Rosauro was a self-appointed authority on nearly every subject. If Joe gave him some medical advice, Rosauro usually countered with conflicting advice. Some of it was culturally based. Once when Joe suggested to a mother that she put warm rags on her baby's buttock to help drain an abscess, Rosauro insisted that this was a "hot" disease, therefore needing something "cold" to fix it.

Dr. Brian Smith sometimes accompanied Joe on his home visits. On one occasion Brian was talking with a young mother about breast feeding. The clinic staff always promoted breast feeding, but the mothers were often reluctant to do so for a variety of reasons. In the middle of this conversation, Rosauro observed that if a mother became angry, she should refrain from breast feeding because the anger would likely be passed to the baby and it would get fussy. Tongue in cheek, Brian and Joe suggested, "*What if the cow had been angry?*" Joe remembers that Rosauro undauntedly declared, "*Cows are not like people. It is very rare for a cow to become angry. In fact, cows sometimes go years and years without getting angry.*"

On June 7, 1981, while Joe was in the States getting married, Rosauro and Blanca, his wife, were baptized into Christ. They began opening their home on Sunday morning for Bible study and communion. This was the beginning of the first church in Josefinos.

Rosauro was later caught up in violence that afflicted Guatemala, but more about that later.

And the Clinic Work Goes On

In a medical evangelism ministry everything and everyone is interconnected. Each and every team member took turns being on call…even the school teacher Lavonne Taylor. She recalls one memorable night she spent at the clinic with Diane Nelson.

Lavonne arrived for her shift and found Diane already busily caring for two patients with malaria. When those patients were treated and sent on their way, Diane turned her attention to a third patient…a three-day-old baby girl named Ana, the firstborn child of Mirna and Cruz. She had not nursed since birth, had a temperature of 103 degrees when she arrived, but it fell to 96 in less than thirty minutes. Something had to be done, and soon. She was so cold. Diane struggled to get an IV into her tiny veins. Once or twice Diane thought the baby had died, but Ana held in there.

Diane talked with the father, Cruz, and prayed with him for Ana. She asked him if he was a Christian, and he replied that he wasn't, but he was interested. Diane talked with him some more about God then later gave his name to Joe Crisp.

Ana made it through the night. Diane taught the father how to tube feed her, and by continually holding the baby, her temperature gradually returned to normal. Feeling comfortable in Cruz's newly acquired skills, she allowed them to go home, but she visited them that afternoon and for several days afterward. Joe Crisp visited, too, and began to study the Bible with the parents.

Lavonne later wrote that *"The baby, Ana, is doing fine and growing now. I know because I held her last Sunday while her mother, Mirna, was baptized in the Subin River. Her father had been baptized the week before. Diane went beyond physical curing to include a healing ministry to the parents' spiritual needs as well as their child's physical needs. Because of this,* **three** *lives were saved!"*

Las Dos Erres

Sometime later Joe talked Billy into going with him to visit another jungle village called Las Dos Erres. The odd name for this village came from the fact that the two men who first settled there each had a first name that started with the letter "R." The word for the plural of "R" in Spanish is "erres," hence the name Two Rs. Las Dos Erres was located deep in the jungle north of the clinic and almost impossible to reach, but Francisco and Igma had recently become Christians in Las Cruces then returned to their land in the jungle to raise a corn crop. They had only one child, a son named Raul. He and Joe had the same birthday…and Joe said he and Raul thought that was really special. Joe felt it was time to visit them.

Joe and Billy set out early, before the sun was up. In the jungle there are only paths to follow, so a Guatemalan was going with them to help them find Dos Erres. They were struck by just how beautiful the jungle was, with orchids growing in the tall trees and ferns and moss making a soft carpet on the ground. Billy remembered, too, that *"It also gave you the feeling of being swallowed up. It was seeing Tarzan movies in real life, at any moment expecting a Johnny Weismuller scream to confirm the fantasy."*

The path slowly disappeared and became a swamp. At first they simply walked in mud, then found themselves wading in it. It began to rain, as it can rain only in the jungle. They thought they were going to drown.

Finally they arrived in Dos Erres and located Francisco's hut. He was delighted to see them, though not surprised. He told them he had dreamed just the night before that they would be coming. The dream was so real that Igma had even prepared a feast for them...of armadillo.

While they were there, they studied also with Tono and his wife, who were Francisco's only neighbors. They lived the next corn patch over. They eagerly studied the Scriptures with Joe and Billy and expressed interest in their returning soon to continue. As Billy and Joe left, they assured the friends that they would return, "Lord willing." Billy said that he had never uttered those words with more conviction.

A week later they made plans to return, but this time they rented a couple of horses to ride. They felt confident they could find Dos Erres this time. But no such luck. They got lost just as badly as before. All day long they followed paths that led nowhere, but they finally made it to Francisco's house before dark. Because they were so hot and tired, they could not muster up any enthusiasm when they heard Francisco's first words to them.

Francisco excitedly told them how "lucky" they were. He had just killed yet *another* armadillo...and wanted to share it with them.

After supper they had a *culto* until late into the night. Tono and his wife confessed their faith in the Lord Jesus and expressed their desire to be baptized. Since there was no water (only mud holes) in Dos Erres, they made plans to go to Las Cruces the next day to be baptized.

Joe and Billy made it home in only three hours the next day because, Billy said, the horses had a better sense of direction than they did!

Meanwhile...Back at the Clinic

It was Saturday night and Ellie, Wanda and Steve were on call. They were hoping for a peaceful night at the clinic, but it was also Saturday night in the Monte Rico Bar. All was peaceful at the clinic...until about 2 AM.

Suddenly they heard a strange sound. When they looked out, they saw erratic lights in the darkness headed their way. As the lights moved closer to the clinic, Ellie, Wanda and Steve were able to make out four figures that seemed to be carrying a fifth. As the figures grew nearer, the clinic staff was filled with horror at what they saw.

The wounded man was blowing a clot out of his nose, making the wound above his eye blow blood bubbles, indicating a communicating fracture exposing the brain, ethnoid and frontal sinuses. His four drunken companions completed the gruesome scene.

Robert wrote in his *Boonie Stomper #6* that "...this was a job that no self-respecting neurosurgeon would have backed away from. Ellie proceeded to clean out the wound. Because of the severity of the wound, she did not attempt to sew it up. Afterwards she tried to explain to the frightened drunken men the critical nature of the patient and that he needed further care and medicines. Reluctantly, the four men left their compadre...then surreptitiously returned at dawn and stole him away while Ellie was taking a shower."

It seems that the fight had started at the Bar Monte Rico because a guy named Pancho had gotten into a fight with the wounded man over Pancho's refusal to pay the fee of Q5 (5 quetzales) to a girl he had just been with. He insisted the price was too high. A barroom brawl followed, and Pancho took a .22 revolver to the head. Just before he felt the impact, he picked up a table and slung it at the victim, who was holding the gun, striking him just above the left eye. The victim fell to the floor, unconscious and bleeding. Pancho managed to sneak out during the commotion and ride away into the night. The victim's four half-lit friends sensed this was a real emergency, so they picked him up and carted him to the clinic a half mile away.

Later that day it was Steve's turn to do home visits, and he was assigned the bar victim. He found the patient bent over in the street with a policeman's M-2 pointed at his head. Steve cautiously approached and tried to explain the seriousness of the man's head wound, but the policeman didn't care. The man's reputation was *malo* (bad) and he had been involved in a brawl last night, the policeman said. He proceeded with the arrest and took him to jail. Not surprisingly, the man later died in jail from meningitis.

In that same *Boonie Stomper*, Robert told the story of another day and another home visit to the Bar Monte Rico. This time Donna and Steve were going together to visit a sick child and her mother. This story illustrates why the words of the song "Anywhere with Jesus" are so meaningful to missionaries.

The person requesting the home visit led Steve and Donna from the clinic through Las Cruces, right up to the door of the Bar Monte Rico. Steve and Donna exchanged glances as they entered the bar and followed their guide through the dance area and into the back where the "working girls" kept their rooms.

The rooms were only about 4' x 6' and had no windows or ventilation. The beds were simply single cots with thin, dirty, stained mattresses and no sheets. Babies lived in the rooms with their mothers. The baby that Donna went to see was sick but was still as "cute as a bug's ear." The mother tried to give her to Donna. Donna almost took her.

Center for Child and Maternal Health

Even before the clinic was open, it was clear that mothers' and children's health problems were rampant. Early on the medical team learned of a baby girl who had died because she had been bottle fed. Mothers could often get formula for free from various sources. They would take it home, mix it with impure water, and feed it to their babies, who would then get very sick. Sometimes they died, as did this baby girl. Some on the team attended her funeral. This experience made them feel the urgency of the situation in Las Cruces.

Ellie, with her training as a midwife and nurse practitioner, became the lead advocate for a Center for Child and Maternal Health. She was tasked with designing the program and facility and raising funds to build it. After the clinic opened, a cursory review of their recent patients with pregnancy problems revealed many challenges. It was clear they needed a facility with an inpatient ward, better monitoring equipment and space for training midwives in better birthing techniques. Ellie set about writing a grant request for funding to present to World Vision.

The proposal requested $100,000 to build a center that would focus on child and maternal health problems. Ellie and Robert spent months gathering the necessary data to write a solid proposal, then even more time putting it together. Ellie included architectural drawings of what they conceived. It was finally ready to submit to World Vision, which they did with great anticipation. Then they waited and waited...then waited some more. Finally, word came back. The answer was, "No." When questioned about it, World Vision said it was clear that the proposal had been written by a professional, a direct violation of funding guidelines.

Ellie was both devastated and angry. She adamantly told them that she herself had written the report as well as the concept drawings. Throughout her professional life she had written a number of successful proposals, so she was experienced in grant writing. She had also consulted with Bob Ewing, an elder of her sponsoring Meadowbrook Church of Christ, who had spent his professional life in engineering and construction. Furthermore, her father had been a builder and her mother had always drawn up the house plans for him. Ellie had grown up in this atmosphere, and as she grew older she began helping her mother with the drawings.

The officials at World Vision were so taken aback by her defense that they promised to give the proposal more consideration. They said they would send someone out for an on-site review.

A few weeks later Ellie was driving her motorcycle back from a home visit, when she ran out of gas. There had been a sudden downpour earlier, so the dirt road was now a muddy road. As she was pushing her motorbike up Main Street, a truck drove by and splashed her with that sloppy, icky mud! She was fighting back tears when she heard another truck coming up the road. It stopped and someone called her name. She lifted her head and saw through her tears that it was Robert in the "Blue Goose." Never was she so glad to see him in her life.

Robert got out of the truck, came over and took the bike from her, then introduced her to the stranger. It was the World Vision representative coming for a site visit. Ellie stuck out her muddy hand in acknowledgement. At Robert's insistence she drove the truck to his house while he finished pushing her motorbike to the gas station.

Needless to say, after meeting her in such circumstances, the World Vision rep found it quite believable that Ellie had done the work on the grant proposal. He could see that Ellie was willing to get "down and dirty!" A few weeks later she received word that the proposal had been funded. Their excitement gave way to sadness when the reality of the need to evacuate became clear a very short time later. Ellie and the others prayed that World Vision would hold their grant money until they were able to return.

Center for Medical Missions Training Finally Begins

From the very beginning, the central focus of Robert's vision was to create a "Center for Medical Missions Training." He knew that this type of facility was wholly lacking in all of Church of Christ missionary training. This goal was included in every aspect of the planning of the Las Cruces clinic. The time had finally come to see it in action...in June 1981.

Six students accepted the challenge to be in the first CMMT class. Two were senior Harding University nursing students, Melissa Redding and Lori Schloffman; Harding pre-med student Meg Finch; Harding pre-nursing student Lesa Cregeen; mechanic Teck Waters (often the most valuable member of a mission team!); and Lelia Jones, a retired school teacher and unofficial grandmother of the group.

The program lasted for six weeks and included four modules: Language, Culture and Missiology, taught by Steve and Joe (followed by working each afternoon with a language helper); Christian Health Care Challenges, taught by Ellie and Robert; and Missiomedicology (a 50-cent word Jon Jernigan created for the act of combining medicine and evangelism), taught by Roger and Ellie. The fourth module, called Jungle Adventures, was optional and was conducted by Dr. Brian and Ruth Smith. Its highlight was a trek through the jungle to visit the recently discovered Mayan Cave of the Inscriptions. More about that later. Because the students came and went at different times, only Melissa, Lori, and Lesa completed all the modules.

In this primitive setting, developing the materials needed for the course was no small feat. Getting the material written was only the first challenge. Getting it typed onto "ditto" forms then reproducing them on the mimeograph machine was quite another. (Oh, how cumbersome it was before photocopiers were available!)

Finally, however, all was done and ready to collate. Ellie tells how the un-collated pages were neatly stacked on desks in the upstairs evangelists' office...when an unanticipated, side-blowing rainstorm erupted one night. By the time the "on call" staff working with patients downstairs remembered that the windows upstairs were open, all the neat stacks had been scattered and soaked. With great effort and tedium, they found all the pages and were able to separate and salvage them. Although the water had thickened and ruffled the pages, they decided that it actually lent an air of authenticity...especially to the Jungle Adventure module.

Students lived with Las Cruces Christian families as they stepped through the course. Melissa Redding remembers being terrified when Steve dropped her off, suitcase in hand, at her host family's house with no introduction or anything. As soon as she met Doña Kita, whose husband was the local dentist, and her three children, her fears were allayed. They all treated her very kindly and as an honored guest. In 1983 Melissa was able to return to Las Cruces to pay a visit to Doña Kita. They were delighted to see each other again.

The purpose of having students live with local families was twofold. First, it was a huge advantage in language learning. If a student *had* to communicate in Spanish, he would have more motivation to try! Also, there was valuable cultural experience to be gained. Despite the differences in lifestyle, food and beliefs, there was much common ground to discover. Getting to know well people of other ethnic groups goes a long way in expanding one's worldview. Students learned early to appreciate the smiles and patience they received that aided communication without words.

The highlight and the hardest part of the entire CMMT experience was the Jungle Adventure. Dr. Brian and Ruth Smith led Melissa, Lori and Lesa into the jungle to visit a Mayan cave filled with Mayan inscriptions. The National Geographic organization had been documenting this ancient relic. The path to it was extremely rugged, so they had rented a couple of burros to ride. There weren't enough for everyone to have one so they took turns riding and walking. They found out very quickly that despite the deep mud they had to trek through, it was easier than fighting the surly burros. The burros made a game of trying to knock their riders off. They would scrape up against big trees, some of which had stickers, then turn so fast the riders would slide right off!

Melissa remembers the deep mud. It was so deep that Lori lost her tennis shoe to the suction. Lori was so tired that she was willing to walk away and leave it there, but Melissa insisted on digging down into 18 inches of mud to find it for her.

They spent the night in the jungle…three girls in a 2-person tent. As luck would have it, there came a massive downpour in the middle of the night. Fortunately for Melissa, she was sleeping in the middle; poor Lori and Lesa got soaked! The girls were thrilled that the trip out of the jungle was much easier. This experience had obviously been planned as an endurance test for the students; and as exhausted as they were in the end, they took pride in knowing they'd passed.

Throughout the month the students had experiences working at the clinic that they would treasure forever. Melissa remembers sewing up multiple machete wounds on an intoxicated man. Dr. Brian instructed her to just start sewing because the man wouldn't feel a thing. Four hours later she finished. The man was still asleep. Another time she had the opportunity to deliver a baby—the woman's thirteenth!

The message of "wholeness" was central to the lessons, and the students seemed to get it. Lesa Cregeen expressed later what I suspect was representative of how all the students felt at the end of the program:

"I can't express the emotion behind the healing and the WHOLENESS the Father is bringing to me. He is profound. I went to Guatemala expecting to serve, and I was served. I went to Guatemala expecting to love and bring people to the Lord. Instead the Lord's people loved me. I went to Guatemala hoping the lost would see the love of Christ in my life and seek for its source. Instead, I saw the love of Christ in your lives, and I am seeking Jesus and to know Him deeply."

This modest beginning spawned an enduring ministry. Of this small group, a third of them (Melissa and Teck) went on to devote several years to medical evangelism. They both went to Belize and Melissa later served in Honduras as well. The program is now called MET, for *Medical Evangelism Training*. The concept of providing field training for future missionaries continues to be a priority for Health Talents.

The Beginning of the End

For well over a year the medical evangelism ministry of Health Talents ran fairly smoothly. Yes, the team had heard news of violence in other parts of Guatemala. And Las Cruces itself was a violent place. With its "Wild West" reputation and pioneer lifestyle, shootings were fairly common, whether over a card game gone bad, a woman, or horse theft. The clinic staff became fairly adept at handling these kinds of emergencies. Little by little, though, things began to change. A sinister aspect to the violence gradually began to impact everyone.

Many of the earliest reports were far away from the Petén. When Alice was in language school in Quetzaltenango, she was aware of instances of university professors being killed and students disappearing. On the day of the funeral for one of the professors, Alice witnessed the grief in the community and felt their fear for what was happening to their country.

Steve and Magda experienced hints of what was to come fairly early on. One evening after dinner they drove back to the clinic. As they neared the clinic site, they found the road blocked by several large rocks. Steve remembers getting out of the truck and moving the rocks out of the road.

The next day some men came to Steve and very quietly, almost in a whisper, suggested that he not move the rocks (for they had been put there by the guerrillas). It seems that there was talk of building a police station out that way, and the guerrillas did not want that to happen so they were protesting. Steve asked them, "Well, what am I supposed to do? I've got to get to the clinic."

The men thought for a minute then again very quietly said, "Maybe we can talk with them." They came back to Steve later and said that the guerrillas agreed to wait until later in the evening to put the rocks out so they wouldn't inconvenience the clinic staff.

The shootout between the military and guerrillas in early September 1981 definitely got the team's attention. That was a reality check for the whole team…when they first realized without a doubt that the war had come to them. That was when they admitted to each other that the time might come when they would need to evacuate. They had their meeting, discussed the situation thoroughly, made their plan, and kept on working.

One night during this period Dr. Brian and Ruth Smith were on call at the clinic when they heard a strange noise. They got up, peeked out the window toward the road, and saw several men pushing a jeep toward the clinic. The jeep had neither lights on nor motor running. They stood in the doorway waiting anxiously, not knowing what to expect. The group came right up to the door, and several men got out and carried a wounded man into the clinic.

Brian and Ruth dutifully provided what treatment they could. When they finished their work, the band of men loaded up their friend and left the way they came…still silently pushing the jeep down the road. Though they never knew for sure, they decided that the group was probably a guerrilla band that did not want its presence in the area known, hence the pushing of the jeep rather than using the vehicle's motor.

After the September shootout, tension began building among the team. There was a new sense of urgency in their work because they sensed that their time in Las Cruces was limited. They resumed their normal activities with a few changes. They began holding *cultos* in the afternoon, for instance, rather than after dark. Unexpected lights or sounds on the road caused them to start…only to laugh at themselves when the lights or sounds turned out to be nothing.

A few weeks after this, Brian and Ruth went to Guatemala City. There they heard about the guerillas taking over the Pan American highway, taking all the bus passengers as prisoners, and burning the buses. They also heard reports of kidnappings and carjacking and leaving people stranded or shot for no apparent reason. They contacted the clinic through the clinic's new shortwave radio and reported what they had heard…and heard in return something about "Yankees" on the bus.

On Thursday before the team evacuated on Saturday Joe Crisp got some disturbing news on that same shortwave radio that he had only been licensed to operate since October 11. Jerry and Ann Hill had been called back to Abilene by their sponsoring church. Ann was calling to ask about public transportation in the Petén, as she had read something in the paper about "bad weather" in the Petén. Roger McCown was in the city and wanted to know if it would be safe to travel by bus to return. Joe told her there had indeed been "bad weather" and that they had come through a "shower" just the day before but that everyone was fine.

This conversation made them understand that their scary bus incident was not an isolated event. Ann could not have read about their particular experience because news simply did not travel that fast from the Petén to the rest of Guatemala. They realized that the violence was becoming more widespread.

By Friday it was apparent that the general level of violence had risen rapidly in just two weeks. They heard rumors of more kidnappings and also of a man being shot in the road somewhere around Palestina. Most disturbing to Joe, however, was the rumor that two men had been kidnapped from Josefinos. One of them was his friend Rosauro.

He, Billy and Steve decided that they needed to check on things in the villages "down the road," as he called it. Their first stop was Josefinos, where their worst fears were confirmed. Two weeks earlier, they were told, men had come and taken away Rosauro and another man. Rosauro's father wept as he related that the other man taken with Rosauro had been killed. Rosauro had tried to escape, but no one knew if he had succeeded.

Joe recalled that the sadness and fear were almost palpable as they drove around. He said he began to understand how terrorism worked. People seemed afraid to come out of their houses.

All of these things weighed on the team as they gathered for that last fateful meeting on Saturday morning. Their hearts were burdened not only with regrets for leaving, but also for those they were leaving behind.

As Joe and Linda boarded the plane to leave a few days later, they saw Rosauro's wife, father and son Tono on the plane. They were headed to the city to stay with relatives. Tono had a very somber look on his face that represented how they all were feeling.

The Rest of the Story

In January 1982, only a couple of months after the team evacuated, Robert and Ellie returned to Guatemala. They found that the political situation had worsened dramatically. Although Las Cruces itself was at that moment relatively peaceful, they were told that the guerrillas had come into town in full force in December, just a month after they left. The guerillas rounded up as many people as they could and had given them an anti-government lecture. Amazingly, however, Robert and Ellie found the clinic and all their houses to be in good order. Former employees and townspeople were guarding their possessions as they clung to the hope the team would return.

Robert was also happy to report to Joe that Rosauro had indeed escaped his captors and had made it to Mexico safely.

J.C. and Mim had chosen to stay on their ranch, and J.C. later reported that in February heated skirmishes had taken place between the government and the guerillas near his house in La Libertad and also near Las Cruces.

On December 6, 1982, it was alleged that government troops entered Las Dos Erres, one of the villages that the HTI team visited frequently. They massacred everyone there except for two little boys…167 people, most of them women and children. Las Dos Erres was in the news again in mid-2012 because authorities finally found, after 30 years of searching, the second of the two young boys who had been kidnapped that day. They were the only survivors. In 2012 Oscar Alfredo Ramírez Castañeda was 33 years old and living in Boston with his wife and children. When investigators came looking for him, Oscar said he had never even heard of Las Dos Erres. Authorities, however, believed he was one of the children kidnapped that day…by the lieutenant of the military squad accused of the massacre.

Authorities believed the lieutenant had kidnapped the boy with the intention of raising him as his own. At the time the lieutenant was not married and was living with his mother. He died eight months later in a trucking accident, but his mother continued to care for the boy and had taught him to revere his "father." Because investigative groups had obtained DNA samples from the remains of those massacred, DNA testing was able to confirm the boy's identity. Based on this evidence, charges are being filed in Guatemala against some of the soldiers involved in the massacre. They have steadfastly denied that accusation.

Evangelistically, the HTI team made a solid impact in the area. During only a year and a half they baptized 26 people and established churches in six different communities: Las Cruces, Josefinos, Palestina, Los Manueles, Rancho Alegre and Vista Hermosa. There were nine scheduled *cultos* each week among them with approximately 75 people attending. This degree of evangelistic success helped assuage their feelings of disappointment at having to leave prematurely. They took comfort in knowing that though they were now gone from Las Cruces, they left behind people with hearts for God.

Major Accomplishment of Las Cruces Mission
In his final report to the Health Talents Board of Directors in 1982, Roger McCown summarized what he thought was the most important accomplishment of the HTI team during its time in Las Cruces:

"The single most important accomplishment, though by no means the most difficult, was the development of a program philosophy which enabled the team to challenge directly traditional ideas and practices in medical missions and provide significant solutions which will endure and serve as models for others. The concept of Jesus as our example and guide in ministries of wholeness encouraged the team to venture into unknown areas in defining the role of medical evangelists beyond the stereotypes present in most medical mission projects. Our recognition of the validity and importance of the time/space union of the twin concepts of spiritual and physical health care provision led directly to useful and effective ways of ministering side by side to restore wholeness to broken lives."

Roger was absolutely correct in his assessment. The model the Las Cruces team developed has become the model HTI has followed ever since. We took it with us to Belize, where it served us well in the program to teach Christian health workers. We brought it back to Guatemala when we returned in 1989 and strengthened it by forging strong partnerships with local congregations. The model they fashioned in Las Cruces, Guatemala, has proven to be a valuable tool throughout the ensuing years.

A Personal Note
About two years later the HTI board sent a small medical team back to Las Cruces to test the "safety" of the waters. I was asked to go along to tend to essential details, like food. Other team members were Drs. Quinton Dickerson, Brian Smith and Mike Kelly, periodontist Dr. John Peden, dentist Dr. Scott Brown, nurses Ruth Smith and Robin Beasley, med tech Louise Griffin, Steve Sherman and Gary McFarland. Although the team initially concluded that the Las Cruces area was safe enough for HTI to consider returning,

it soon became evident that our initial perceptions were incorrect. Therefore, the HTI Board made the decision to not reopen the Protalsa clinic at that time.

1983 team: Kneeling...Dr. Scott Brown; Front row...Mim Reed, Marie Agee, Ruth Smith holding baby Mim, Melissa Redding, Dr. Mike Kelly; Back row....J.C. Reed, Dr. John Peden, Robin Beasley, Louise Clites, Dr. Bryan Smith, Gary McFarland, Dr. Quinton Dickerson, Steve Sherman

That trip, however, remains embedded in my heart to this day.

For the first and only time in my life, I felt true fear in a political situation. Driving from the airport in Santa Elena to Las Cruces was only the beginning. Each time we neared a new community we had to stop at a guard shack manned by an armed civilian militia and present our passports and state where we were headed. This was only a couple of years after the two nuns in El Salvador had been kidnapped and murdered. I thought about them one day as we were driving down a long, winding mountain road when we encountered a canvas-backed military truck. I consciously thought to myself, *"We could literally disappear off the face of the earth, and no one would ever know what happened to us."*

My other lasting memory is the sadness I felt in knowing the fear and insecurity the people of Las Cruces lived with on a daily basis. I felt this sadness most keenly during the day because several local men, armed with heavy-duty guns, patrolled the perimeter of our clinic. The mayor of Las Cruces had promised that he would keep us safe, and he kept his word. Day and night these armed men from the community guarded us. Some of them even sat right outside the doors of the upstairs rooms where we slept each night.

The highlight for me came, however, during our devotional at the close of our first day of seeing patients. There was no electricity at the clinic, so we worked until dark, then with flashlights in hand, filled our plates with food our cook had left for us. We gathered in the outside patient waiting area to eat supper together under the stars. I remember how we laughed when we realized that Dr. Mike Kelly had gotten the fried chicken feet.

When we finished eating, we began to reflect on the day, sharing stories of our patients, praying and singing. We stood together, joined hands and began to sing the last song of the night...the most appropriate one I know for that situation: "Anywhere with Jesus I can safely go."

As we sang, we became aware of another sound that filled the air. It was our Guatemalan guards singing with us in Spanish as they encircled us...their big guns still hanging around their necks. We unclasped our hands, widened our circle to include them, and then rejoined hands forming a circle of love and trust. Some of us were so overcome with emotion that we could not help but let the tears flow. This was one of the most intense mountain-top spiritual experiences I have ever had. It is one thing to sing of believing God's promise of safety when you know you are going home to the security of your country and the comfort of your family. It is quite another to sing that song from the depths of your heart when you are living in the midst of a civil war...and have nowhere else to go.

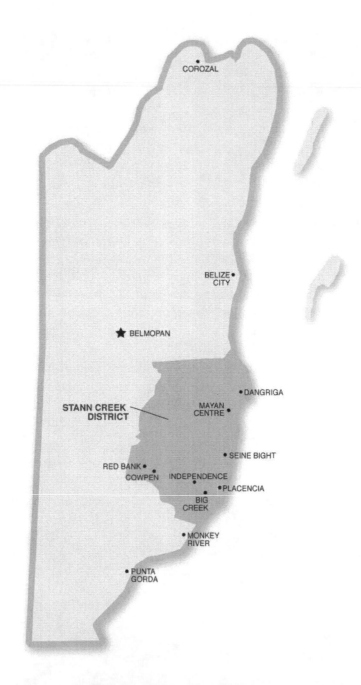

COUNTRY OF BELIZE

Chapter 5: The Belize Years

1984-89

Period of Transition

As soon as the dust settled, the HTI Board turned its focus to the future. The Board asked Ellie Evans and Pam Caffey, also a nurse from Jackson, Mississippi, to investigate alternate sites. The selection criteria included medical need, political stability, receptivity to change, government willingness to work with HTI, legal processes required, existing resources for medicine and supplies, cost of living and language.

In February 1982 Ellie and Pam filed a report entitled "Alternate Countries Profile." Here they listed in great detail a review of 10 different country options, including Belize, Dominican Republic, Haiti, Honduras, Ivory Coast, Jamaica, Liberia, Martinique, Mexico and Panama. After Pam and Ellie submitted their report to the Board, Pam wrote a letter of inquiry to Dr. Stuart Kingma, Director of the Christian Medical Commission, which was a division of the World Council of Churches in Geneva, Switzerland. She told him of the research she and Ellie had done and asked for his counsel. He responded in April 1982.

Dr. Kingma methodically went down the list Pam had sent and responded to each country individually, citing whether or not he felt it to be a good prospect. He gave various reasons for his opinions, from political instability to less than desirable opinions of U.S.

groups working in their country. He ruled out Haiti, for instance, because there were more than 300 non-profit groups already working there. In the end he suggested only two countries: Belize and Liberia.

The Board took his recommendations to heart and charged Dr. Robert Clark with assembling a team to make a two-week site visit to Liberia. Robert, Ellie, and HTI Board member Dr. John Peden were among those on that team. They traveled to Liberia in July 1982. The targeted site was on the grounds of an active gold mine that employed 150 workers. While they were there, they conducted mobile health clinics. They were all a bit shocked when the village witch doctor came to be treated! In the end, however, the Board decided that receptivity to change was very low. They learned that the Assembly of God was doing poorly in its evangelism efforts and that the Catholic Church had not had a conversion in the past 32 years. A final major consideration in ruling out Liberia was its great distance from the U.S., as this would limit the number of university students able to come for training.

The Board then turned its attention toward Belize.

Clarks Separate from Health Talents

Dr. Robert Clark found the pain of seeing his dream of establishing a Center for Medical Missions Training in Guatemala disappear before his very eyes too much to bear. Doris said that she believed he never really recovered from that deep disappointment. As excitement about Belize grew in the HTI organization, Robert realized that he was not ready to do it again. He and Doris made the difficult decision to separate from Health Talents. They continued on in Atlanta, where he was working and worshipping with the Decatur Church of Christ. When his spirit recovered, they moved to Catacamas, Honduras, where he started the organization known as *Predisan*, a vibrant ministry that continues to this day.

Plowing the Ground of Belize

In April of 1982 Charles Bates, President of Health Talents, began researching Belize. He and Ralph Jones, a former missionary to Belize, made an initial trip there. They met with the

Honorable Assad Shoman, Minister of Health, Housing and Cooperatives, in Belmopan. Charles explained to the Minister the evangelistic nature of HTI and what services it could provide the people of Belize. The Minister's initial response was cool, and he said bluntly, "*We have too many missionaries here already.*"

Charles immediately replied, "But wait, we bring much more than that. We are *medical* evangelists. We can treat your sick plus train some of your own people to be health promoters and care for their own." Mr. Shoman paused a moment, then replied thoughtfully, "We'll be back in touch."

Ralph Jones attended the August 1982 HTI Board meeting and shared with them his long personal history of living and working in Belize. He strongly urged the Board to consider locating the next CMMT in Belize. After much discussion, the Board voted to send a survey team to Belize in the fall to evaluate the possibilities.

Thus, in October 1982, Ellie Evans, Roger McCown and Joe Crisp made a fact-finding trip to Belize. They returned with a favorable impression of the country, noting that Belize offered many of the factors advantageous for another Center for Medical Mission Training:

1. **Health needs:** Tropical disease present, making it an ideal place to train health promoters.
2. **Close proximity to United States:** Airfare at the time ranged from $210 to $250 round trip.
3. **Government appeared cooperative and English was the official language**, although Creole, Spanish, Maya and Carib were also prevalent.

As a consequence of this positive report, Charles wrote a formal proposal to the Honorable Assad Shoman. In his proposal Charles requested that HTI be given official permission to establish a Centre for Medical Missions in Belize. (He used the British spelling for "center," as Belize is a British colony.) He mentioned in the letter that he had met with several Ministry of Health personnel previously, who had expressed interest in the HTI project. Charles reminded them that HTI could make a substantial commitment to their effort to training Belizean community health workers.

Because of internal problems within the Belizean government, Charles received no response to his letter for some time. Ralph Jones had intermittent contact with the Ministry of Health, however, who assured him they were still interested in HTI's help. Finally, the Minister of Health invited HTI representatives to his office to discuss the proposal on June 22, 1983.

Dr. Quinton Dickerson, Dr. John Peden, Bob Netherton, Wanda Miles and Ralph Jones traveled to Belize to meet with him. During that meeting, Dr. Antonio Casas, the Chief Medical Officer, said to the group: "*Malaria control is our number one problem, and we are having a huge problem with it. You help us with that, and we'll let you do whatever else you want to do.*"

Dr. Casas explained that they were experiencing a great surge of malaria cases (1 in every 25 people) in Belize, unlike anything they had seen in recent history. More importantly, it was expected to worsen if nothing was done. In fact, he said, the estimate for 1983 was that there would be 8,000 new cases of malaria. This was a huge number in a country with a population of only 145,000.

Dr. Casas proposed that HTI conduct malaria control training classes, beginning in October 1984. Their goal was to train 200 people in the basics of malaria detection, treatment and prevention. They wanted to train one "volunteer collaborator" for every 30 households (about 200 people). These VC's, as they were commonly called, would then share their knowledge with their communities. The government's target area encompassed 50 villages—30,000 people. They wanted to conduct this training in the two Southern districts where very little malaria education had ever been done.

There was no mention of evangelism, but it implied that if the malaria training program went well, they would open the door wider to HTI and its core mission.

As they considered the Ministry of Health's proposal, it became clear to the HTI Board that an October start date was impractical. After the Las Cruces clinic in October 1983 Dr. Quinton Dickerson, Dr. John Peden, Steve Sherman and Melissa Redding (who didn't realize she was being recruited to be a missionary in Belize) traveled to Belize to meet with Dr. George Price, the new Minister of Health. Their goal was to present HTI's counterproposal. At the conclusion of the meeting, all agreed that a starting date of June 1984 was feasible and that the first year's training would best be done in the northern part of Belize where logistics and language were less of a problem.

Steve Sherman, Melissa Redding and Bill Searcy met with Dr. Antonio Casas again in January 1984 to present HTI's official letter of intent. They also presented to Dr. Casas a draft copy of the proposed training manual. Dr. Casas expressed gratitude that HTI continued to be interested in the malaria project and promised blanket licensure to all U.S. medical personnel upon proof of state licensure. He gave assurance that all equipment and supplies needed for the project or by team members would be allowed to enter the country duty free.

Raymond Shackleford was a surveyor by trade who had a heart for missions. He was also a member of the Cahaba Valley Church of Christ in Birmingham, Alabama. Charles solicited his help in compiling the material for the malaria training manual. Raymond diligently gathered relevant material from entomologist Dr. Michael Williams, Dr. Mike Kelly, Louise Griffin, Jon Jernigan and the Centers for Disease Control. The resulting manual was quite comprehensive. It began with a recitation of the "Life Cycle of Malaria Parasites" and included sections on how one could become infected with malaria, how to identify it and how to treat it.

Raymond also created and Doris Clark illustrated a supplemental education piece. He entitled it "The Story of Ramon and His Family…The Malaria Problem in Belize." This simply-told story was spiral-bound so it could be easily used to teach the volunteer collaborators, who would then use it to teach others in their communities.

At the conclusion of the meeting, Dr. Casas requested that HTI send an entomologist to Belize to conduct vector research. The Ministry of Health specifically wanted to know if there was resistance to DDT in the mosquito population. HTI subsequently contacted entomologist Dr. Cecil Simmons of the University of Mississippi in Oxford, Mississippi, who volunteered his services. He made an initial trip to Belize in the spring of 1984 then returned that same summer to conduct his research. Dr. Simmons' research ultimately showed that DDT was still a viable weapon against the mosquitoes there.

Steve and Magda Sherman were committed to leading the new Belizean mission, so they moved to Corozal in February 1984. Melissa Redding soon joined them, and Bill Searcy followed a short time later. When official word came down to start the program, they were already in place and began laying the groundwork for malaria control training.

Magda, Steve and little Melissa in Belize

Malaria Control Training

First Malaria Control Training team – 1984

In the States, Charles Bates began recruiting volunteers for the teaching team. Since it was such a clearly defined project for a specific period of time, it wasn't long before he had a full team. It was a good team of young, enthusiastic volunteers, including Kathy Bates (Charles' daughter), Linda Crooks, Lynn Schmittou, Joy

Gillett, Thomas Meade, Phil and Faye Heffington (who brought along their four children), Karen Hicks, Becky Amole, Janine Content, Mike and Glenda Cobb, Russell and Kristi York, Jayne and Randall Harley, Bill Searcy, Melissa Redding, and Steve and Magda Sherman.

The group gathered the first week in June 1984 for intensive stateside malaria training at Wood Junior College near Starkville, Mississippi. Entomologists Dr. Cecil Simmons and Dr. Mike Williams, lab tech Jon Jernigan, and Raymond Shackleford presented the malaria material.

The team also studied cross-cultural communication under the tutelage of Joe Crisp, Steve Sherman, Bill Searcy and Dr. Philip Slate. At the end of the week the group was ready! They headed to New Orleans to catch the plane to Belize.

Me? Malaria??

An ironic side note here is that the very week the team was at Wood College studying how to recognize, treat and prevent malaria, I was engaged in my personal battle with it. I had obviously contracted it during my trip to Las Cruces in malaria-plagued Petén eight months before. A medication I had been taking at the time had evidently suppressed its presence in my system for eight months. When it awakened, it came at me with a vengeance! My fever rose as high as 105 degrees as it raged in my body. It brought with it teeth-rattling chills. The importance of what we were doing suddenly became quite clear (and quite personal) to me! Fortunately, my doctor immediately recognized what I was experiencing and provided the appropriate treatment. Within a week I was well. Again, God had impressed upon me the importance of our mission.

Structure of Malaria Control Training Classes

The general outline for the training program of Belizean volunteer collaborators was that the sessions would be divided into two-week segments and take place in 13 different training centers. The government-selected students would come from many different villages. Each team would teach four different groups for a week at a time, and each would be followed by a summary session and graduation. Each graduating student was to receive a certificate of completion.

In between the two-week sessions, the trainers would participate in public service activities, such as going into schools to educate students and meeting with town councils. To generate interest and excitement among the students, the trainers would have poster contests in the schools then award prizes to the winners.

These activities turned out to be exactly what was needed. The school children loved the poster contests, most likely because of the prizes. The townspeople attending the meetings seemed enthusiastic about the team members' presence and the services they were providing. It was clear that the Belizeans were well acquainted with the malaria problem and eager to combat it. They continually expressed their gratitude to the malaria teachers for their help.

To advertise the malaria prevention effort, electrical engineer/artist John Pleasant, another member of the Cahaba Valley Church of Christ, designed a sign to advertise the malaria control program. The signs were 9"x16", made from tin, painted a bright yellow with black lettering and a giant yellow mosquito with a black line across it. They were definitely attention-grabbing. We had 200 of these made and posted throughout Belize. On a visit I made to the area several years later, I was surprised yet delighted to see some of them still hanging.

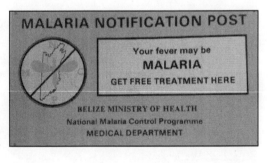

Living conditions could be rough yet varied for the malaria control volunteers. Electricity and indoor plumbing were often scarce commodities. On one end of the spectrum, Karen Hicks, Kathy Bates and Becky Amole lived with a family in Progresso that literally took them in and made them part of the family. They shared meals, games and conversation—so much so that Karen said it was hard for them to leave.

Mike and Glenda Cobb, on the other hand, stayed in what used to be a village market that was now boarded up. It was rather stark, they said, but clean. Sort of. Obviously it wasn't clean enough because they spent several hours sweeping, spraying and mopping so they could feel better about staying there. They made a bed by pushing two counters together and then placed their air mattresses on top. A final touch was mosquito netting. They hoped it kept them safe in the night from the very mosquitoes they were teaching about!

They ate their meals at the home of Mrs. Norma, who lived a short distance down the road. Hers was a small, modest green house, but she had a *color television* in the "eating" room. In retrospect, Glenda wondered why she paid so much attention to food in her journal. But because she did, we are able to get a more complete picture of what their time in Belize was like.

Glenda recorded that they paid $10 a day for their meals: $3 for breakfast, $4 for lunch, and $3 for supper. They generally had scrambled eggs with tomatoes for breakfast. They often had soup for lunch made from chicken, cabbage, noodles, potatoes and lots of seasoning. Their hostess made a drink from the "sour sap" tree, and Glenda said it actually tasted pretty good. They most often had rice and beans for supper.

Kristi and Russell York described their accommodations in San Luis, a small community located in the northwestern corner of Belize near Mexico, as rugged. They lived with a Mayan family of 16 people in a two-room house with a stick/thatch kitchen. The heat and mosquitoes were their worst challenges. The daily temperature averaged 100 degrees and hordes of mosquitoes made them understand clearly why malaria was a problem. Their diet consisted of small portions of eggs, rice, beans and tortillas. They laughingly said that the combination of living in a sauna and eating very little created the perfect weight loss program.

Classes finally began, and as the malaria volunteers settled into the routine, they quickly felt good about their progress. They sensed a good level of excitement among both those being taught and others in the community. Although many of the students had had malaria themselves, it was readily apparent that much misinformation abounded. The students in one particular class seemed especially elated to learn that one could contract malaria *only* from a mosquito bite. Curious, the teachers asked how they thought one contracted it. Their answers ranged from drinking contaminated water, eating contaminated foods, to even just touching the sweat of an infected person.

Melissa Redding told the story of one of the volunteer collaborators, a young woman of 25. She had contracted malaria some time earlier and had gone to the hospital for treatment. On the first day of her hospitalization, despite being six months pregnant, she was given nine Chloroquine tablets and four Primaquin. (The correct treatment according to the Pan American Health Organization is three Chloroquine tablets and two Primaquin, and even that is dangerous for a pregnant woman.) The next day she aborted her baby. The doctors told her it was from the malaria. She had believed them.

Only while sitting in class and learning the correct treatment dosages as well as signs/symptoms of toxicity did she understand what had actually happened to her. She had had a medication-induced abortion that might have been prevented with proper education. Melissa said that as the woman told her story her whole class became pale, then angry.

Over the course of that summer, 100 people received training in how to identify, treat and prevent malaria. The Belize Ministry of Health was pleased.

As a follow-up to the malaria control training, Louise Griffin, a medical technologist from Fort Deposit, Alabama, spent a week in Belize City in late October 1984. The purpose of her visit was to conduct a three-day workshop for laboratory technicians from various outlying districts. During the seminar she demonstrated to them the correct method of preparing and reading blood smears to aid in malaria detection and diagnosis. Her classes consisted of lecture, visual aids, hands-on demonstrations and the reading of known and unknown blood smears. This training was vital in the battle of reducing the rates of malaria infection in Belize.

Invitation to Expand Ministry in Belize

The Belizean government announced in late 1984 that the rate of newly diagnosed cases of malaria had dropped 25% as a result of HTI's malaria control teaching! Because the malaria training project was such a success, the Ministry of Health's confidence in the Health Talents organization grew.

On October 31, 1984, Steve and Magda Sherman and Bill Searcy met with Dr. Errol Vanzie and David Gibson, Permanent Secretary of the Ministry of Health. Dr. Vanzie thanked them for a job well done then invited HTI to conduct another malaria control training program in 1985. Additionally, on behalf of the Belize Ministry of Health, Dr. Vanzie extended an invitation for HTI to plan and execute a full-time health care project in South Stann Creek District in Southern Belize.

After careful consideration of the request and evaluating the HTI team's capabilities, the HTI Belize team recommended to the HTI Board the following response:

- HTI accept the invitation to create a program of health care in the South Stann Creek district that fits within a 3-5 year program.
- Recruit 1-2 medical doctors, 2 additional nurses, 1 lab tech, 1 additional evangelist, 1 administrator, and 1 mechanic.
- Program would include curative, promotive and preventive health education.
- Commence project in August or September 1985.
- Although target area is small in population, project should be expected to have a country-wide impact on the church.
- Coordinate project with Belize Health Ministry.
- Conduct another series of malaria control training classes as requested.

The Board concurred and the Belize ministry was born.

Time was short to assemble another malaria team, so Charles Bates set to work immediately. Three volunteers were repeats from 1984: Kathy Bates, Becky Amole and Thomas Meade. The other 1985 volunteers were Katherine Dean, Kim Morgan, David Burch, Earnest Baragona, Celia Lett, Teck and Debra Waters, and Jeff and Noretta Jackson.

This 1985 training program focused on the Cayo and Stann Creek districts, located in the south of Belize. In order to more easily direct the program, the Shermans, Bill and Melissa moved to centrally located Belmopan. They followed the pattern set the year before of training 100 volunteer collaborators in week-long sessions for six weeks. As in the previous year, the volunteer trainers received a warm welcome in the villages.

The trainers would again reside with local villagers, but on occasion glitches arose in the plan. Katherine Dean said that now and then she and Kim would find themselves without a plan for a meal. She recalled that various fruits were always available, including "those big green balls" that grew on trees. No one ever knew their name, but she said they were quite tasty. Katherine added that having no one provide your next meal was sometimes a blessing—in a land where the most popular foods were pig tails, pig snouts, rat, tepescuintle (a large rodent) and chicken feet.

Again, the malaria control volunteers proved themselves to be a hardy lot as they dealt with a variety of inconveniences with both the living conditions and the food. There were other types of inconvenience as well. One of the most memorable was at the site of a river crossing just north of Belmopan. The only way across the river was by an unmanned ferry raft. Most often it seemed that the raft would be on the wrong side of the river when someone came to use it. That meant one of the team members had to get into the water, swim across to retrieve the raft and drag it back for the others to use. The swimmer would then spend the rest of the day trying to dry out in the Belize humidity.

Despite all these unpredictable experiences, by the end of the summer this team had trained another 100 volunteer collaborators in the basics of malaria control.

Belize History

Belize is the former British colony, British Honduras. About the size of New Hampshire, Belize is situated on the Caribbean Sea at the southern end of Mexico's Yucatan Peninsula and northeast of Guatemala. Most of the country is heavily forested with various hardwoods. Mangrove swamps and cays along the coast give way to hills and mountains in the interior. Although Belize had received its independence from England in September 1981, Guatemala continued to claim it until 1992. For years the maps of Guatemala I bought in Guatemala showed the border expanded to include

Belize. The Brits kept a small military force of 2,000 in Belize City for years...to guard against a possible invasion by Guatemala.

Politically, Belize is a stable country with two political parties and a British parliamentary system of government. English is the official language, but several different ethnic groups reside there, and they speak Mayan, Garifuna, Creole and Spanish.

Brief History of the Church of Christ in Belize

The Church of Christ in Belize had been established several years earlier, with some degree of success. Those early efforts seemed to have not included much leadership training, however, because when the missionaries left, the churches gradually slipped into decay. When the Health Talents team arrived, there were only five actively meeting churches in the entire country. They were located in Belize City, Corozal, Punta Gorda, Dangriga and Orange Walk. None were very large, and the last two were quite small with only 2-3 members. There was no Church of Christ in Independence until the HTI team arrived.

The Belize Mission Officially Begins

The HTI Board named Steve Sherman as project director, Bill Searcy as evangelism coordinator and Melissa Redding as medical education supervisor. With this plan, the new Belize project began to take shape. The immediate goal was to train volunteer community health workers in thirteen districts in the south of Belize. This would be done through both classroom instruction and hands-on training in mobile medical clinics. They would use an integrated program of primary health care and evangelism to accomplish this, following the model that worked so well in Las Cruces. All team members were to be equal participants in every aspect of the program.

In 1985 Steve Sherman summarized the general scope of the CHW program:

"CHW classroom training will begin in March 1986. Starting in June 1986, mobile clinics will be held every other week to all the target communities without permanent clinic facilities. Towards

the end of 1986, one mobile clinic each month will be phased out depending on need so that by 1987 mobile clinics will be held once a month in each area with a second follow-up each month to emphasize home visitation and community teaching. Follow-up for acute illnesses will be done throughout the month by HTI personnel. As the teaching program for the Community Health Workers (CHWs) finishes, much of the mobile and teaching routine will be picked up by each CHW in their respective village, and by the middle of 1988 mobile clinics will be cut back to once every 8 weeks as is currently provided by the PHNs and/or RHNs at present in the District."

Bill Searcy described the evangelistic goal as one that would *"plant and establish self-sufficient, evangelistic Churches of Christ with the ability to convey the Gospel message in a manner relevant to their particular culture in strategic villages in the area."*

Since the work was to be done in Southern Belize, they had to move again. This would be the third in-country move for the Shermans, Bill, and Melissa. They had lived in Corozal upon arriving in Belize in late 1983, then about a year later moved to Belmopan to direct the malaria training program, and now in the fall of 1985 they were moving again. This time they moved south, to the South Stann Creek District.

Independence was the largest and southernmost community in the district. Because it was central to the targeted work area as well as the closest to the airplane landing strip in nearby Big Creek, they selected it to be the administration center. Being near the airport was important because the roads in Belize were so bad. Being near it would make travel in and out of the area easier and make receiving visitors more convenient.

Farther south the country was dotted with numerous tiny communities with charming names and cultures: Monkey River Town, Placencia, Cow Pen, Red Bank and Seine Bight. Melissa, Steve, Magda and baby Lisa settled in Independence. Bill (and later his new wife, Kathy Heitman) chose Seine Bight.

The houses were quite different from the ones in Las Cruces and rental houses were difficult to find. Because Independence was near the coast, the houses were built eight feet off the ground to allow for the occasional hurricane storm surge. Most were built using the slap board tongue and groove method. After much searching, Steve and Magda finally found one to rent, but they were puzzled by what they found shortly after moving in. Above every outside door and window ledge they found a double-edged razor blade. Because they had a baby in the house, they gathered them all up and disposed of them. It took several months to find out why the razor blades were there. They finally learned that it was to protect the family from any evil spirits that might try to enter the house at night.

Melissa finally found herself a house to rent as well. It was a small wooden house that had been built for use by banana farm workers. It had window openings, but no glass in them. When Melissa's mother saw it for the first time, she said that it reminded her of pictures she had seen of slave quarters—except slave quarters were bigger!

Melissa lived in that house by herself for a while, but Celia eventually joined her. It was a good thing, too, because one night as Melissa lay sleeping, she awoke to see a dark arm come up over the window ledge. With her heart pounding, she quietly reached over and clasped her machete in her hand, and with a quick *whoosh* she slashed toward the window! The arm disappeared...and never returned. Fortunately.

Charles began recruiting team members again. The Decatur Church of Christ in the Atlanta area had been prepping a team to go to Liberia for two years. Suddenly Liberia was no longer an option. The team of five included Celia Lett (nurse), Teck (mechanic) and Debra (nurse) Waters, and Jeff (nurse/evangelist) and Noretta Jackson. They were "all dressed up with no place to go" when they heard about Belize. They initially signed up to be malaria control volunteers in 1985. That experience went well, so they made a request to their sponsoring congregation to join the new project in Belize.

The geographic area the government asked them to cover was spread out. It was also multi-cultural:

- Independence – Hispanic culture; population 2,000
- Monkey River Town – Creole (located beyond the cypress swamp); population 250

- Cow Pen – Hispanic/Creole; population 500
- Seine Bight – Garifuna (descendants of survivors of an African slave ship that crashed onto the Belize coastline in the 1800s); population 700
- Placencia – Garifuna; population 400
- Red Bank – Mayan (immigrants from Coban, Guatemala, in the late 1800s when the Guatemalan government seized their land and gave it to German immigrants to grow coffee); population 300

By February 1986 most of the team had arrived. The target area was quite large geographically, so the team decided there were advantages to splitting up. Nurse Celia Lett and pharmacist Russel Whisenhunt moved to Monkey River Town out by the cypress swamp, Teck and Debra Waters stayed in Independence, and Jeff and Noretta Jackson settled in the coastal town of Placencia. Evangelist/linguist Wayne Braun, family nurse practitioner Jean Enochs and teacher Becky Amole arrived in March 1986, and they all set up residence in Independence. MARK apprentices, Tim (artist) and Dawn Smith, arrived in September 1986, and they settled in Independence, too.

The four very different cultures in the area presented two major challenges: many languages to navigate and widely different cultural responses to the Gospel message. In the end, the team felt that any success they might have achieved was limited because of working with so many different cultures.

Front row: Lisa Sherman, Steve Sherman, Bill Searcy, Wayne Braun, Noretta and Jeff Jackson with baby Trudy, Teck and Debra Waters. Back row: Magda Sherman, Becky Amole, Melissa Redding, two visitors, Russel Whisenhunt and Jean Enochs

Settling In and Learning the Ropes

As I mentioned earlier, Independence was near the small airstrip that was the main thoroughfare for visitors. In addition to making travel more convenient, the airstrip served as a staging area for marijuana shipments. Steve knew that for certain because he and Magda had witnessed one such transfer.

One day Steve noticed that as a small plane was landing, a pickup truck waited on the far end of the runway. In a surprisingly short amount of time the driver transferred his cargo to the plane. When the pilot took off, he neglected to raise his landing gear, which caused him to nose dive into the ground at the opposite end of the runway. The last they saw of the pilot, he was running away from the airstrip as fast as he could! The pickup that had just unloaded its goods sped up to the pilot, slowed down long enough for him to climb aboard, and sped away.

Suddenly, out of nowhere came hordes of young boys on bicycles. They descended on the plane like vultures! Out of the plane came big bundles of marijuana that the boys hauled away, balancing them on their shoulders as they rode away on their bikes. Rumor had it that one of them found a briefcase containing $15,000 under the pilot's seat.

Finally, after three hours the police showed up. There was nothing left in the plane by this time but gasoline. Gasoline was hard to come by in Independence, so it wasn't surprising that about an hour later Steve heard a knock on his door. When he opened it, there stood two policemen with containers in their hands, saying, "Want to buy some gasoline?"

On the other hand, villages like Monkey River and Seine Bight were so remote that they were accessible only by water. Bill and Russel eventually purchased boats to expedite their travel. Tales of Bill and his boat are legendary. Rather like Ernest Hemingway and the fish in *The Old Man and the Sea*, Bill and his boat had a love/hate relationship. He related a specific incident.

One day in 1987 Bill had driven his boat from Placencia to Big Creek early in the afternoon to pick up some people. Although he waited until dusk, they never showed up. Since he had come early in the day, he had not thought about bringing a flashlight. His boat was running fine, so he left in the dusk to head home.

On open sea about halfway back to Placencia, Bill felt the motor lose power. He throttled down but it didn't help. He remembered that sometimes when the motor acted like that a clip that attaches the gas line to the motor had come off, causing the motor to stall for lack of fuel. So, he pushed on the clip to pump more gas into the motor. What happened next was terrifying!

When Bill turned the key to start the motor, an explosion blew the hood off the motor and sent flames all over the place! Instinctively, he jumped over the center console and steering wheel and ducked low onto the floor. When he finally peered up, he saw the motor engulfed in flames! He also saw that the motor hood had come back down and landed on the motor but was not in its correct alignment. He surveyed the situation as quickly as possible to decide what to do next. He looked over at the gas tank and determined that if he could get to it and disconnect it before the whole thing blew, he could prevent total disaster. He took a deep breath, jumped back across the console, and disconnected the gas line in one motion! When he could breathe again, he positioned the hood over the motor correctly to extinguish the blaze.

For the next few moments he simply sat in the drifting boat listening to his heart beat as he looked at what he imagined was a ruined motor. He suddenly realized he was drifting out to sea! To make matters worse, a storm was brewing and the wind and waves were growing stronger by the minute. The thought of winding up in Honduras (or worse) threw his mind and body into action. Knowing the water wasn't particularly deep where he was, he first put a long pole into the water in an attempt to slow the boat by lodging it into the sea floor. The wind's strength was too much, however, and his pole snapped. Next, he threw his anchor overboard.

It didn't stop the boat, but it did slow it down enough so he could jump out of the boat to try to drag it back. His feet touched bottom, thankfully, and he found himself in chest deep water. He knew that he wasn't the only being in the water, however. There were also likely sharks, barracudas and stingrays nearby. His adrenal level shot up so that, little by little, he was able to drag the boat to a nearby island that was about the size of a small house. He got out of the boat, tied it to a coconut tree, sat under it for a while and prayed.

Not wanting to be stranded on a tiny island in the coming gale, he returned to the boat and tried the motor again. After several attempts in the dark, he saw that if he left the hood off the motor it would start. Thus, with only partial power, he finally made it back to Placencia safely.

In the next day's light he discovered the problem. A small screw had worked its way off the carburetor and allowed gas to spew all over the motor when Bill tried to start it. Because the starter was bad, when he cranked it a spark from the starter had ignited the fuel that had pooled underneath the motor hood. That was what had caused the explosion. Amazingly, he found no serious damage to the motor. It would survive to create other boating adventures for him.

Laying the Groundwork

The Ministry of Health had identified 13 villages for training. It was important for the team to meet with those 13 village councils face-to-face to gain support for the program, so Bill and Melissa began making the rounds in November 1985. Steve and Magda (with baby Lisa) and others took part in these meetings as well.

All three entities, the Belize Ministry of Health, village health committees and the HTI team began to work together to select the CHW candidates. The appropriate candidate would be someone already working in his or her village in some minimal caregiving capacity and who was willing to volunteer time to take the training. All CHWs were volunteers initially, but the best ones would eventually be hired by the government. By March 1986 all 30 community health workers had been selected. HTI was to provide direct supervision of the CHWs during the training period, but upon completion of the program, a Belizean nurse appointed by the Belizean Ministry of Health would supervise them.

Community Health Worker (CHW) Training

The Christian Health Promoter training was expected to take 18 months to 2 years. The combined physical and spiritual focus emphasized HTI's three-legged health program (curative, preventive and promotive care) integrated throughout with spiritual health discussions. Various HTI team members took turns teaching when the 30 CHWs gathered in Independence every three months. Public health professionals from the Belizean government also taught some. The hands-on training took place using a one-on-one method in mobile clinics.

The Belizean Ministry of Health requested that HTI create a comprehensive instruction manual, one that could be used in this immediate program and in future training sessions. Jean Enochs was central to this effort. In addition to her BA from Lipscomb, she held a string of degrees (BS in Botany, an MS and PhD in Botany and Plant Pathology from Purdue, both a BS and MS in Nursing from Vanderbilt, and a post-Masters Degree in Community Health Nursing from Indiana University). She had also taught biology for 14 years at Michigan State University. Needless to say, she was well qualified to compile the training material for the community health worker classes.

Using the *Where There Is No Doctor* as a guide, Jean worked tirelessly to compile and produce culturally appropriate training materials that would effectively communicate basic health principles. Artist Tim Smith worked diligently to illustrate many of the lessons. This book was entitled *A Handbook of Christian Health Promotion*.

Classroom Training Begins

With the training sites determined, volunteer collaborators selected, and the instruction manual prepared, classroom training began in March 1986. All 30 students showed up at the community center in Independence, brimming with excitement at this opportunity to expand their skills. Little did they know that this was not going to be your typical health care class.

The first lesson was "Introduction to Christian Health Promotion: What Does the Bible Say about Life, Health and the Church?" This introduced the "holistic health" concept. Holistic health includes all aspects of a man's being. Jean Enochs used Luke 2:52 to illustrate that the case for holistic health and Christian health promotion is biblical:

"And Jesus grew in wisdom (mentally) and stature (physically), and in favor with God (spiritually) and man (socially)."

She further defined the rationale for Christian health promotion:

"The concept of holistic health is based on the recognition that health does not depend primarily on the health professions. Primarily the health of individuals, families, communities and the nation is dependent upon their own beliefs and behaviors.

Jean Enochs and Teck Waters present a CHW lesson.

Christian health promotion focuses on salvation, the restoration of a healthy relationship with God, and on the implications of salvation for all our relationships. Relationships with each other in the church and the family, with one's own body and mind, with the social and vocational world, and the whole creation are changed by salvation. God, who is holy and loving, the creator and healer of the earth, invites us to join in the salvation of His creation. Christians respond by following Jesus in drawing close to God and serving each other and our neighbors in holiness and love. We promote the healing of the world by living active, godly lives because of our faith in the healing power of God."

Throughout the program, Jean put emphasis on practical topics:
General Record Keeping
Immunizations
Nutrition/Breast Feeding
Growth and Development
Oral Rehydration
Personal Hygiene
Water Sanitation
Communicable Diseases
First Aid and Disaster Planning

Family Life Education
Hypertension
Diabetes
Family Spacing
Dental Health
Environmental Hazards (specific to communities)

As CHWs progressed through the training, they were responsible for sharing what they learned with others in their villages. The ideal way to share was, of course, in context. When a mother brought her poorly nourished child to see the CHW, the CHW would counsel her about how to reverse the child's malnourishment. The CHW was expected to keep a notebook record of these teaching opportunities, and HTI team members would review them when they visited the villages.

Mobile Medical/Evangelistic Visits Begin

Nurse Deb Waters treats an injured man at clinic as Melissa makes a home visit.

Mobile medical clinics, with accompanying home visits, began in June 1986 and were a vital part of the curriculum. Actual hands-on training and follow-up took place during these visits. This is where the *rubber meets the road*, so to speak, and the students had to put into practice what they had learned in the classroom. The classroom training also included emphasis on self-evaluation because CHWs worked alone. They needed to be able to recognize both their strengths and their weaknesses. When HTI trainers were satisfied that a CHW was proficient in a given area, they would authorize him or her to proceed with using that skill set. HTI provided medicines to the CHWs so they could distribute them to their patients free of charge.

From the outset in the mobile clinics, the CHWs were expected to register patients, pull charts and perform the initial screening. The HTI medical team treated patients only after this was done. Eventually the CHWs would be responsible for both triaging and treating patients, as the HTI team looked over their shoulders. By the end of the two years, the CHWs would be qualified to treat patients independently.

Jean told of a time she participated in a mobile clinic Mayan home visit. Jean listened as her student taught the mother how to make oral rehydration salts for her two sick children. The two-room stick house with a thatch roof had a kitchen with a fireplace made of packed earth. It had a small compartment for warm coals, and a supply of dry grass to start the fire. They first boiled water in a wash tub over the fire, let it cool, and then added a 3-finger pinch of salt and a scoop of sugar to a pint of the water. After stirring it well, the father gave some to the 4-year-old, who drank the whole thing and asked for more!

The mother sat in a hammock hung near the floor holding the baby and giving him the solution by the teaspoon. The elderly Mayan grandfather squatted in the doorway, watching the whole procedure. Jean wasn't sure what he thought, but when the little girl asked for more, she hopefully thought that he would be convinced of its benefit. This was very important because in the Mayan culture the men make all the decisions, and if the father or grandfather did not think it was helpful, the mothers would not be allowed to use the new treatment.

Jean was especially hopeful that the ORS treatment for diarrhea was acceptable, because diarrhea was a major cause of death for infants and children in Belize. She was aware that at least three children had died from diarrhea in Independence during the previous month alone. This reality highlighted the need for education on how to treat it.

Cultural beliefs like the one mentioned above presented many challenges to the team. Another example was in the Mayan community of Red Bank where there was a huge problem with worms. The HTI team presented educational classes on basic hygiene and even built outhouses for them, but the people wouldn't use them. When Steve Sherman questioned them about it, they told him that their pigs wouldn't have anything to eat if they used the outhouses.

A Balancing Act

As the team members moved about meeting local people and conducting mobile clinics, they were pleased with the welcome they received. Despite any initial suspicion or hesitancy the people may have felt, they were generally accepting of the team's presence. The team had especially felt acceptance with the malaria training program. They attributed that acceptance to the fact that the people were acutely aware of the increasingly large malaria problem and were grateful for the help that the HTI team had come to provide.

There is always the risk, however, in any medical evangelism ministry that local healthcare providers might feel competition with the North American medical professionals. In the south of Belize this was not a huge problem because medical professionals were few and far between there. There were a few nurses and midwives and most seemed welcoming, but there was one nurse who was NOT happy at first about the HTI team being there. Unfortunately, she happened to be the head nurse for the entire country. Everyone called her *Nurse Vargas*.

Steve had an unpleasant encounter with her one day. He had been asked by the Ministry of Health to serve on a national health committee, and he agreed to do so. One day when the meeting was about to begin, Nurse Vargas came into the room and spied Steve sitting quietly. She began yelling at him in front of all the other committee members. *"What are you doing here? Who do you think you are?"* she shouted. Gulping hard to catch his breath, Steve quietly responded, *"I am here at the government's request, and I have a job to do."* She sat down and said no more. Ultimately and fortunately for HTI, she came around and proved to be quite helpful to HTI's ministry.

On another occasion an issue arose about well-baby checks. Evidently, the government nurses in some of the villages were feeling competition from the HTI mobile medical teams when HTI team members worked with local CHWs in their mobile clinics. After discussing this at length with Nurse Vargas, Steve agreed that HTI would do well-baby checks in Trio Bladden and Cow Pen only. The government nurses would do them in all other villages in the target area. This would give the government nurses more contact with the CHWs, which was badly needed.

Because they birth the babies, midwives are vital to small communities. Most do a reasonable job. Many midwives looked upon the HTI team presence with enthusiasm because they saw it as an opportunity to learn from them. The attitude of a few, however, showed it was wise to be cautious.

Melissa especially remembers the midwife in Independence. On the surface the midwife was very pleasant. When her own daughter gave birth, she invited Melissa to assist so she could see firsthand the local customs and rituals of birthing. She had even allowed Melissa to "catch" her grandchild. Just beneath the surface, however, Melissa sensed a quiet resentment of HTI's presence. Melissa suspected it had to do with fear of competition, so she tried hard to avoid delivering babies in Independence unless the midwife was out of town. It wasn't always possible, though.

One Creole couple who were members of the church in Corozal had recently moved to Independence. Their oldest daughter was 26 years old and pregnant with her third child. She was intent upon having the new white nurse deliver her baby. She arrived in labor one day at Melissa's house. She labored for a while, but her pains gradually subsided then stopped. As she readied to go home, Melissa pointed out the midwife's house and urged the pregnant woman to go there when it was time.

The next night...in the middle of the night...the young mother returned in full labor. Her family had brought all the necessary supplies with them and proceeded to spread the plastic over Celia's bed. (Celia was out of town.) Magda Sherman got out of bed and came over to Melissa's to help. Sure enough, about 4:00 in the morning the woman gave birth to a bouncing baby girl. Melissa wanted to breathe a sigh of relief but could not because she couldn't get the placenta to pass. While she worked to get it to release, she and Magda prayed that the mother would not bleed to death. Melissa knew she would be in huge trouble if that happened. The placenta finally did deliver, and the mother promptly named her new baby Magdalena Melissa, for both Magda and Melissa.

The anxiety Melissa felt was quite real. She knew that serious consequences were a reality if something went wrong, especially if the local midwife was not an ally.

Melissa went on to deliver seven babies during her time in Belize…all girls…and all of whom were named Melissa.

Evangelism Opportunities

Rodney and Marina – The team had ample opportunities to talk about spiritual matters. Melissa seized upon an early opening through her relationship with her new neighbor. The house Melissa rented happened to be next door to a couple named Rodney and Marina. They had five little boys, who immediately claimed Melissa for their own. Marina and Melissa bonded quickly and enjoyed a warm, satisfying friendship.

It began with Marina mentoring Melissa on laundry. Melissa was already well educated on the use of a scrub board, but Marina found her wanting in knowing the correct way to hang wash on the line. She politely took Melissa under her wing and proceeded to teach her that laundry was to be hung out to dry by type and length—from shortest to the longest. According to this rule, you would not necessarily hang a pair of socks together if one were longer than the other. Length would trump and determine where on the line you would hang it. Such things are important in some cultures.

As they got to know each other, Melissa learned that though Marina had been raised to be a good woman, she had no real church background and did not attend church. A major reason was that in the Belizean culture one could only become a Christian if you were married. Co-habitation was not accepted in the church. At all. She and Rodney were not married. They had never married because, also in Belizean culture, a husband must provide his wife a home…and Rodney had not been able to do that thus far. Like Melissa, they were renting their house. Eventually Rodney was able to purchase a house for his family and they got married. Melissa made the wedding veil that Marina wore in the ceremony on May 28, 1988.

While Melissa and Marina lived next door to each other, they began having religious discussions. Marina soon invited some friends over so Melissa could teach them about the Bible, too. Thus began the first of many Bible studies Melissa conducted while she was in Belize. Many others on the team had similar experiences. In addition to Bible studies, Becky Amole taught adult literacy classes. It was a very effective way to integrate into the community.

Shortly after Rodney bought the house and he and Marina were married, Marina finally became a Christian. Rodney did likewise about a year later. They eventually had a total of eight children, seven boys and one girl. Marina and some of her children are faithful servants in the church in Independence even today.

I cannot leave Rodney and Marina without sharing a touching story Melissa told me about Rodney. Rodney fished for a living, as did most of the men in the village. Each day he and others would motor out to sea in their little dinghies to catch what fish they could eat or sell. On this particular day the sky was clear and beautiful and the waters calm. They began to fish and chat from boat to boat when one of them spotted a pod of whales coming directly toward them. The men were suddenly filled with fear, knowing their little dinghies were no match against excitedly curious or aggressive whales! The whales seemed to be coming directly toward them. Their fear began to grow. With hearts pounding, to a man they lay down as low as they could in their vessels and held their breath so as to not attract undue attention. They lay there, listening to the sound of the whales approaching.

When the whales reached the boats, they swam around and around them, splashing water into the boats and onto the cowering fisherman. It was becoming clear that the whales were simply curious, but the danger of one of them upsetting their boats was still very real. Rodney heard one big one swim right up to his boat and felt it rub against the side of his boat, lingering there for a few moments. In an act of pure human emotion, Rodney quietly lifted his arm from the bottom of his boat and began to pet the whale. He could feel the whale respond to his touch. In that incredible moment Rodney said later he felt that he and the whale were alone in the universe, just the two of them. After another minute or two the whale turned suddenly and swam out to sea, with the other whales trailing. Rodney went home that day with a real "fish tale" to tell.

Margarito and the Maya Center Bible Studies – Bill Searcy tells that in his effort to bond with the people of his village, he participated in Bible studies at the Maya Center with Margarito, the local church leader. Bill was initially proud of the fact that there was always 100% attendance when he preached on Friday nights. He finally had to reluctantly admit to himself, however, that his marvelous preaching wasn't responsible...it was simply the only show in town. Everyone in town came. No matter *who* was preaching!

One week Bill was planning to preach on Philip and the Ethopian eunuch in Philippians 3:13. He asked Margarito if there was anything in the Mayan culture that related to the concept of forgetting what lies behind and reaching forward to what lies ahead. He used the example of a foot race where the runners stretch and focus all their energy on getting to the finish line. Margarito said there was such a concept, and he related the following story:

"The Maya don't understand foot races as you do, but they do go to the river to spear fish. When they spy a big fish, they chase it with all their might! They pay no attention to the cuts and scrapes they receive from rocks, sticks and logs in the water, nor do they worry about the places where snakes frequent the water. Their eyes are solely on the fish, and they use their last ounce of energy and their last breath to lunge for the fish and spear it. This final lunge that often resulted in nose bleeds is the concept of reaching forth for the prize of the upward call of God in Christ. Our brothers and sisters in Christ are like the friends on the shore correcting us and directing us to the goal."

Bill used that illustration in his sermon that night, but he modified it to acknowledge other cultural sensitivities like men needing to provide for their families. He told a story of a Mayan man named Antonio whose family was hungry, so he went fishing. Then, as he described the fishing event, he led to the idea that we stretch forth to become like Christ and onward to the resurrection. Jesus is the fish that we should focus on and lunge for.

Typically, when he was through speaking, Bill would ask Margarito what percentage of what he had preached the people understood. This night, however, he didn't have to ask because Margarito quickly volunteered that the audience had really "gotten" the message. They understood it because they had experienced it so often in their own lives. Bill thought to himself, *"Bull's-eye!"*

VBS on Steroids!

Belize was full of children. In fact Wayne Braun cited in a 1985 report that the percentage of children under the age of 20 in Belize was 58%. He noted that because of these numbers it was not surprising that fully two-thirds of those in attendance at the Corozal church at that time were children. This sheer size of this number of children prompted the next Bible-teaching effort: Vacation Bible School.

Some things just stay with you...like this children's song:

> *Father Abraham had many sons*
> *Many sons had Father Abraham*
> *And I am one of them*
> *And so are you*
> *So let's just praise the Lord!*
> *Right arm...*

This song will forever take me back...to 1986 and the Church of Christ in Independence, Belize. The little church was filled with a sea of Belizean children singing at the top of their lungs! Every day at the start of our VBS program we would sing all six long verses, and when we finished the last verse, we would fall into our seats exhausted!

What ultimately turned out to be one of the longest-lasting and most effective ministries ever in Belize started out without a lot of fanfare. Observing that there were very few activities for children during their summer vacation, the first malaria control teachers taught a Vacation Bible School in Corozal in 1984. It was not pre-planned, but rather cobbled together at the last minute. All the supplies had to be bought in Corozal, and the flannel graph figures were made from Pellon®, the interfacing fabric for sewing garments. The VBS lasted one week with a daily attendance ranging from 50 to 70. It was wildly successful.

Quiet, mild-mannered Thomas Meade made his debut as assembly leader, and teachers Karen Hicks, Melissa Redding, Becky Amole, Kristi York, and Jane and Randall Harley did the teaching. Bill Searcy, Jeanine Content, and Linda Crooks helped wherever they were needed.

Because this first attempt had been so successful, Magda Sherman and Carolyn Maddux conceived the idea of inviting churches from the U.S. to bring VBS teams the next summer. Since Belize was an English-speaking country, language would not be a problem. The advantages seemed obvious. The first advantage would be to provide an opportunity for U.S. church members to experience mission work firsthand. Secondly, they would get a better understanding of Health Talents and its ministry in Belize. It was a win/win idea for all.

They invited only a few Churches of Christ to take part in 1985: Otter Creek in Nashville, Meadowbrook in Jackson, Mississippi, and Highland and White Station in Memphis. Taking a week each, these churches conducted Vacation Bible School for an entire month at the Corozal Church of Christ. Carolyn Maddux from Otter Creek agreed to be the coordinator from the States, and Becky Amole assumed the role of Belizean coordinator. Magda served in every way she possibly could. She ran errands, gathered supplies, hauled people and on and on— always with precious baby Lisa in tow. Frank Maddux volunteered to be the chief cook and bottle washer for the entire month. This turned out to be way too big a task for one person. Carolyn later wrote a comprehensive summary of the summer, which I will summarize here:

Carolyn opened her 1985 VBS report by saying that *"We wanted to show that a relationship with God can be very real and can make you different, but not weird."* They wanted to emphasize God's love for the world. The teachers wanted the children to know that whether or not you have lots of money or only a little, God loves you; whether you have an advanced education or almost no education, God loves you; whether you live in a big house or a little house…God loves you. He just loves you, and He wants you to be with Him.

Another goal for VBS was to make it an encompassing experience for the children, not just two hours of structured Bible lessons each morning. The visiting teams wanted to share their lives for the whole week. With a different group coming in each week, the lessons might be different, but they were all about the same Jesus. The common theme throughout the month was "Jesus, Our Champion." They used a variety of activities to stress being a champion for Jesus.

First, there was singing. Oh, my, was there singing! As I mentioned earlier, my fondest memories with the children was how much they enjoyed singing. Carolyn felt the same way. She remembered that the teachers taught the students songs, but the students also taught the teachers some, like "Alabare." It is a simple song in Spanish with a great message about the apostle John seeing a number of the redeemed. There was also one about the King and flags:

> *There's a flag flying high in the castle of my heart*
> *when the King is a resident there.*
> *Fly it high in the sky, let the whole world know*
> *that the King is a resident there.*

Secondly, there were puppet shows and Bible stories. That first year the Corozal VBS rented space in a large building next door to the church. The rooms were small—the noise level high. There were so many children that every class was huge! One class had 36 kids in an 8' x 10' room. Becky Amole had the smallest classroom…5' x 10', yet every day she somehow managed to make space for 16 to 18 children.

Even this large building couldn't hold all the children when they divided into classes. So after the singing and puppet shows, everyone would pitch in to move the benches out of the building and under the trees. These outdoor classes actually turned out to be the most efficient classroom space: less noise and more room. There was a daily concern about rain, but it fortunately held off until the afternoon each day. The morning classes lasted an hour, when they had to reverse the moving process to shift back inside for assembly and break time.

Belizean kids are no different from kids in the U.S. They think that the best part of a good VBS is the refreshments. They were not disappointed. During that first VBS, Marge Keedy from Otter Creek in Nashville baked cookies or brownies every night, then served them to the children the next morning with Kool-Aid to wash them down. This was no small undertaking, because anywhere between 100 and 150 children came every day for VBS.

One day the teachers learned about a local treat that the children loved, called Ideals. These were a frozen fruit-flavored ice (similar to frozen Kool-Aid) packaged in a sandwich-type baggie. The children would tear out one of the corners with their teeth then proceed to suck the ice out as it melted. The teachers asked Randolph Baptist, the preacher at Corozal, about them, so one day he bought Ideals for the snack. They became the regular snack after that, although the Marge-made brownies served with reconstituted dry milk were without a doubt the most popular snack of all.

The children were so excited about all that was happening that even when VBS was over in time for lunch, some of them never went home. One young boy named Junior was one of them. At nine years of age, he seemed very sad and neglected. He would not talk or smile when VBS started, but he hung around the team members constantly. He would attach himself to one of them each morning and would stay with that person from breakfast until they made him go home at 10:00, 11:00 or even midnight.

All that personal attention paid off for him. By the end of the month, he was talking and laughing all day. Everyone began to realize how smart he was, and they discovered he spoke three languages. They had already recognized how polite and appreciative he was. His mother seemed to look at him with new eyes when she saw how the others took to him. Randolph Baptist took him under his wing, and Carolyn left wondering what the Lord would do with Junior in the future.

Besides VBS time there was afternoon organized game time where they played volleyball (with a string stretched between two trees for a net) or baseball (where they used a wiffle ball, a 2"x4" for a bat and coconuts for bases!) Sometimes the teachers taught hygiene lessons and even shampooed heads for lice.

Drugs were a big problem in this community, so it was heartening that the two most popular and effective activities among the teenagers were the coffeehouse and the Corozal Chorus. Three nights a week the teenagers in Corozal were invited to come to

Nestor's Hotel. And come they did—about 40 to 60 each night. Here they enjoyed activities like movies, games, puppet shows (both watching and performing) and singing. During the third week, Pam Watkins from Nashville organized a teen chorus and taught them four-part harmony. On Thursday night of that week, then again by popular demand on Friday morning, they gave public performances.

Carolyn said that she and the others believed that the coffeehouse was particularly effective in making their presence known in the community. By the end of the month, in addition to the crowd of teens, many of their parents stood in the entryway to watch. Afterward, they would talk with the teachers about the films, VBS and the church.

Some of the other activities focused on adults themselves, such as literacy training, Bible studies, and the showing of the Faulkner-Brecheen Marriage Enrichment Series.

By 1986 HTI was really growing, and Charles Bates was finding it difficult to balance his regular job as a Research Metallurgist at Southern Research with the day-to-day activities of Health Talents. The Board decided it was time to give Charles some relief. The HTI Board asked Mike Cobb to be the Stateside Coordinator for Health Talents. Along with his wife Glenda, Mike had been on the first malaria control team. He attended the Cahaba Valley Church of Christ in Birmingham, Alabama, as I did. When Mike began talking about taking a team from our church to participate in the VBS program in 1986, my family and I once again jumped onboard. I didn't have to be talked into it this time.

That summer the HTI team in Belize expanded the program to include Independence and Punta Gorda in southern Belize, where they had all just moved. Cahaba Valley was scheduled to go to Independence. Our team flew from New Orleans on TACA Airline, which we commonly referred to as *"Take a Chance Airline!"* That was similar to the popular moniker for SAHSA Airline, a Honduran line: *"Stay at home...stay alive!"*

In addition to the original four teams and Cahaba Valley, groups from two other churches came that year: Decatur Church of Christ in Atlanta, and Park Row from Dallas. The original four teams went back to Corozal, while Cahaba Valley, Park Row and White Station went to Independence. Small teams made up of some team members from Cahaba Valley and the HTI ministry team went to Punta Gorda. All in all, the Belizean children enjoyed nine weeks of VBS that summer.

Above and below: VBS in Independence

The size of the visiting teams varied. We had 19 on our team, but some had as many as 30. Ours was made up of half teenagers and half adults, with two younger children along with their parents. Unlike Corozal where hotels were available for housing the teams, the Independence and Punta Gorda teams stayed in private homes. Jean Enochs received the "Golden Houseparent" award for housing four teenage girls from our team!

We also gave Ideals to the children as snacks. There were a couple of downsides to them, I remember. One was that when the children finished sucking all the sweetness out of the baggie, they simply tossed the empty baggie on the ground. What a mess! We instituted a new daily activity: picking up the trash around the church building. (It never really caught on as a fun activity, as you might guess.) The second downside was that most of the children had rotten front teeth from all that sugar.

Friday Night Youth Nights

Another activity that arose very naturally with the permanent Belize team that lived in Independence was Friday night youth night. Melissa and Celia began inviting the teenage girls from the church to their house every Friday night to hang out. About six of them would come every week. While they were there they would cook supper together, sing, do crafts, study the Bible, paint fingernails, and do all manner of girl stuff. Week after week they would come. Week after week Melissa and Celia made ready for them. Teck and Wayne did the same thing for the teenage boys, although I doubt they painted fingernails.

These youth nights were invaluable. They provided a forum for all kinds of discussion, religious and otherwise, and in the process created lifelong friendships. Many of these young people became strong Christians and are the backbone of the church in Independence today. Melissa remembers Alita, in particular.

Melissa first met Alita when Alita was only seven years old. Although wet and filthy from doing laundry by the side of a dirt road, Alita was smiling and waving when Melissa arrived at her house. Alita's mother was one of the CHWs, and Melissa had come to meet with her. Alita and Melissa bonded immediately and had many adventures together through the years, including the many Friday evenings that Alita spent at Melissa and Celia's house for Youth Night. Alita was smart as a little whip at only 4 feet tall, and

Melissa found her to be a special young lady. Melissa eventually came to believe that Alita was the reason God sent her to Belize. Melissa said, "*It wasn't all easy. But it was all joy.*"

Melissa with Alita and Kevin Joyce

Alita was baptized at the age of 15 during the 1992 Vacation Bible School in Independence. Because of Melissa's influence, Alita eventually went to high school then on to St. John's College in Belize City. She married a young man named Kevin Joyce from Nashville, who had been working with the church in Independence while she was in college. She and her husband now have a family of their own. They are faithful members of the church and are raising their children in the Lord.

Alita is only one example of many changed lives in Belize. She is who she is today by the grace of God… and because HTI and Melissa went to Belize.

Children's Ministry in Summary

Looking back it is clear that VBS was a brilliant idea. At its height 14 different congregations sent teams into Belize, some multiple times. It is important to note, how-ever, that the VBS program continued for some time after HTI left the area. The effort clearly had a positive effect on participating stateside church members and their teens. Aubry Burr from the Meadowbrook Church of Christ had been a regular on her church's team for a few years. Belize meant so much to her that when she made the decision to be baptized, she wanted to be baptized there. She later served with HTI in Guatemala.

In Belize VBS accomplished good on so many levels that were critical. In a country where the HTI team soon learned it was not socially acceptable for men to be religious, the challenge to bring Christ to the area was huge. In an area of the country indifferent at best to religion, it was a start. If you can reach the children, you plant seeds for the future. That is exactly what ultimately happened.

The church in Belize today, especially in Independence where the team spent so many years, is populated with many of the children who grew up going to Vacation Bible School week after week during the summer and to Friday Youth Nights at Melissa and Celia's house and Wayne's house. As Jesus himself said, *"Let the little children come to me."*

Belize Epilogue

Wayne Braun was the last team member to leave. Melissa went home in February 1990 and Russel later that same year, but Wayne continued on. He moved to Belmopan in 1992 with his soon-to-be-adopted son, Leland. When the adoption process was complete, he returned to his native Seminole, Texas.

Steve and Magda had been the first to leave in late 1988, after completing five full years of service in Belize. They moved back to Guatemala but were in the States in January 1989 for the birth of Amy, their third daughter. She joined sisters Lisa and Sarah.

The others returned to the States to pick up their lives where they had left off. Teck and Debra went to Harding so Teck could finish his degree; Melissa got her nurse practitioner degree; Celia moved to Honduras to work with *Predisan;* and Bill and Kathy Searcy eventually moved to Kenya with their three children. Bill chose to stay and raise their three children there after Kathy was tragically killed in an automobile accident. The Jacksons returned home to Indiana and Becky Amole to Missouri. She later married a Belizean man. Jean went back to the States but continued her work on the community health worker's manual that the government had requested. When she completed it, HTI sent numerous copies back to Belize where we understand it is still being used today.

Everyone took home with them the feeling that they had made a difference. Though it had been a long and sometimes difficult five years, with baptisms coming fewer and further between than they would have liked, the team left knowing their efforts to minister spiritually as well as physically had paid off. The strength of the church in Independence today is testament to that. Not only is the church strong both in theology and numbers, with the help of the Park Row Church of Christ in Arlington, Texas, it started its own primary school that is still functioning today.

Additionally, they felt confident that Belizeans had benefitted from the educational programs they conducted. Both the malaria training and the Community Health Worker training programs impacted the quality of life for many. In fact, just before leaving Belize Steve received a letter from Dr. Vanzie, the Chief Medical Officer of Belize, saying just that. He thanked the HTI team for their service and for the good they had done in Belize. He also referenced the great relationship that the HTI team and the Ministry of Health had enjoyed. Having been on the front line for the past five years, Steve and Magda took personal satisfaction in knowing that the Ministry of Health was pleased with their efforts.

Chapter 6:
Back to Guatemala...from Rural to Urban

1989-2002

Clinica Promesa

Guatemala's civil war was now in full swing. The newspaper was filled with stories of bridges being blown up, villages decimated, and people dying. By now much of the violence had spread to the countryside rather than the city. Many times it was impossible to tell which faction was worse: the guerrillas or the army. Regardless, the Mayan Indians were caught in the middle. No matter what the prize of war might have been...they were the victims and they paid the price.

To escape the unrelenting violence, Mayan Indians began moving in droves to Guatemala City. Steve and Magda Sherman had become aware of this during their frequent visits to Magda's family. As the five-year contract with the Belize Ministry of Health drew to a close, Steve and Magda began to consider returning to Magda's home country, in part because of a letter they had received from Nery Castillo the year before. An elder in the Zone 12 Iglesia de Cristo in Guatemala City, Nery had written asking them to return to help the church. The influx of refugees was becoming a major challenge, and the church leaders felt that a medical evangelism clinic would help them better respond.

Steve discussed the possibilities with the HTI Board. In August 1988 he, Jon Jernigan and Dr. Irene Gordon traveled to Guatemala to survey the situation. They returned convinced that the idea of operating an urban medical evangelism clinic in conjunction with the Zone 12 church had merit. They wrote a proposal to present to the Board. Steve knew it would be a stretch for the Board because HTI had no experience with an urban clinic. To bolster his case, he included four specific rationales:

1) The Zone 12 church was experiencing revived energy because of the influx of refugees from the countryside.
2) There was a huge middle class gap in the Guatemala City religious community. Most churches in Guatemala were simply too poor to put forth effective ministries.
3) The people of Guatemala were in the midst of a great religious conversion. Steve said in his proposal that every four minutes a Guatemalan was converting from Catholicism to Protestantism.
4) The Zone 12 Iglesia de Cristo was serious about proceeding with this plan. They had already purchased a dilapidated school in a centrally located part of town that would allow for growth and better position them to minister to the refugees.

In November 1988, Steve presented his case, citing facts and figures about how an urban clinic could reach more people and meet more needs than a rural clinic could. He pointed out that in many cases, because of the shifting demographics, the patient population would be the same.

The Board listened carefully and in the end agreed to adopt Steve's proposal. Mike Cobb announced it in the April 1989 *Mission Moments* newsletter. It was to be a partnership with what would become the Zone 11 Iglesia de Cristo after the Zone 12 church moved to its new location. Nery agreed to be HTI's government representative.

HTI Board in Guatemala to formalize agreement with Zone 11 church

Steve and Magda moved to Guatemala in late 1989 and spent the first few days trying to determine if it would be feasible to re-open the Las Cruces clinic. That proved to be inadvisable because the area was still too unstable.

Within Health Talents, everybody felt it; it was good to be back in Guatemala. Excitement was rising about an urban clinic, but there was much to do. After again ruling out re-opening the Las Cruces clinic, Steve's first task was to find the best location for the new clinic. He surveyed the area and found a suitable building to rent in the block behind the Zone 11 church's newly-acquired property. Steve discovered in his research that this medical clinic would be the only one in a 20-block radius.

The building needed work, so Steve set about remodeling it…just as he had ten years before in Las Cruces. He brought not only that experience with him but as much material from the Las Cruces clinic as he could. He hauled windows, doors, and cabinets down from Las Cruces and installed them in the new clinic.

Steve and Magda searched for a name for the clinic to reflect the promise we have in Christ—one that would send out a message of hope to all who came. They settled on *Clinica Promesa*...Clinic of Promise. The clinic's mission would again be that same three-legged stool of health promotion, disease prevention and curative services, wrapped in spiritual caring. They would, of course, once again train health promoters.

But what is a clinic without a doctor? Steve found one. She was a pretty, dark-haired young woman named Dr. Luz Esperanza. He also hired a young man in the church who was still in medical school. Sergio Castillo was Nery's younger brother. Sergio agreed to work part time as his schedule allowed until he graduated in 1990. Soon afterward Dr. Raul Chenal joined the team as its first dentist. With these personnel in place, the clinic opened in October 1989.

Clinica Promesa in Zone 11 Guatemala City

Word spread quickly. In no time at all patients began streaming into the Clinic of Promise. By March 1990 Dr. Esperanza had begun training seven community health promoters in the basics of health care.

In the spring of 1990 measles came to Guatemala. Measles can be deadly in marginalized populations where there is severe malnutrition and poor sanitation. That represented much of Guatemala. It was common knowledge, confirmed repeatedly by nutrition studies, that child malnutrition in Guatemala was the worst in Central America. Thus, thousands of children were infected with measles and many died. The Ministry of Health was in a tight spot. Although they had an ample supply of measles vaccine that had been donated by World Vision, they did not have the needles and syringes to administer it. They turned to the multitude of non-profits working in Guatemala and asked for help.

HTI supporters responded generously. Almost immediately we were able to send $10,000 to Guatemala to buy needles. This brought the clinic appreciative recognition from the government. Clinica Promesa then began holding vaccination clinics to help.

Things settled down once the measles crisis was over, and by late summer the Promesa team began to identify sites for mobile clinics. By fall they had selected four. In the last quarter of 1990 they began seeing patients in those sites one day a week, while continuing to see patients at Clinica Promesa four days a week.

I have mentioned before the value of mobile clinics. Time, distance and money often kept people from seeking the medical help they needed. Many lived so far out of town that they had to walk a mile or two just to catch a bus into town, then change buses to get to the clinic. When they chose not to make this trek, their physical maladies often become worse. In the most serious cases, by the time they sought treatment it was too late. There was much resistance to being hospitalized. The perception of most of the Maya was that one only went to the hospital to die. They believed this because, in truth, most of the people they knew who had gone to the hospital had died there.

An advantage from the spiritual perspective was that mobile clinics provided the opportunity to get local churches involved. HTI's policy was to hold clinic in local Churches of Christ wherever possible so the physical/spiritual connection would be apparent to all. Having the clinic in a church and with some of its members present to talk and pray with patients did two things: it gave the medical clinic credibility in the community and, even more importantly, raised the visibility of the local congregation. This helped to change the perception of the church from being only a place of worship to being a place of refuge, a source of help. This opened the door for local follow-up. We had seen this played out in dramatic ways in Las Cruces.

Halfway through that first year, Dr. Esperanza resigned and moved to California, leaving Dr. Sergio Castillo to become medical director. Even with this unexpected event, by the end of the first year of Clinica Promesa's operation, Drs. Esperanza, Castillo and Chenal had together treated more than 5,000 patients.

Changing of the Guard Stateside

In early 1989 HTI Coordinator Mike Cobb and his wife Glenda learned they were going to have a child, so Mike notified the HTI Board that he wanted to resign. His position as the stateside coordinator for Health Talents for the previous three years had required a great deal of travel. Neither he nor Glenda felt that would be acceptable after the baby came.

With this news, the Board began the search for a new coordinator. I mentioned it to my minister at Cahaba Valley at the time, Robert Montgomery. He immediately said, *"Why don't you apply for Mike's job?"* I responded, *"Robert, in case you haven't noticed, I am a woman."* Robert immediately came back with one word, *"So?"* I quickly added, *"They aren't going to hire a woman."*

The next morning Charles stopped by my house to drop off some work, and I told him what Robert had said. (Here is where Charles and I have different memories of this exchange.) I remember Charles looking very uncomfortable and abruptly excusing himself and walking out the door. The next morning, however, he returned. He walked in my front door and said very strongly, *"Robert is absolutely right. There is no one better for this position than you. I am putting your name up for the job!"*

I was a reluctant applicant. During my official interview, I kept protesting. *"What about meeting with elders across the country? What about mission committee meetings? What about speaking in churches? No woman in the Church of Christ has ever tried to do a job like this. How are we going to do this?"* After I'd exhausted all my defenses, they held fast. They told me, *"Do all that you can do. When you need help, let us know and one of us will be there to help you."*

The next thing I knew, the Board voted unanimously to hire me as Mike's replacement. My first day of work was to be June 1, 1989. This would be only two days after Joanna, my youngest child, graduated from high school. The timing of this whole thing was unbelievable. My desire from as far back as I can remember was to be a stay-at-home mom as my mother had been. Although I had held many part-time positions and volunteered extensively in both my church and the children's schools, I had never worked full time from the time my son David was born. The incredible timing of this convinced me that it was meant to be.

The ABC Program

Her name was Osiris. She was a tiny, black-haired Mayan girl whose body was wracked with hepatitis when her father brought her to Clinica Promesa one day in early 1990.

José Cayax arrived with Osiris in his arms and several other children in tow. At two years of age, Osiris was the youngest. As Dr. Sergio examined Osiris, José told his story. He had brought his family into the city seeking refuge from the violence in the countryside. When his wife died suddenly of pneumonia, he was left with five little children to raise alone. The only work he could find was filling potholes in roads for a mere $1 a day. His oldest son, fourteen-year-old Wilfrido, was working, too. He earned $1.43 a day as a servant in a private home. Erilda was his second child, and though only nine years old she acted as mother for the family, cooking meals and looking after her younger siblings. They were living in a cardboard shack in a slum area of Guatemala City.

Jose Cayax and his children in front of a later house

Magda was there when José came in, and the sight touched her deeply. The plight of this small, illiterate man trying desperately to care for his motherless children brought tears to her eyes and pain to her heart. It drew forth in her a resolve to help him, and in so doing reactivated a long-held dream.

Before she came to work for Health Talents, she had been employed by World Vision in Guatemala City, where she worked with their child sponsorship program. As inexperienced as she had been at the time, she kept imagining other ways to conduct such a program. As she considered Jose's situation, these thoughts resurfaced in her mind. And with that, the ABC program was born. ABC is a Spanish acronym for the aid and benefit of Christian families: Ayudar y Bienstar de las Familias de Cristianas.

Magda outlined the basic goals of the program and shared them with Ana Virginia Castillo, wife of Nery Castillo, and Carolyn Maddux. Carolyn was on the Missions Committee at the Sherman's sponsoring church, the Otter Creek Church of Christ in Nashville. Magda and Ana Virginia co-directed the program for a time. Carolyn proved to be a staunch supporter and faithful advocate of the ABC program until her death many years later.

Their first resolve was that the program be spiritually based. Knowing there were literally millions of destitute children in Guatemala, they had manageability concerns. It became clear that the best way to stress spiritual growth yet maintain manageability was to limit acceptance to children of members of the Church of Christ in Guatemala. The overall goal was simple. ABC would provide three basic things: sustenance and regular medical and dental care so children could thrive physically, an education through regular school attendance, and a spiritually nourishing church community.

They knew that these three things combined would greatly increase a child's chance of growing up to be a self-supporting adult. Their underlying hope was to break the cycle of poverty in the Church of Christ in Guatemala. They knew that with more resources, the local church could broaden its efforts to serve others. In so doing, they would see the church's influence magnified in the community. Long term, the ABC program could literally change the face of the church in Guatemala.

Magda and Carolyn knew the best way to fund the program was to offer Christians in the United States the opportunity to serve as sponsors. They would make it clear that ABC children were not orphans, but rather children of struggling parents. Most of these parents were illiterate and working at manual labor jobs for a pittance.

What made the structure of the ABC program different from most child sponsorship programs was that in order for a child to be accepted into the program, the parents had to make certain commitments. Since the basic core of ABC was spiritual, the first requirement was that the parents had to commit that their family would continue to be a part of their local Church of Christ. If they did not, their child would be removed from the program. HTI believed deeply that the spiritual training the children received at church was central to long-term success in life. This training would help children to learn who they are...and *whose they are*. The confidence they gained through this knowledge would serve them well.

The second major commitment was that parents had to promise to keep their child in school. This, too, was critical because it would ensure their child would learn the basic skills required to become self-supporting.

The third commitment was that their child would keep the required twice-a-year medical and dental checkup appointments. Through this he would receive preventive care in the form of immunizations and dental cleanings.

Like every successful program, ABC included incentives. Upon registering in the ABC program, each child was given a notebook to record his progress throughout the year. The children carried their book with them to dental and medical visits so their visits would be recorded. Their school teachers likewise recorded their grades and attitudes at school. Church leaders would make similar notes about church attendance and attitude.

Students earned points throughout the year in each of these categories as well as points for writing thank you letters to their sponsors. It is important to note that each student competed only against himself. The greater number of points a child accumulated, the bigger the prize he could win. At the end of each year the ABC staff in Guatemala City tallied each child's points. The big day was the annual Christmas party where all the ABC children and their families gathered for the presentation of prizes won!

I know, you're thinking dolls, soccer balls, or iPods. Granted, there was the occasional bicycle. The actual prizes the children received, however, were more likely to be new backpacks for school, a bed to sleep in, or a dresser to store their clothes in. What was exciting about this, you might ask. It's all a matter of perspective. Many children in ABC slept in hammocks because they didn't have a bed. What few clothes they had were simply stacked in a corner because they had no dresser. The children took pride in winning such a valuable prize for their family. It was no surprise that the children were motivated.

These basic parental commitments proved to be winners, especially the one about keeping a child in school. In the Mayan communities particularly, children frequently dropped out of school after third grade in order to work in the coffee fields to help provide for the family. With the ABC program providing a monthly food allowance, the parents felt free to allow the children to stay in school. Not surprisingly, there were still children who did not want to go to school and who tried to quit. We were ecstatic when we began getting reports of parents *insisting* their children stay in school so they could continue to get the help that ABC provided. This had rarely happened in the Mayan community!

The medical and dental help the children received proved invaluable. As time went by it became obvious that the ABC children had better teeth and physical conditions than other children in their villages. In one dramatic case ABC played a vital role in getting a little boy a kidney transplant. In others ABC was able to arrange for cancer treatment. Had it not been for the ABC program, we might never have heard of these seriously ill children.

The ABC food subsidies helped tremendously as well. Because most ABC families subsisted on only $30 to $50 a month, many ABC families' daily diet consisted of only rice and beans (or less). The added sustenance and milk that ABC sponsors provided most likely averted untold numbers of cases of severe malnutrition.

Christians in the United States eagerly accepted the ABC program and continue to do so today. The program began with only 20 children from 1 congregation and has expanded to more than 750 children in 37 congregations in 2013. The internal ABC structure has been refined and strengthened through the years. Local church leaders in Guatemala are more involved and more keenly aware of the responsibility they have to mentor the children to adulthood. They have eagerly accepted that role.

Overall, the ABC program has been a resounding success, from basic education to spiritual care. In village after village children are graduating from high school where none had ever done so before. White-headed church leader Don Pablo is the ABC coordinator in San Basilio. He told Board member Harriette Shivers, Charles Campbell and me when we visited there several years ago about five students from his village who were graduating from high school that year. His eyes welled up with tears as he said, *"No one from here has ever been able to do that before! Finally, someone from San Basilio will grow up to be something besides a ditch digger."*

Alex Gonzalez was one of our first shining ABC stars. He and his two siblings were indeed orphans when they went to live with their grandmother after the deaths of their parents. Their father had been killed in a car wreck, then six months later their mother died from cancer. The grandmother lived near the Zone 18 Iglesia de Cristo in Guatemala City, so the children began attending services there. With his twinkling eyes and pleasant personality, Alex became a leader in the youth group. When he graduated from high school, he applied for a Bates Scholarship that would allow him to go to dental school. One year into dental school he knew that it was not for him. But because the scholarship program required him to work for HTI one year for each year of scholarship, he began working in the HTI office in Guatemala City.

It wasn't long before everyone was impressed by his work ethic. When his first year was up they offered him a job, and he has been with us ever since. He is now HTI's Director of Finance in Guatemala.

Nidian Patricia Poz is another former ABC child. She will be graduating from medical school soon, and this is no small feat. As a Quiche woman in Guatemala, the chance of her accomplishing her life's dream of becoming a doctor without help was miniscule. Truly ABC is making a difference.

Visiting Mobile Medical Teams Begin

Things were rocking right along at Clinica Promesa. The medical team was treating patients both at the base clinic in Zone 11 and in mobile clinics. They soon noticed a consistent pattern. There were always huge crowds when they held mobile clinics. Steve and Magda began to think that perhaps the time was right to carry out another basic tenet of Health Talents…that of providing opportunities for North American Christians to use their talents in service to God.

As we clearly saw with the Belize VBS ministry, there are advantages to occasionally bringing in teams of U.S. volunteers. Hosting teams of medical professionals meant that more patients would receive the medical treatment they needed. Secondly, it would provide opportunities for medical professionals to use their God-given talents in medical evangelism. This "giving back" enhances one's relationship with God in a way few other things can. The third was less obvious but no less important. Visiting team members would see firsthand the need that exists for medical evangelism. Hopefully, once they saw it they would be more willing to support it.

The Board set a target date for the first clinic: November 6-14, 1990. The Board approved it, and I set out to recruit a team.

My first attempt was at the Abilene Christian lectureship in Abilene, Texas. I was armed with shiny new trip brochures, and I was ready. I remember expecting to have to beg and grovel to get people to sign up. But, boy was I wrong! The very first person I "accosted" was Dr. Jim Haller, a dentist who lived in Abilene.

I made my pitch and stepped back…ready to counter the resistance that would surely come. After all, I was asking him to commit a week of his life to do what he does in comfort in Abilene…in a totally unfamiliar and uncomfortable setting. I was asking him to travel to Guatemala to practice dentistry without the guarantee of electricity, comfortable chairs, or even adequate supplies. Oh, and on top of that, he wouldn't be able to drink the water.

God had clearly heard my prayers as I handed Dr. Haller a brochure. He read it carefully, asked me a question or two then said, "Where do I sign up?"

Dr. Jim and his wife Barbara have gone on HTI trips every year since then. They even brought

Dr. Jim Haller holding one of the first teeth he pulled in Guatemala

their airline pilot son, Rob, along on several occasions. They have been some of our most loyal team members. I will be forever grateful to Jim, though, for responding positively that day because it taught me a lesson. People want to serve God...and will respond positively when they are made aware of specific needs and of concrete things they can do to make a difference. That meeting with Jim that day in Abilene empowered my personal ministry in a dramatic way. I was able to move forward with confidence to recruit the rest of the team.

First Mobile Medical Team Arrives

On November 6, 1990, the first of HTI's visiting mobile medical teams arrived in Guatemala. Because it was a symbolic beginning of a new outreach, it seems fitting to list the names of those hardy souls who signed on. Dr. Jim and Barbara Haller were there, of course, along with HTI Board members cardiologist Dr. Quinton Dickerson, gastroenterologist Dr. Billy Long, and periodontist Dr. John Peden. Other medical doctors on the team were Drs. Steve McCormick, Rick Carlton, Eric (and Kris) Fortmeyer, Jim (and Annette) McCauley, Timothy North, and Harold (and Fran) Sutton. The dentists included Drs. Conrad Whitefield (and son Mark), Jim Grigsby, and Robert (and Mary Lou) Shumaker. Dental hygienists/assistants Susan Gulley and Renee Hopkins had come to help Dr. Peden. Optometrist Dr. Van Smith came with his teenage daughter Ashley. Non-medical team members included Rick and Susan Harper, Joe Belew, Bill Robertson, and Lipscomb Biology professor Dr. Willis Owens. I was team leader.

When we arrived in Guatemala, Steve and Magda welcomed us with great warmth. They had arranged for a Clark Tours bus that took us to the Sheraton Hotel where we spent a short night. The next morning we left the hotel at 5:15 for the drive up to Chocolá. We had never heard of Chocolá and we were all excited, yet nervous. Only a few of us had ever done anything like this before.

Guatemala was still involved in an escalating civil war, but few of us knew much about it. That ignorance didn't last long. As we made the drive in the early morning light, we drove past a bridge that had recently been blown up by guerrillas. It was one of the few pieces of physical evidence our group would see of the turmoil going on in Guatemala that was largely unseen by the outside world.

The drive took four hours. We divided into three groups for clinic. The largest of these was held at the school in Chocolá. I remember the crowds were huge. The doctors had to have two translators each…one to translate English to Spanish…and another to translate Spanish into the Mayan Quiche…and vice versa. It was cumbersome to say the least, but the patients were welcoming and kind so that made it easier.

People came with all types of maladies, many of which we commonly suffer from here—things like upper respiratory infections, arthritis and cancer. Still others came with malaria, worms and tuberculosis. I remember a 14-year-old girl with a badly clubbed foot. Her foot was so badly twisted she could barely walk. But she was still smiling.

A patient I will never forget is one whom I affectionately remember as "Wife on a Rope." Dr. Quinton Dickerson and I were with Dr. Mike Kelly in the tiny pueblo of San Juan Moca, and Quinton was seeing patients on the front porch of Armando's house, one of Mike's health promoters. The house was small with a wide, covered front porch surrounded by trees that created a gentle breeze. The yard in front was filled with nursing mothers sitting on wooden benches, toddlers toddling around and older children climbing trees. The noise level was high.

All of a sudden, people took off running in every direction, the kids in the trees climbed higher, and a hush settled over the area. The courtyard was empty. Quinton and I looked at Mike questioningly. Mike quietly replied, *"The crazy lady is coming."*

Suddenly a young woman charged out of the forest into the clearing with a haunted look on her face. She appeared to be about 20 years of age. A much older man followed about six feet behind her, holding the end of a rope. Our eyes naturally followed that rope. We were shocked to see it tied around the waist of the young woman.

Mike explained that the man's wife had died, leaving him with several children. About a year ago he had married this young woman. She had recently given birth to twin girls, and then almost immediately began having schizophrenic-like symptoms. She had begun stripping off her clothes and standing out in the middle of the road throwing rocks at her neighbors. She was clearly unable to care for herself or her infant girls. Mike had asked the husband to bring her to see him that day so he could give her some Haldol.

Watching Mike as he talked with the husband filled my heart. He was so tender and kind. The husband held on to the rope and kept a watchful eye on his wife as he listened to Mike. When Mike finished his presentation, he prayed with the man. The husband was clearly grateful, not only for the medicine but for the kindness and respect he felt from Mike. I have never seen this couple again, but I have never forgotten them. They symbolize to me the very real harshness of life that exists in the world and the extent people will go to in order to cope when coping is all there is left to do. Whenever I hear someone complain at length about some small medical problem, I find myself remembering the "wife on a rope."

Fiesta in Xejuyup

We worked hard all day on the little sleep we'd had the night before, and before we knew it, it was dinnertime. It was then we learned we were to be the honored guests of the village of Xejuyup, where Dr. Mike Kelly's clinic was.

It was nearly dark by the time our pickups made the slow climb up the steep mountain to Xejuyup. When we arrived, we were greeted by a sea of color! What a wonderfully warm welcome it was! The sea of Mayan Indians awaiting our arrival seemed endless, with the women dressed in their traditional brightly colored *juipiles* (blouses) and *faltas* (skirts) and the men in their plaid woolen skirts and sandals.

Smiles are universal, which was a good thing because no one spoke English and only a few Spanish. Most spoke only Quiche, and none of us spoke that. As we were greeted from every direction, people began pressing bowls of hot soup into our hands. Upon examining mine, I recognized beef chunks, onion and carrots, but there was another vegetable that I'd never seen before. It looked a little like a potato. I later learned it was a relative of squash and a member of the gourd family. It was called *güisquil* (pronounced wees-queel). With my first bite I discovered it was delicious and have loved it ever since.

I saw that there weren't enough bowls to go around, so I hurriedly finished my soup and gave my empty bowl to one of the men standing nearby. He nodded in thanks as he grabbed a cloth to wipe out the bowl and clean off the spoon. He quickly refilled it…and handed it to someone else. *Gulp*. I was glad I had eaten first. At least I think I had.

The next challenge was where to spend the night. Not to worry. Dr. Kelly had it all arranged. We drove back down the mountain to Santo Tomás, the town at the base of the mountain. Unlike Xejuyup, Santo Tomás was a ladino town. It was much larger and even had a town square, which is where most of the team spent the night.

I was among the fortunate few escorted to local homes to sleep in a real bed. The others literally settled down for the night in the center of town on a concrete pad that had a half wall and a chain link fence around it. They went to sleep under the buzz of mosquitoes and watchful eyes of half the town!

It was a long night and a relief when morning eventually came. We drove back up the mountain to hold clinic in the community center in Xejuyup. Local church members had already hung blue plastic sheets to create exam cubicles. The cavernous room had a stage at one end that we used for the dental clinic and the pharmacy. Dental was on one side…pharmacy on the other. We did this to help with crowd control. Rather than pressing in on the workers out of curiosity or waving their prescriptions, patients awaiting their turn in the dental chair or medicine stood on the floor below the stage.

Once we got everything settled, I had a chance to look around. I recognized people I had seen the night before, and I was again almost overcome by the beauty of it all. In the midst of such obvious poverty, they appeared anything but poverty stricken dressed in their lovely traditional clothing. Sadly, this was merely an illusion. Beyond their big smiles I couldn't help but notice that most of them had teeth missing.

Xejuyup family waiting to see a doctor

Halfway through the morning I felt a moment of panic. A Guatemalan army squad of a dozen or so men dressed in camouflage came in through the main door, bearing big military firearms. Having just seen the blown-up bridge, I was frantically wondering why they were here! I watched as Pancho Hobbes, a local missionary from Quetzaltenango who had come to help translate, went over to speak with them. He then looked over at me and motioned for me to come.

I climbed down off the stage and walked over to where he was standing next to the stern-looking man who appeared to be the squad leader. Pancho said, "*Marie, this is Captain So-and-so. He wants to meet the "jefe.*" (This means boss in Spanish.) He then turned to the captain to introduce me. I stood there thinking, "*Oh man. I'm going to die! I will never be seen or heard from again!*"

Instead, the captain smiled and extended his hand to acknowledge the introduction and explained why he had come. No, he hadn't come to run us in. He said that some of his men had serious dental needs, and he wondered if we could help them. I'm afraid I made a fool of myself as I eagerly told him we would do whatever we could! I felt such relief that I wasn't going to disappear after all.

We spent the last day of that clinic week in Canalitos and Margaritas, two slum areas of Guatemala City where Clinica

Promesa held occasional clinics. The final tally of patients seen during the three days of clinic was close to 1,500.

There were many more adventures on the trip, but the most important thing about that first clinic was its success, measured by the sizable number of people who came to be treated and the abundant interaction between local churches and HTI. The team had provided ample evidence that mobile clinics were both needed and valuable.

Clinics, Clinics and More Clinics

When we returned to the States after that first clinic, we were excited about what had taken place. We took time to evaluate what worked and what didn't work. Noting that there were many more positives than negatives, we scheduled two clinics for 1991. In 1992 we hosted four.

Those early clinics were fraught with experimentation. Some ideas worked; others, not so much. We learned early on the perils of trying to do too much. On one trip we experimented with holding clinic at two sites in the same day with only one team. What happened was inevitable. We closed up the clinic at Site #1, leaving hordes of disappointed unseen people, only to drive several miles away to host another clinic. At day's end, we again drove away, leaving yet another horde of people still unseen. Fortunately, we were good at math and saw immediately that we were leaving twice as many unhappy people than we would have if we had stayed in one place all day. We also acknowledged that we would be able to see more patients by avoiding all the set up/shut down times.

We soon learned the importance of using a numbering system. By having the local church distribute a specific number of numbered cards ahead of time, we could specify the size of the patient load and limit the risk of unruly crowds. Those holding cards were guaranteed to be seen. This system ensured as well that we would see the sickest patients rather than those just wanting to come see a gringo doctor in action.

Another method we tried was combining a mobile medical clinic with vacation time: a few days of clinic then a trip to Tikal. That proved to be unpopular with churches that provided support for some volunteers. Even though the volunteers were expected to cover their personal vacation expenses, the perception of missions committees sending people on "vacation" was just too much, so we stopped doing it.

Belly Button of the World

We did make occasional unplanned side trips, however. Some of them lifted the veil on the Mayan culture and gave us a peek inside…like our visit to the "belly button of the world."

It was the summer of 1992 when a mobile medical team was on a bus returning from Quetzaltenango. The guide suddenly turned to me and asked if we would like to stop and visit a witch doctor's cave. *"Well, of course,"* I told him!

A mile down the road, the driver slowed the bus to and pulled off to the side as far as he safely could. The area was mountainous so the roads were very curvy. All 40 of us got off the bus and followed the guide down a steep, winding trail. We laughed and talked as we walked down and around the mountain, at least a half mile. It gave us time to imagine what we were about to see. What we saw was much different from what any of us expected.

Witch doctor's cave

I literally gasped when it came into view. Rather than being the small, rock-lined hole in the earth I had expected, there was a gigantic, soot-covered hole in the earth lined with rock... and smoke was pouring from it! We readied our cameras as we got closer. Then we heard a voice. There was someone IN the cave. Our ears immediately tuned in to the sounds.

When we came close enough to see inside, we saw a Mayan witch doctor doing what witch doctors do—chanting incantations around the fire. Kneeling beside the fire, his barefoot female Mayan assistant was placing various items into the fire in synchronicity with his incantations. We spied incense, chicken feathers, grass, cigarettes and corn husks. Dozens of little flickering candles were scattered around the floor and lent mystery to the dark recesses of the cave.

The witch doctor obviously was not pleased with our cameras. He immediately wagged his finger in disapproval, so we respectfully put our cameras away. (Fortunately, some of us had already gotten a couple of good shots!) We watched in respectful silence for a few minutes as he performed his ritual. The guide told us that according to local folklore that cave had been used for such rituals for the past several hundred years. That explained the thick layer of soot.

As we turned to leave, I was struck that in viewing the ceremony as an outsider it seemed like such a pointless ritual. It had obviously evolved out of fear and hopelessness, sort of a man-made religious experience designed to provide a sense of control over life's circumstances. As team member Dr. Dan Wilson later wrote, *"They were unaware that the void they felt in their hearts was the size and shape of the Risen Savior."*

We turned to go back to the bus and I found myself walking next to the guide. I asked him a question that had been burning in my head. *"Was he a good witch doctor...or a bad witch doctor?"* The guide quietly replied, *"Both."*

Planning Logistics

These clinics took a tremendous amount of time and effort to organize and execute. Stateside, I had to recruit team members, gather documentation, make flight arrangements and collect money.

Steve and Magda had even more complex tasks. First, they had to determine where we would hold clinic. Since it was in the days before cell phones, they had to travel to different villages to communicate with local church leaders about hosting a clinic. Once the sites were determined, Steve and Magda had to submit that information, along with the professional documentation I had forwarded to them, to the Colegio de Medico office to get official governmental approval. This was crucial because the visiting medical professionals worked under Dr. Sergio's medical license, and we did not want to jeopardize his licensure in any way. The HTI Board was determined from the beginning to always obey local laws. There was simply too great a risk to Dr. Sergio and to our visiting healthcare professionals to do otherwise.

Steve and Magda also ordered medicines, bought food for the team, arranged transportation, hired translators and secured lodging. Once this was done, Steve would send this information to me...and I would relay it to the team. Most of the time, the system worked. Occasionally, however, Steve left out a few critical details.

The November 1992 trip was one such example. Steve sent word that he'd secured the old German hotel in Chocolá as a place for the team's lodging. I had seen the old hotel when we had driven through Chocolá on our way to Santo Thomás. It was right next to the aqueduct that dripped water on the top of our bus when we drove under it. But I had never been in it. I knew it had been built in the late 1800s to accommodate the multitude of visitors who came to tour what was at the time the *only water-powered coffee processing plant in the entire world*. That plant had long since gone out of business, leaving little reason for visitors to come to Chocolá. The hotel had stood empty since then except for the occasional migrant worker. I questioned Steve about that. He admitted that although the hotel had not been in use in recent years, it was well built and had *plumbing*...as well as lots of interesting architectural details. I relayed that information to the team...and am still trying to live it down. Dr. Jeff Bennie was on that team, his first trip with us.

At first glance, the hotel didn't look too bad. It had a certain charm about it with its cupola perched on top and gingerbread details all around. The group eyed it curiously as they walked up the wide wooden steps to the dusty porch and entered the old building. As we weaved our way through the halls to our rooms, we began to sense we were in trouble. It turned out there were only three or four rooms fit to use, so each housed at least six cots lined up side by side with barely space to stand in between. In an effort to reassure herself as well as the rest of us, one woman muttered, *"Well, at least the cots look comfortable enough."*

The windows, however, were another story. They *were* screened…at least partially. The center of each screen, however, was rusted out, leaving a hole (as one team member described it) *big enough to throw a dog through.* Someone pointed at one of the windows and said, *"Look at that interesting architectural detail!"* Everyone looked at me and laughed. This wasn't the worst part.

That honor was reserved for the ladies' bathroom at the end of the hall. We were relieved to see that there were indeed flush toilets. And, yes, the flushing mechanism worked *most* of the time. There was a bucket to refill the tank when it didn't. But the plumbing leaked—badly. The constant dripping from the tank caused water to stand at least an inch or two deep on the bathroom floor. Fortunately, it was *incoming* fresh water! Someone found several large planks and positioned them on the floor so we could keep our feet dry. Navigating all of that in the middle of the night was quite a challenge.

Some village ladies cooked for us in a room downstairs. The food was basic rice and beans, but it was tasty. There was no dining table. At each meal we would have to find a spot on the edge of the porch to sit while holding our plates in our laps. It was hardly the Sheraton.

All in all, it was pretty depressing, and Dr. Bennie seemed especially burdened by it. I noticed him because he seemed to function well during clinic hours, but the minute we went "home," he simply lay on his cot reading, not talking or interacting with anyone. I was convinced he would never be back.

Surprisingly, he did return. A couple of years later he joined the HTI Board as a director and even served as president of the HTI Board for two terms. He still serves as a member of the Board today…but he takes every opportunity to remind me of the *"interesting architectural details"* of his first trip.

Man with No Nose

I spotted him on this same Chocolá clinic. He was an elderly Mayan man wearing the traditional wool skirt, white shirt, hat and sandals. When I first noticed him, he was about 50 feet away. He caught my attention because he had a cotton ball perched on the end of his nose. I chuckled to myself and sidled up closer to see why.

When I got close enough to see, I was hit by a moment of nausea. I saw that rather than a cotton ball **on the end of** his nose, he had a cotton ball **instead** of a nose. Really!

At that very moment, he turned to enter an exam room, and I never saw him again. During the flight home, I sat by Dr. Jeff Bennie. We were chatting about the week when I suddenly remembered the man with no nose, and I told Jeff about it. He excitedly replied, "*I saw that man! He was my patient.*" I eagerly asked him to tell me more. Here is the story as it was told to him.

Sometime earlier, this elderly man had developed a bad sinus infection. Because he lived in an area with no medical care, he couldn't go to the doctor. Pressure from the sinus infection finally got so bad that he went to the only health care that *was* available to him: a witch doctor. The witch doctor took the only tool he had available, a broken Coke bottle, and lanced the man's sinuses to let them drain. The witch doctor's action certainly relieved the sinus pressure, but the bacteria causing the infection spread into the man's nasal tissue and literally ate his nose away. True story.

Frog in the Brain

Another witch doctor story involved Steve Sherman. During clinic, Steve was often called upon to provide spiritual care. The diagnoses were not always what they seemed, but they provided the perfect segue to conversations about God. Such was the case in one of our early mobile medical clinics in Guatemala City.

A fortyish-looking woman approached the doctor when her number was called. The doctor asked her what was her biggest problem *today*. (We learned that it was important to be specific about time. Otherwise some people would list every complaint they had endured for the past five years!) The woman responded that her head hurt. After a brief physical exam where the doctor found no presence of sinus congestion, he asked her if she had migraines.

She said quietly and quite clearly, *"No, I have a frog in my brain."*

The doctor gulped and motioned for Steve to come over. After hearing her self-diagnosis, Steve sat down beside her and asked her why she thought she had a frog in the brain. She looked Steve straight in the eye and said, *"A witch doctor put it there."*

This time Steve paused, then countered with, *"Do you believe in God?"* She replied that she did. He continued, *"Do you believe that God has more power than the witch doctor?"* Again, she nodded. Steve pressed forward. *"Well, let's pray that God will remove that frog from your head right now."* They did and she left the clinic feeling freer and less burdened than she had in days.

Chapter 7:
Surgical Ministry Arises

1990-93

Steve Sherman, Nery Castillo and Dr. Mike Kelly met in Retaluleh the weekend of August 25, 1990, to discuss expanding the HTI ministry. This was only a couple of months before HTI's first mobile clinic. Mike had been urging HTI to include the Suchitepequez Department of Guatemala in its ministry and had, in fact, convinced Steve to bring the team to Xejuyup when it arrived in November. They discussed establishing a base of operations from which mobile clinic teams could be sent out. Village leaders in Xejuyup had recently offered Mike land and labor to build a medical clinic there. He thought that might work as a base clinic.

After much discussion that weekend, the three agreed on three things: (1) there was indeed logic in expanding HTI's ministry into Mayan country, (2) a base clinic would be very useful in that endeavor, and (3) Xejuyup was too remote to be considered as a base clinic because it was not easily accessible. Mike insisted that any clinic built should include exam rooms *and* a surgical operatory. Mike explained that he had seen far too often the desperate need for surgical care among the Indians. The need was desperate because the Mayan Indians had virtually no access to surgery in Guatemala. The reasons for that were simple: expense, language difficulties, and widespread social discrimination against them.

In December 1990 Steve submitted a proposal for consideration by the HTI Board to build a modest facility to serve the expansion into Mayan country. His proposal described a facility that would serve as a staging area for mobile clinics and include two surgical operatories. He proposed that these operatories be used four times per year for one- to two-week periods by visiting North American medical professionals. He added that the building could also be used to train health promoters, as a site for local churches to hold retreats, and perhaps at some point house an alcohol rehab program. This was the first recorded mention of HTI venturing into a surgical ministry.

The Dr. Mike Kelly Family

Dr. Mike Kelly, his wife Julie and children Patrick, Katie and Brian lived in Santo Tomás, just down the mountain from his clinic in Xejuyup. He also regularly conducted mobile clinics in the surrounding area. Mike and I first met in October 1983 on the Las Cruces test clinic. He and Julie had earlier spent a couple of years in the Cameroons in Africa.

The time spent in the Cameroons plus Mike's Las Cruces clinic experience had inspired them to join the Clinica Cristiana team in Quetzaltenango in 1985. This was the clinic that Dr. Richard Rheinbolt had started in the early 1970s. His team had evacuated about the same time the Las Cruces team did. Dr. Mike and Dr. Bruce Smith moved to Guatemala in 1985 to operate that clinic, although it had never truly shut down because health promoters had continued to run it. In the absence of a physician, however, they were often limited in what care they could provide. Mike and Bruce worked together sometimes at the clinic itself and each also traveled to outlying areas to conduct mobile clinics. Xejuyup, about two hours away, had been one of them. It was a Mayan village where 1500 Indians resided, but several thousand more lived within a radius of only a few miles.

As Mike spent more time in Xejuyup, he became convinced that the size of the population and the extent of their health needs warranted more regular care. He and Julie decided to relocate to be closer to it. When Mike learned that an HTI mobile medical team might be coming to Guatemala, he encouraged Steve to bring the team to his area. Steve agreed...and that's how we wound up in Xejuyup. That was when our long and rewarding association with Mike and Julie began and the first seeds of surgery were planted.

Stepping Out in Faith

The HTI Board reviewed Steve's proposal and agreed to it in principle, but many questions remained. For the next couple of years the idea germinated. While the mobile medical clinics continued on a quarterly basis, the HTI gears continued to grind toward establishing a surgical ministry. Finally the proposal to proceed with surgery took root, and in October 1992 the Board officially mandated it. Simultaneously, they initiated the Great Physician campaign to raise $260,000 to purchase land and build a facility. There was some preliminary discussion of the value of proceeding with surgery in a temporary facility even before we built our own facility. The most immediate question that kept running through my mind at the moment was *"WHERE would you do surgery?"*

When you work in the God business, however, you don't have to wonder long. God makes it happen. There had been very few times in my life when I felt as though I was witnessing the "hand of God" in action—in real time. What happened next made a true believer out of me. God can and does answer prayer.

When I returned home after that meeting, I called Mike Kelly to make him aware of the Board's decision. We talked about the need to find a temporary facility. Mike called me two days later to relate the following story. He began with, *"You won't believe this, but...!"*

He told me that the evening after he and I had talked he was having dinner with his family when there was a knock at his door. Three men from Chocolá stood on his porch. (Chocolá is located in the Suchitepequez Department of Guatemala, about 10 miles nearer Guatemala City than where the Kelly family lived in Santo Tomás.) The men told him they represented the health committee in Chocolá and had a proposition for him.

Mike went outside and sat down with them to hear what they had to say. Their message was clear and simple. *"We have some buildings in our community that we would let you use if you would agree to do a medical work in Chocolá."* Remembering our conversation about needing a suitable place for surgery, Mike told them he would come by the next day after work to check it out. He did. And as soon as he got home from there, he called me.

Now understand that Mike is not, and never has been, an excitable guy. He is a lot of wonderful things, but giddy with excitement is not a way I would ever describe him. Mike is of sound judgment—all the time—very disciplined, and steady as a rock. I would trust him with my life. This time, however, I heard glee in his voice.

"*It is perfect for what we want to do,*" Mike excitedly exclaimed! He described the three buildings being offered. They were each about 30' x 100'. One was already designed to be a dormitory; one could easily be modified to house two surgical rooms with enough open space on one end of it to serve as a patient ward; the third building had exam rooms and a large room that could be used as a pharmacy. There was even indoor plumbing.

When I arrived in Guatemala a few days later, Mike took me to see it, and I was pleasantly surprised. Though I had been in Chocolá several times, I had never been down the road to where these buildings were located. It was quite charming actually. The three main buildings were nestled closely together in the midst of a little community. Though the concrete-block structures had been built in the early 1970s, they appeared sturdy. The walls were lined with louvered windows all around that let in the cool breezes from the surrounding trees. Two buildings were parallel with about 40 feet between them, while the third was perpendicular to the first two. A T-shaped covered walkway connected all the doorways. Yes, I thought. This would work.

Steve surveyed the property as well and agreed that with only slight modification, it would serve us well. He and Magda soon set about preparing the property for use by a surgical team. They had to first do massive cleaning in the facility because of its years of non-use. For a cost of only $25,000 Steve remodeled one of the buildings to create two functioning operating rooms. They bought furniture for the dorm. In July 1993 Dr. John Peden brought a group of young people and adults from the Donelson Church of Christ in Nashville to give everything a coat of fresh paint. That group had more fun painting than any I'd ever seen! They seemed excited to be a part of something so promising. I began to believe that we were really going to do this.

Searching for Land

Sometime after the decision was made to initiate a surgical ministry in October 1992, we began looking for land to build our own surgical clinic. In mid-1993 before we began conducting surgical clinics in the borrowed facility in Chocolá, we found a plot of land that seemed suitable. It was in the very area that Steve Sherman had suggested in his proposal. It was located in the Suchitepequez Department of Guatemala, about 100 miles southwest of Guatemala City. The plot was on the northern side of the road that led from the western coastal highway inland to Chicacao and contained the essential components for establishing a surgical clinic: a consistent supply of electricity, an excellent water source, and it sat on a main bus route.

Because of the Great Physician campaign, we had money in the bank to buy it. Steve was careful to stay out of sight while Nery did the negotiating. The owner settled on a price of about $50,000 for 7.8 acres. We thought everything was set. Not quite.

A few days had gone by when Nery received a phone call from the owner. He said he needed to back out of the deal because word had gotten out that he was about to sell the land and he was worried he would be robbed. Nery told him that if word had gotten out, the owner himself must have done the telling, because Nery knew that he had told no one. Reading between the lines, Nery felt that this was merely a ploy to manipulate him into offering more for the land. Once Nery made it clear he was willing to walk away, the owner called back the next day saying he was ready to sell.

The land came with a bridge already built over the creek.

The bridge on the property had an interesting history. We were told that many years ago a Guatemalan general was convinced that the main road was to be rerouted through this land, so he proceeded to have a substantial yet decorative bridge built over the creek…in tribute to himself. Obviously, the general had been wrong, but his ego saved HTI a great deal of money. I told this story one day on the bus with a mobile medical team, and a voice from the back saying, "So, what we have here is a tribute to *general stupidity!*"

By the summer of 1993, HTI had completed the purchase. We now had the land but not nearly enough money to build a clinic yet. The Board was determined to operate on a cash basis, so the Great Physician campaign continued. By the time the construction fund reached $125,000 we thought perhaps we had enough, so we requested a construction estimate from a firm in Guatemala City. Sadly, the estimate was for twice the amount we had in the bank. The Board decided we should proceed with erecting a storage building on the property, which we would need anyway once construction began. Steve designed it to be multi-functional with a warehouse, a couple of offices and a bedroom and bath for the watchman. This design allowed it to be used for mobile medical clinics in the interim. We gave permission for a new church in the community to begin holding services in that building. And we kept on raising money.

Surgery Clinics Begin

At the October 1993 Board meeting, the Board took stock of the situation. We now had a place to do surgery; Steve had remodeled the building to make it suitable for surgery; the Donelson group had brightened everything up with a fresh coat of paint. The Board decided it was time to begin. Though we did not yet have our own building, we had raised a sizable amount toward that goal and knew the actual experience of performing surgery in such a setting would be of value in designing our own facility. Because eye surgery was the least invasive, the Board decided to begin with that and selected the first weekend in December 1993 as a starting date. It was only six weeks away.

I remember that when the vote was taken and the motion to proceed with surgery passed unanimously, all eyes of the Board members turned toward me. Someone said, *"Well, Marie, let's make it happen."* I felt numb and thought, *"How in the world does one actually go about DOING surgery in a foreign country?"*

We had a place to do surgery...God had seen to that. We already had a reconditioned operating microscope...Dr. Theo Kirkland had seen to that. But we needed so much more. We needed surgical tables, surgical lights, patient beds, and untold numbers of things that I didn't even know the names of. How do we find those, God?

As word got out about our first surgery clinic, my phone began to ring. One of the first calls was from someone who had 25 hospital beds. Did we want them? A surgeon on the Board called saying he had some surgical instruments. Healing Hands in Nashville had a couple of surgical tables they offered. Dr. Dan Brannan in the Biology Department at Abilene Christian called saying he had two used 1950 MASH unit autoclaves that we could have. Another call was from a retiring physician in Dallas who wanted to donate his entire office of equipment and supplies. By this time my head was spinning!

Clearly God was making sure we had what we needed, but how were we going to get it all to Guatemala? Knowing for a year that we were headed in the direction of surgery, I had been accumulating boxes of surgical supplies and storing them in my basement. Several hospitals had been routing their discards my way for some time. My house had a full basement and it was so full of medical and surgical supplies that there was only a narrow walkway from the outside door to the staircase leading into the house. The question of logistics was looming larger all the time. The pressure was on from another source, too—my husband. He wanted his basement back.

The immediate challenge was to gather those items in Abilene and Dallas, plus my basement, and transport them to Nashville where Healing Hands would prepare them for shipment. What I needed was an 18-wheeler.

I suddenly remembered a high school classmate who worked for a national trucking firm, so I called him. He said they were a union shop and did not have much leeway for donating services, but he named another truck line that was non-union and suggested I call them. I checked my local phone book and was excited to find a listing for it. When I dialed the number, a man answered.

I explained who I was and what kind of help I needed. He introduced himself as the new local manager, saying he'd only been in Birmingham two weeks. Without hesitation, he volunteered to send a truck to both Abilene and Dallas then to my house to clean out my basement. The last stop would be Healing Hands in Nashville. I thanked him profusely, hung up the phone, and almost cried. It was once again becoming exceedingly clear that God was blessing this decision to provide surgery for Mayan Indians in Guatemala. How else could I interpret the ease at which everything was coming together? And it wasn't over yet.

Chris Jingles and Healing Hands arranged for the Air National Guard in Tennessee to ship all of our supplies to Guatemala on a cavernous C-5 plane. I drove to Nashville to be there when they loaded the shipment onto pallets. It was such an exciting day! There must have been 30 soldiers participating, and they all seemed enthusiastic about their work. I especially loved the moment when I met the general in charge. When he learned who I was, he bodily picked me up and stood me on the back of a flatbed truck, then called out to his soldiers. When they stopped what they were doing and turned to listen, he pointed up at me from his vantage point on the ground and said, *"Guys, she is the boss. Do whatever SHE says!"* I loved it.

A week later I was in Guatemala with a mobile medical team when I received word that the plane would be arriving while I was still in Guatemala. I said to Board member Dr. John Peden who was also a part of the team, *"We just have to be there when it lands!"* He agreed.

Steve and Magda took us to the airport to meet the plane. I was as excited as I have ever been—even more than in my best Christmas ever as a child! We had all worked so hard to get to this moment, and it was truly joyous. We really were about to begin doing surgery in Guatemala.

Exhausting work, but all was ready by the time the eye surgery team arrived. Incredibly, this had all happened in a space of only six weeks. There seemed little doubt about who was directing this. It absolutely had to have been a God thing.

CHAPTER 8:
CHOCOLÁ SURGERY CLINIC IN ACTION

1993-2001

First Eye Surgery Clinic

All was ready on December 4, 1993, when HTI's first surgical team arrived in Chocolá. Two ophthalmologists came: HTI Board member Dr. Dan Wilson from San Angelo, Texas, and Dr. Larry Patterson of Crossville, Tennessee. Others included Jurdean Reed, an eye surgery nurse from Birmingham and Dr. Roy Wilson, Dr. Dan's father. It was a small team, but deliberately so. The first clinic needed to test the waters before we jumped in head first.

By the end of the week they had performed eye exams on 150 people and operated on 25 of them. Half of that number was for cataract removal; the other half was to remove pyterigiums. There were some dramatic moments. In the middle of one procedure a patient began yelling, *"I can*

see!" Another patient came back for his post-surgery exam, and when he was told that all was well, he raised his arms high and praised God for his gift of new sight. Legend has it that one elderly woman literally jumped off the table when her eye patch was removed, shouting to everyone as she ran out the door and down the road, *"I can see! I can see! Praise God Almighty, I can see!"* What a wonderful beginning.

First GYN Surgery Clinic

Preparation for the first gynecological surgery clinic began at my kitchen table in Birmingham. HTI Board members Dr. Jeff Bennie from Nashville and Dr. Ken Mitchell from Pensacola, Florida, met at my house to sort out details. Gynecological surgery is vastly more complicated than eye surgery, so planning was critical and starting small a must. They agreed to schedule only 10 patients for surgery.

As a first step, Ken called Dr. Henry Farrar, the Church of Christ *master of medical evangelism*. He had been performing surgery in Nigeria for years. If anyone could give him good advice, it would be Dr. Farrar. Dr. Farrar was happy to provide many important particulars. He ended the conversation by reminding Ken that he wouldn't be able to fix everybody. He told him, "Some will die, but they would have likely died anyway. Many will be improved, and their lives will be better. Besides, you are not in control anyway." Truer words were never spoken.

There were only five people on the team: Gynecologists Dr. Ken Mitchell and Dr. Roy Kellum from Jackson, Mississippi; Dr. Jeff Bennie was the anesthesiologist; and surgical nurses Lisa Cantrell from Jackson, Mississippi, and Alton Aldridge from Nashville.

They arrived in Chocolá just as the second eye surgery team left in February 1994. Dr. Jeff Bennie had gone a week early to prepare the operatory as much as possible and to assist the eye team. That eye team was from Brookwood Hospital in Birmingham, Alabama. Drs. Tom McKinnon, Bo Ackerman, Wade Joiner, and HTI Board member Theo Kirkland were the ophthalmologists. Jurdean Reed was again the eye surgical nurse. Jurdean had come our way because of my fellow church member Dr. Theo Kirkland.

He had been with her on a mission trip to Mexico and quickly realized how good she was. He told me that if we were going to be doing eye surgery there was one person I definitely HAD to meet. It was Jurdean. And he was absolutely correct. Jurdean proved to be a mainstay in our eye surgery ministry and went to Guatemala time and time again, year after year, to support the ophthalmologists.

Jurdean was so dedicated that she continually gathered salvageable supplies she knew would be needed and somehow managed to get them sterilized for use in Guatemala. Since we had only one (reconditioned) operating microscope, she would often borrow a portable one from the hospital where she worked and carry it back and forth to Guatemala. She was quite the "take charge" nurse, and everyone learned quickly that she deserved their respect because she ran a tight ship in the operating room. I have heard many doctors say after having worked with her only one time that they would not come again unless Jurdean was there! Her assistance was so valuable that shortly before she passed away from brain cancer in 2008, we dedicated the eye surgery operatory to her.

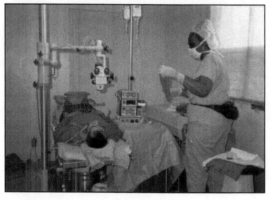

The GYN team members arrived on Sunday. Ken described the experience:

"Our operating room was primitive. The ceiling was reinforced with sheet rock but the edges were still uncovered, and when the wind blew, the bat guano fell from the ceiling and blushed the wall like make-up. Our lighting was a gooseneck lamp with an incandescent bulb in a chrome reflector. It was hot and did not focus the light at all. Roy was the assistant on that first case, and we encountered a 'bleeder' under the bladder that could not be easily controlled, especially considering that the exposure was limited with our light and the table. I am sure it divinely stopped as

did her post spinal headache which I will relate in a moment. We did ten vaginal hysterectomies, all for prolapse. With vault suspensions. The electricity went out daily. A long extension cord carried power down the hall while the noisy generator protested outside the back door. I remember a mangy dog that made its way into the theater in the middle of a case, the smell of the Clorox from the washing, and the smell of the burning trash which seemed to always be upwind of the windows.

"After Roy and Jeff left, I stayed a few more days to watch the patients post op, not knowing what kind of morbidity they might suffer. The first patient had a severe post spinal headache that was pounding when she sat upright and relieved when she was supine. I remember Mike Kelly coming for breakfast. It was my idea to do an epidural blood patch which I had seen but never performed. Basically you take blood from her arm and place it outside the dura to 'patch' the leak. I remember praying with Mike about these details, asking God to help us. So after breakfast we made our way to the bedside and I asked her to sit up again to verify her symptoms before the procedure. Thank God...He protected her from my trial. She said the headache was gone, so we all had reasons to celebrate His Goodness. All ten patients recovered nicely."

Lisa Cantrell kept a journal that week at Chocolá, and she expressed amazement at the doctors' willingness to get fully involved. Roy and Ken didn't just operate on the patients and Jeff didn't just put patients to sleep. Roy scrubbed instruments and Ken Mitchell mopped the blood up off the floor between surgeries. Dr. Jeff Bennie played supervisor and often sorted through boxes to help Lisa and Alton find the supplies they needed to set up the operating rooms. Lisa and Alton "assisted" them! The humbleness and dedication exhibited by everyone on the team set the behavior standard for these clinics.

Although Dr. Quinton Dickerson was not on this team, he too significantly impacted team dynamics. On an early mobile medical clinic another team member called out to him across the room, saying, "Dr. Dickerson." Quinton stopped in his tracks, turned to look at the person who called, and said, "No. Just call me Quinton. Down here we are all the same. We are all here to serve the Lord."

I was not present on this GYN surgery trip, so I had to rely on second-hand reports. Knowing this, when Ken returned home and developed his film, he mailed me a handful of pictures. I eagerly opened the envelope when it arrived and almost fainted! Staring back at me from the first photograph was a gigantic prolapsed uterus. I had never even seen one before and certainly had no idea they could be that large. (We no longer see them that large because the women are able to get help much sooner now.) After that, whenever anyone questioned me about the need for surgery clinics, I would offer to show them that picture!

Regular Surgical Clinics Begin

By February we had successfully completed two eye clinics and one GYN surgery clinic. All had gone fairly well, despite the primitive conditions. We had proven to ourselves that we could do this, so we moved forward with scheduling another eye surgery clinic for April 1994. We felt ready to begin in earnest.

Unfortunately, we weren't prepared for what happened next.

Guatemala became a very turbulent place for gringos in the spring of 1994. Out of nowhere, there were ugly rumors being whispered throughout Guatemala. The rumors alleged that gringos were stealing Guatemalan children to sell their body parts for cash. A woman photographer from California was severely beaten to the point of unconsciousness for simply carrying a camera and wearing a backpack as she walked alone through a Mayan village. The people suspected her of having a baby in her backpack. Another North American woman was attacked while sitting in an outdoor cafe in Esquintla having coffee. It was not a good time to be doing surgery in Guatemala. We cancelled both the eye and the mobile medical clinic that had been scheduled for April.

September 1994 GYN Surgery Clinic

By September things had calmed down enough that the U.S. State Department lifted its Travel Advisory for Guatemala. We felt comfortable bringing in another team. This time we planned to conduct a combined GYN surgery/mobile medical clinic. I was so grateful that Dr. Ken Mitchell agreed to come again and be the surgery team leader. At least he knew what a surgery clinic should look like. I certainly did not.

By today's standards, it was a small team of only 19 people. But it was a start. This was our first "full-sized" surgery team, so I will list those pioneering souls who signed on. Because there were so many unknowns, each had to have had an extra measure of courage and faith to want to be a part of such a dramatic new ministry in a foreign country. The team included gynecologist Dr. Ken Mitchell; general surgeon Dr. Phil Bates; orthopedic surgeon Dr. Jeff Lawrence; dermatologist Dr. Alan Boyd; internist/Spanish speaker Dr. Rugel Sowell; surgical tech Richard Yates; nurse anesthetist Eddie Milam; RNs Betsy Keene, Kristi Morris, Bonnie Spink and Joyce Strickland; and others whom we have come to call "compassionate caregivers."

Compassionate caregivers did everything from scrubbing instruments to caring for patients and mopping floors between surgeries. This group included Pat Dwyer, Molly Germash, Bob Hatch, John Himmelrick and his daughter Lynn, Don Reeves, Allan Seaman and me. Many of these people still participate in HTI clinics today, 20 years later.

Our first case was especially touching. With the backdrop of child kidnapping rumors, a young mother fought her fears to bring her baby to our surgeons for help. I had noticed her early that morning holding her year-old baby close as she leaned against a tree. Her guarded eyes darted back and forth as though checking to see if she was safe. She wouldn't make eye contact with anyone. Despite the already warm morning, her baby was wearing a knitted cap that tied under the chin. I wondered about that.

The baby's name was the first called for surgery. Wilmer, it was. I followed him and his mother inside, curious to see what was under the cap. As she removed the cap for the doctor to examine her child, I saw the problem. Just below Wilmer's right ear on his neck was a cystic hygroma, a genetic defect that causes an abnormal lymphatic lesion. It was the size of a silver dollar. The mother stood silent as she watched, looking pale despite her dark skin. Her eyes gave evidence of the terror she was feeling inside.

I stayed nearby to comfort her when Wilmer went into surgery. She spoke only Quiche, so there was no verbal conversation between us, only smiles and hugs. When Dr. Bates called for Wilmer, I motioned for her to carry him to the operating room and hand him to Eddie, the CRNA. At that point her tears began to flow. I encouraged her to linger for a few minutes to watch through the window as Eddie put little Wilmer to sleep. I found a couple of chairs for us to sit in just outside the door to the operating room to allay any fears she might have about Wilmer disappearing. We sat there together quietly throughout the surgery.

When it was over, the surgeon came out and told her through an interpreter that Wilmer was just fine and would be out shortly, she smiled so broadly that she looked like a different person! When she finally saw Wilmer, she was at peace.

I was struck by how she was like any mother I had ever known. Despite her fears, she did what she had to do to get help for her little one, even handing him over to the very people rumored to kidnap babies. She had figuratively climbed a mountain and crossed a deep sea to get help for her baby. God had blessed her for it—Wilmer would be just fine.

By the end of the week, the team had performed 16 hysterectomies, 17 hernia repairs, two cyst removals, one tendon repair and one thorn removal from an arm. This made a total of 37 procedures, which was quite a formidable load for a small team that had only four nurses on it! Once again I felt God's presence.

Steve and Magda had again made all the on-site arrangements. A new requirement demanded that they submit in advance a list of everything the teams would bring with them. This was substantial because in those early surgical clinic days **we had to bring with us almost everything we needed!** Everyone who came had at least one extra suitcase filled with surgical supplies. On one early trip, I personally checked 13 duffle bags full of medicine and supplies! This was obviously before 9/11. It was also before many groups had begun doing surgical clinics around the world, so it was still a bit of a novelty. The ticket agent who was to check my bags quizzically asked why I had so many. I explained what we were doing. He was so touched that he did not charge me anything extra! He said, *"You deserve a break for doing that."* I took his response as another sign that we were on the right path.

The Shermans managed the surgical clinic while continuing to manage Clinica Promesa in the city, which by now was a fully functioning clinic. In 1994 they were treating nearly 500 patients a month and had two full time evangelists on staff to ensure that spiritual care was part of the treatment plan for each patient. Twenty of their patients had requested baptism in 1994.

There began to be a rhythm to the surgical clinics. The surgical clinics soon developed a strong following, and recruiting became easier as word began to spread. Most people who participated once wanted to do it again…and they all had friends who wanted to come. As rugged as the experience was, most everyone thought it was a wonderful experience. I thought so, too, but sometimes I wondered why.

The last 12 miles of road to Chocolá was rugged, with deep ruts and huge rocks that jarred you to the bone as the bus made its way over them. In the rainy season there was mud…lots and lots of mud. In 1998 the bus in which we were riding was overcome by the mud and sank, jolting sharply to one side. One of the surgeons, Dr. Brian Camazine, flew out of his seat and landed on top of me where I was sitting on the other side of the bus! He injured his thumb but worked all week despite the swelling.

We had to slog through that mud the rest of the way to the clinic. The cots we slept on were not at all comfortable and sagged more and more on each subsequent visit. We slept several people to a room, which afforded little privacy. Because of the building design, if anyone in the dorm snored, we all heard it! Village ladies cooked our meals in a primitive outdoor kitchen with a dirt floor.

Outdoor kitchen at Chocolá

The patient ward was small so all the beds were jammed up so close to each other there was barely room between them. Oh, did I mention the barking neighborhood dogs that frequently made their presence known at 2:00 in the morning?

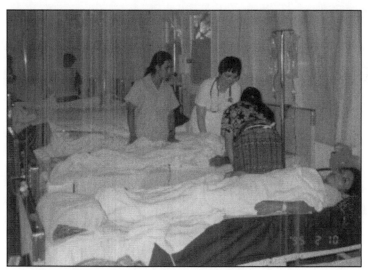

Nurse Bonnie Spink tending patients in the crowded ward

Those were some of the negatives. There were many positives, with the most important one being the fact that our surgical facility in Chocolá was located right in the middle of a rural residential area. There were no fences, only corn rows surrounding it. Quite simply, this meant we were part of the community itself. As children came and went freely (sometimes *too* freely), we learned to keep our belongings out of reach of the little arms and sticks that sometimes poked into the dorm room windows. Adults often wandered over to chat, and we got to know our neighbors. Our basket-making neighbor graciously gave demonstrations and sold his baskets to us for a pittance. They would bring us little presents, like a live chicken, bananas, mangoes, eggs or bread. We felt appreciated and safe.

The thing that brought us the most satisfaction, however, was the feeling that we were making a difference in the world. We saw women who had been forced to live for years with prolapsed uteri that had gotten so large they couldn't sit and in some cases were even infected. Some men had testicular hernias as "big as a backpack," as one surgeon characterized it. We clearly provided physical relief for these people.

One of my favorite healing stories involved a 4-year-old blind Mayan girl. Her Mayan grandparents had brought her in with hopeful hearts. They did not show it because Mayans don't display much outward emotion. They explained to the doctor that their granddaughter had been born with cataracts and had never been able to see. Dr. Michael Balok examined the frightened child. Even though she could not see the crowd of people watching, she could hear them. It made her clutch even more tightly the little Pretty Pony she brought with her. It was purple with a pink mane, and like they all did, it came with a little comb.

After examining her, Dr. Balok agreed that he would remove the cataracts but cautioned the grandparents and those of us in the room not to expect too much. He explained that sometimes eyes that have never seen cannot be repaired because the brain had come to believe that the eyes couldn't see. There was no way to fix that.

The next day he performed the surgery. Then we had to wait a day to allow for the swelling to recede. Finally it was time to remove the bandage. As Dr. Balok prepared to do so, anticipation grew among the waiting crowd. I was in another building at the time when suddenly someone ran in the door calling my name. I ran toward them asking what was wrong. *"She can see! She can see!"* was what I heard in reply. I broke into a sprint as I headed toward the hospital. As I came through the door, Dr. Balok saw me and said, *"Watch this, Marie."* With that he held up the purple Pretty Pony and slowly moved it across his little patient's line of sight...and her eyes tracked it! She was seeing her world for the first time.

Through my tears, I saw other faces glistening, too. It was such an incredible moment—even her stoic grandparents were smiling! To be privileged to give the gift of sight in the name of our Lord to someone who has never experienced it is precious indeed.

Most patients openly expressed gratitude to God for the relief they received as soon as they were awake enough to do so. I was happy to note that they always thanked God before they thanked any of us. That seemed completely appropriate.

Sadly, there were people we were not able to help. One man appeared to be in his 50s. He had a beautiful full head of white hair and a huge abdominal hernia. It was so big that he was living with considerable pain because of it. After the surgeon examined him, he asked me to help him explain to the man that we did not have the capability at Chocolá to repair a hernia of that size. One that size brought with it a great risk of complications, and we did not have the equipment to manage those complications. When the doctor turned to leave, the man broke down and cried like a baby.

I remember a colorfully dressed young Mayan mother who appeared to be in her late 20s, who came with an abscess on her breast. She had two or three very young children with her. When Dr. Sergio uncovered her breast, he and I were both stunned. What she thought was merely an abscess was clearly malignant. The tumor had eaten its way through her skin. Dr. Sergio explained the seriousness of her condition to her then wrote a referral note so she could be seen at the National Cancer Hospital in Guatemala City. He urged her to go there at once. She covered herself up, took the note, quietly thanked us and left. We strongly suspected she would go home and do nothing...except die.

One night about 3:00 in the morning, we heard a vehicle drive into the compound. Almost immediately one of the night nurses came looking for Dr. Ken Mitchell. Two anguished parents had brought their 17-year-old daughter in to see a doctor. She was clearly in great distress. Ken conferred with the parents to gather information about what might be wrong and quickly determined that the young girl likely had a severe case of food poisoning. Ken related to me later that it was clear to him the moment her saw her that the young girl was near death, and in fact she did pass away within a few minutes.

The father was visibly shaken and the mother wailed in grief. There was nothing more to be done, so they simply wrapped their daughter back up in the blanket they had carried her in on, took her outside and laid her in the back of the pickup. The mother and father climbed in beside her, and they rode away into the night.

At the same time the young woman was dying, there was stark fear in the cooks' quarters. In the Mayan religion, an owl is considered a harbinger of death. Earlier in the evening the cooks had heard the hoot of an owl, and they had been shaken at the time. When the pickup arrived in the night, the cooks were truly afraid and hurriedly got out of bed and gathered up the two babies present. One belonged to one of the cooks; the other was Melissa, Dr. Sergio and Veronica's infant. They placed them on a bed that the cooks then encircled…and prayed. Hard.

Remember evil eye? In the Mayan culture infants are believed to be especially vulnerable to it. Despite the fact these women were Christians, they had grown up in a culture filled with fear of evil spirits. In an interesting combination of faith in God and an instinctive reaction to the symbols of their time, they did all they knew to do that night to protect the babies. They prayed to God for protection from the Spirit of Death.

Chapter 9:
Dr. Mike Kelly and Clinica Cristiana

1990-95

Unlike most North American missionaries, Mike and Julie did not leave Guatemala during the 1992 period of the child kidnapping rumors. They felt that they were well known enough that the people they ministered to would never believe them to be guilty of such horrendous acts. They were right, as the following story shows.

One day Mike heard a chilling rumor about himself. He heard that some people associated with the Catholic Church in Santo Tomás were claiming that he had stolen some idols from their church. As the rumor gained traction, the men of Xejuyup heard about the charge, and they were fiercely indignant! They decided to take the matter into their own hands to stop what they considered to be an insult to their beloved Dr. Kelly.

The next day a group of 20 or 30 of them, dressed in their traditional woolen skirts and armed with machetes, marched en masse down the mountain to Santo Tomás and made their way through the streets until they arrived at the Catholic Church. When they entered the building, the startled people there demanded to know what they wanted. Without flinching, their spokesman said, *"We have heard the rumors you have been spreading about*

Dr. Kelly stealing your idols. We are here to tell you that that is simply not true. Dr. Kelly would **never** do anything like that. And if you think you are going to go after him, just know that you have to go through us first." End of rumors...and end of story. Mike felt vindicated. And extremely grateful.

Dr. Mike and Florinda

Mike knew her; everybody in town knew her. Her name was Florinda. Everyone knew her because she had the reputation of the Woman at the Well. (John 4) She was a pretty, vivacious young woman with three children, each by a different man. She was pregnant yet again with another child by the third man, who was not her husband. None of them had been. Despite her troubled life, she seemed happy and was always smiling.

That particular afternoon Florinda came to see Mike at the clinic. She was in the room at the end of the hall, and as he walked toward the open door of the room he could see her sitting there laughing with her children. When he entered the room, Florinda turned to face him and smiled broadly. As he looked into her eyes, Mike said it was as though at that very moment God had permitted him to peer into the depths of her soul. What he saw was pure agony.

A moment of heavy silence hung in the air as they looked at each other until Mike said softly, *"Florinda, what do you have to be so happy about?"* She was so taken aback she couldn't speak. Instead, big tears welled up in her eyes and slowly cascaded down her cheeks. In moments she was sobbing. Mike sat down beside her and held her as she cried. When she calmed down, he asked her, *"Aren't you ready to find out what really makes life worth living? Aren't you ready to learn about Jesus?"*

Florinda nodded in reply. Mike asked Marta, his trusted health promoter, to study with her, and in no time at all Florinda asked to be baptized. A short time later the man she was living with was also baptized and they were later married.

This story had taken place several years before Mike told me about it. Mike told me with gentle humbleness that every year since then Florinda had brought him a cake on the anniversary of her baptism to thank him for changing her life.

This is one example of why Dr. Mike Kelly was so loved and respected. He is a man of God who considered it a privilege to do the work he felt called to do. His patients felt his love and respect for them and responded in kind. When he and Julie returned to the States in 1995, they left a big hole in Xejuyup, Guatemala. I have been with Mike and Julie on some of their return trips to Guatemala and witnessed the warm greetings and tight hugs their former patients showered on them. They clearly still feel a great love and affection for Dr. Mike and Julie, even after all these years.

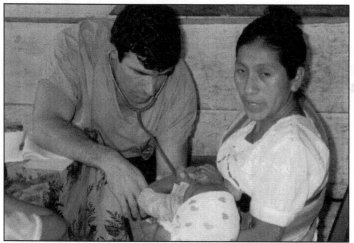

Dr. Mike Kelly...doing what he does so well

Clinica Cristiana and Health Talents Become One

In June 1994 the elders from the Church of Christ at Falls Church in Virginia announced to the supporters of Clinica Cristiana that after a year of serious study and consideration, they had made the difficult decision to ask Health Talents to assume the administrative responsibilities of Clinica Cristiana. The HTI Board had agreed, and the transfer would take effect on July 1, 1994. The Falls Church elders stated that the change of hands was made easier because of Mike Kelly's long association with Health Talents. They also noted that one of the elders, John Johnson, was already serving on the HTI Board. They reassured their supporters that the transfer would have no impact on U.S. missionaries. Mike and Julie would continue to receive their support from Falls Church.

This was an exciting step for Health Talents because up to this time HTI's mission had been more focused on medical and spiritual care and less on community development. Clinica Cristiana helped us broadened our scope. The Clinica Cristiana had been much more involved in community development for some time with its latrine, smokeless stove building and rabbit breeding projects.

Along with Mike and Dr. Bruce and Beth Smith, U.S. missionaries working at Clinica Cristiana during this time included Pancho and Lera Hobbes, Gene and Janice Luna, and Ken and Eileen Shoop. Pancho, Gene and Ken were evangelists, and Ken also oversaw the Appropriate Technology division. Pedro Batres was a highly respected evangelist from Nicaragua who also worked with them.

They all wore multiple hats, but every one of these folks made time to travel down to the coast periodically to translate during HTI's mobile clinics. We were so grateful for them. They were talented, God-loving and hard-working. Lera Hobbes had four children, but for years she made time to serve in the church, translate for HTI, and work as the clinic bookkeeper.

Clinica Cristiana had a network of Guatemalan health promoters, both medical and dental, that they had trained to treat both physical and spiritual ills. In the three different medical clinics associated with Clinica Cristiana, the doctors and health promoters treated an average of 1,200 patients each month. Evangelism was such a large component that in 1994 one of the dental health promoters, Carlos Deleon, *alone* baptized 30 people. Carlos had been a raging alcoholic when somehow he made contact with Dr. Mike and Dr. Bruce. They treated him, counseled with him and brought him to the Lord. He was already a trained dental technician who had worked for the government for 10 years until alcohol got hold of him. After Mike and Bruce helped him get his life back, he worked as a clinic staff member. In his spare time he regularly operated two different Alcoholics Anonymous groups.

Ken and his Appropriate Technology team placed 1,525 latrines in nine different villages and built 137 ceramic stoves that year, too.

Dr. Jim and Mary Rackley from North Carolina joined their ranks in 1994. Dr. Jim served as medical director after Mike moved to Santo Tomás and Dr. Bruce and Beth Smith returned to the States. Mary was an R.N., and it had long been her and Jim's dream to serve in overseas missions. They arrived in 1994 and were a godsend to the clinic. Due to unexpected health concerns they had to return home in 1996.

John Wright joined the HTI team in August 1993. As he was completing language school, the Clinica Cristiana/Health Talents merger was taking place. The Board asked John to oversee the administrative duties. He assumed the role of bookkeeper when the Hobbes family returned to the States in 1995 after 10 years in Guatemala. As a young, fun guy who was also a former MET student (Class of 1989), he was of particular benefit as MET coordinator. He, Steve and Mike worked together to guide students through the program each summer. Additionally, the Board asked John to serve as surgical clinic coordinator to provide some relief for Steve and Magda. A major purpose of MET is to inspire young adults to consider full time missions as a career, which John did. He initially made a three-year commitment but ended up serving in Guatemala four years. John definitely left his mark on the hearts of many people when he left.

Dr. Mike and Julie and their children returned to Stillwater, Oklahoma, in 1995 after 10 years in Guatemala. They felt it was time to introduce their children to life in the States. Julie had begun homeschooling the children when they moved to Santo Tomás, so 8-year-old Brian had never been to public school. Patrick, the oldest, excelled in the family's phys ed class, so he was eager to compete in track. Their PE class consisted of getting up at 5:30 every morning to run as a family up and down the mountains. No small feat! When Patrick joined the track team at his high school in Oklahoma, he set state records that to my knowledge have yet to be broken!

Clinica Cristiana was under the umbrella of Health Talents for a number of years. Eventually, however, all the North American missionaries serving there returned home, and the local Guatemalan board requested that they manage it themselves. Health Talents honored that request.

Chapter 10:
Call to Nicaragua

1993 - Present

In 1993 we received a letter from the Rene Polanco Iglesia de Cristo in Managua, Nicaragua. Two of the ministers and a physician in the congregation requested HTI's assistance in establishing a medical clinic in their church. In response to their letter, Roger McCown, Dr. Quinton Dickerson, Dr. John Peden and I traveled to Managua to meet with them and discuss it further. Over dinner the night of our arrival, José Garcia de la Llana, Noel Romano, and Dr. Gabriel Gonzales outlined their proposal.

Nicaragua had only recently come out from under the embargo that the U.S. government had placed around it on May 1, 1985. The embargo was lifted in March 1990. The purpose of the embargo was to undermine the rule of the Marxist Sandinista government that had come to power in 1979, sparking a civil war that raged on and on. While the embargo was in place, travel from the U.S. was restricted, so few North Americans had any involvement with Nicaragua. John Johnson was one of those few who did. On my first visit there, I was struck by the many symbols of revolution on display. This one was at main intersection from the airport into Managua. The man holds a hoe in one hand and a rifle in the other, symbolizing the common man fighting for freedom.

An attorney by profession, John was also an elder at the church in Falls Church, Virginia, that supported the Kelly family. He later became a member of the HTI Board. During the 1980s he worked for the federal government negotiating treaties with countries in Central America to allow the U.S. to put satellites in the airspace above them. Wherever he went, he attended a local Church of Christ and was well acquainted with the Rene Polanco congregation in Managua. Once when he visited there, José and Noel told him of their dream to have a medical evangelism ministry in the church and showed him their clinic. It consisted of one room with a storage cabinet in it. Inside the storage cabinet there was one shoebox full of medicine. That was it. But John was impressed with their vision. He handed them $500 that day and prayed God's blessings on their dream.

José told me years later how offended they had been at the time. They had not wanted John's money, but rather wanted his help to connect with a North American congregation that would make their dream possible. John, however, believed more in "empowerment" rather than charity. He believed that the Rene Polanco leaders were capable of making their own dream happen.

Even though the church leaders had not appreciated John's response to their petition, they ultimately realized it was just the push they needed. It helped them understand more clearly their own responsibility in fleshing out their vision. They began sharing that understanding with the congregation. The members of the congregation immediately set about saving every penny they could for construction and soon had enough to do some modest remodeling of their building. Members of the church brought what they could to contribute...a sack of cement, a length of rebar, a few Córdobas (Nicaraguan currency). This building process energized their entire church.

By the time they requested additional help from HTI, the church was in *full ownership* of the medical clinic vision. When HTI received their proposal, John provided Health Talents with a solid recommendation for it.

Their plan was to establish a small clinic in the church building that would be operated by Dr. Juliana Mena, José Garcia's wife. What they wanted from Health Talents was logistical help in the form of donated medicines, equipment, and funds to buy a neighboring property that would give them the needed space to better function. They hinted that their ultimate goal was for Health Talents to oversee the project.

Like John Johnson had been, those of us meeting with José, Noel and Dr. Gonzales were impressed with their plan. It seemed to have been well thought out. We were also impressed with the extensive level of evangelizing that appeared to be taking place in the church. It was an example of how adversity makes one stronger. Since the embargo had prevented outsiders from coming as missionaries, the Nicaraguan churches knew that if evangelizing was to be done, they would have to do it. And they did.

We made only two promises that day: to consider their proposal and to bring a mobile medical team to Managua to check out the potential. The first mobile medical team went to Nicaragua on November 4-9, 1994, and it was a resounding success. We treated nearly 2,000 patients in three days. We've gone every year since.

After reviewing their proposal and after completion of that first mobile medical team, the HTI board felt that with minimal logistic support the Rene Polanco church could establish and operate a clinic without HTI involvement. There were several medical doctors in the congregation who could rotate in clinic, and Jose was a very capable administrator. Their evangelistic zeal was already proven. They did not need much help.

For the past 20 years HTI has been taking one mobile medical team a year to Managua. In addition to conducting clinic at Rene Polanco, we travel to outlying villages where we typically treat between 1,200 to 1,500 people during the few days we are there.

Some of these sites are very primitive, such as Nuevo Horizonte. At the close of the week, we leave any leftover medicine with the Rene Polanco clinic.

Dr. Alan Boyd (Ctr) with preachers at Nuevo Horizonte, Nicaragua

Dr. Alan Boyd, Dr. Charles Jarrett, Dr. David Weed, pharmacist Larry Owens, Gary Tabor, Grace McIntyre, and Steve Fox have dedicatedly comprised the core of the Nicaraguan team for the last several years. Others come and go, but these folks go every year. For many years pharmacists Dave Ellis and Guthrie Hite were the dedicated mainstay pharmacists of the team until they retired. Grace McIntyre recently decided she could no longer make the trip, so she ceded her place to Robert Taylor, one of the ministers at the Waterview Church of Christ.

The 2013 Nicaragua Mobile Medical Team

Our initial assessment of the talent and ability at Rene Polanco proved to be correct. Their clinic is now an officially licensed medical/dental clinic that meets all the government standards. HTI, the Waterview Church of Christ in Richardson, Texas, and some individuals have provided financial help from time to time, but by and large Rene Polanco is operating its own ministry.

A typical mobile clinic day at the Rene Polanco church building

Jose Garcia also coordinates the Children's Breakfast Program. In 2002 the church began serving breakfast and a Bible story to 30 neighborhood children aged 4 through 10. It now operates at two different locations every Saturday morning with about 135 children attending. Through the efforts of Grace McIntyre the program became a ministry of the children of the Waterview Church of Christ in Richardson, Texas. Dr. Charles Jarrett shared news of the program with his church, the Church of Christ of Bethlehem in Spencer, Tennessee, and in 2009 they began supporting the program as well. The breakfast program has become a vital ministry in Managua because of the help it provides and access it affords to neighborhood families. Several parents have attended church services and many have come to know the Lord because the church first fed their children.

Another amazing ministry at Rene Polanco is the deaf ministry. In order to start the ministry several years ago, Jose had to learn sign language. Today there are easily 25 mostly young adults in the class…and it has produced some baptisms (and a few weddings) along the way! This is such an amazing ministry in a place where so few opportunities are available to the deaf.

As John Johnson said so long ago, *"Empowerment is better than charity."* Rene Polanco is a golden example of that.

CHAPTER 11:
CHOCOLÁ CLINIC CONTINUES

1994-2002

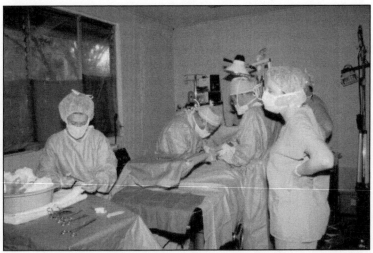

Dr. Brian Camazine and surgery team at work in Chocola

The surgical ministry continued at Chocolá. The size of the teams grew as confidence in the program increased around the country. We developed a core of committed volunteers for the quarterly surgical clinics and that aided tremendously in stabilizing the program. Those committed volunteers helped mold the surgery ministry into what it is today. They came with a passion to use their talents to serve God. They helped define what physical problems were treatable at Chocolá, aided in setting parameters for what procedures would be used, and diligently participated in the search for needed equipment, supplies and people. Despite the risk of omitting someone, I need to give a special "shout out" to some of these people who were so important during the first couple of years of HTI's surgical ministry. They include HTI Board members Dr. Quinton Dickerson, Dr. Ken Mitchell, Dr. John Peden, RN Vicki Ratts, and Dr. Dan Wilson. Other medical personnel included Dr. Jeff Bennie, Dr. Roy Kellum and Dr. Danny Minor, and Dr. Larry Patterson (who all later became HTI Board members), CRNA Eddie Milam, RNs Neva and Glen Berkey, RN Connie Campbell, RN Lisa Cantrell, RN Nancy Carlisle, RN Betsy Keene, RN Cathy Love, RN Martha Oyston, RN Jurdean Reed, RN Bonnie Spink, and surgical tech Richard Yates. Their personal participation, guidance and especially their enthusiasm helped shape the structure of the surgical ministry in invaluable ways. Years later Glen and Neva Berkey moved to Guatemala and volunteer their skills during surgical clinics. What a blessing they have been to us!

There were others with no medical training that played pivotal roles. Gary Tabor was one of those. He spent several years serving on the HTI Board as a "work horse." Whenever there was a job to do that did not require medical expertise, Gary was there. From working as a dental helper to being a part of the *Guatemala Grunts* team to helping install the water filtration system at Clinica Ezell and even playing chauffeur in Nicaragua, Gary was always willing to work.

Alfred Anderson was another. Alfred is a college-educated soybean farmer from Clarksville, Tennessee. Alfred first came on the September 1996 clinic, announcing he was willing to do whatever we needed him to do. Since he was a farmer, I assumed he was mechanically minded and asked him to be in charge of sterilization. This was a crucial task because without sterile instruments the surgeons were "dead in the water." Remember those donated 1950s Army MASH Unit autoclaves? They worked but were temperamental to say the least. Alfred accepted the challenge and promptly set about to charm them. The first thing he did was to name them Willie and Matilda, then proceeded to work his magic. They behaved better that week than they ever had! We told Alfred he must have a gift. Their working smoothly was certainly a gift to the surgical team.

Alfred quickly became a legend among Chocolá team members because he could repair anything, like Bovie machines and OR suction pumps. What magnified his legend, however, was that he learned how to work the autoclaves to his advantage. Bear in mind that we had no hot water in Chocolá. Any warm showers to be had resulted from solar water heaters that team members brought. We would fill them up in the morning and lay them out in the sun. By evening they were typically warm enough to at least take the edge off the normally icy cold water that came from the faucet. That bit of warmth was such a blessing. Hot water was such so valued that some of the worst moments of tension we had at Chocolá occurred when someone used someone else's bag of warm water!

Alfred took note of that and realized that he could be of service to the team by heating water in the autoclaves at night. He good naturedly began bartering it off to people who had forgotten to fill their bags that morning. A Payday candy bar here, a bag of M&Ms there, and before you knew it, Alfred was in business. The hot water he offered made him the most popular man on campus!

His legend extends even today at Clinica Ezell, where you will find him still tending autoclaves. A few years ago Alfred began coming twice a year, but now *he* brings the snacks! He places them on the counter in the autoclave room so others can share. He and Eugene Campbell, Connie Campbell's husband, are also our emergency autoclave crew. They have made several trips to Clinica Ezell to either perform maintenance on the autoclaves or install new ones. Alfred has proven his worth over and over, so the Board invited him to join their ranks in 2010. They were pleased when he accepted their invitation.

Life After the Kellys

We knew that it would be a challenge to find a replacement for Dr. Kelly when it came time for him to leave. He had a large clinical practice that would definitely need coverage. God answered our prayers and provided several people to serve in Mike's stead. Following is a brief description of each one:

Dr. David and Jeri Hurley

After the Kelly family moved back to the States in early 1995, pediatrician Dr. David Hurley volunteered to operate Mike's clinics for a year. He, his wife Jeri and their 3-year-old son, Nathan, were a godsend. David and Jeri already spoke Spanish, which made for a smooth transition, and they even moved into Mike and Julie's house! David filled that void as smoothly as anyone possibly could. Nathan was such a little charmer that seemingly everyone in Santo Tomás knew who he was. And he came to love Guatemala's *helados* (ice cream).

Dr. Sergio and Veronica Castillo

HTI's awareness that the Hurley family was scheduled to leave in July 1996 prompted them to ask Sergio to move to the coast, as we refer to it, so there would be continuing clinic coverage. We suggested that he and his family could live in one of the houses on the Chocolá property. He and Veronica readily agreed and made the move. A retired physician, Dr. Angel Juarez, took Sergio's place at Clinica Promesa.

Having Sergio and Veronica in Chocolá was helpful for many reasons. Most important was that Sergio could keep the Xejuyup clinic running, but another advantage was that he and Veronica gave more careful attention to the facility itself. I could tell a difference almost immediately. Veronica's touch in organization and cleanliness was apparent to all.

Dr. Tony Rector Family

In January 1996 Dr. Tony Rector contacted HTI and expressed interest in becoming a part of the HTI Guatemalan ministry. He was a family practice physician from East Texas who had been on multiple short term mission trips to Honduras. He was now feeling the pull to full-time missions. His wife Dana and three children, Calli (14), Aaron (12) and Brady (8) were all excited about going.

We had some concerns about their going to Guatemala because of the ages of their children. We talked seriously with them about this and also asked them to undergo professional counseling with veteran missionary counselor Dr. Clyde Austin of Abilene Christian University. In the end we felt they would do well and agreed for them to go. The entire family was delightful with their positive attitudes, flexibility and an obvious dedication to God.

There were two immediate obstacles to their leaving. They needed to sell both their house and Dana's business, a successful kitchen shop. They put them both up for sale with a prayer that if God looked favorably on their decision to make the move, He would see that the house and business sold. They both sold immediately. So, in the fall of 1996 they moved to Santo Thomas, Guatemala, for two years. Again, they moved into the same house where both the Kellys and Hurleys had lived. Tony already spoke some Spanish and that aided in the transition. Dana left her mark by dramatically changing the menu served during the surgical clinics from all Guatemalan to a combination of Guatemala/U.S. fare that remains popular to this day.

Terri and James Wheeler

Physician's Assistant Terri Wheeler came to HTI with years of orthopedic surgery experience. She expressed interest in joining the ministry team when she was single and made a survey trip in 1996 that confirmed her desire to move to Guatemala. The Board was very interested in her expertise, knowing she would be valuable during the surgical clinics. Soon afterward she met and married James, a certified public accountant, and he committed to go with her to support her in her life's dream. In early 1997, after only three months of marriage, they moved to Santo Tomás. Between surgical clinics, Terri treated patients in the Xejuyup clinic with Sergio and Tony Rector. They divided the workload, with some going on mobile clinics while others stayed at the base clinic.

Appropriate Technology Missions

Charlie Pulliam: We had our first intern in Appropriate Technology during 1996. Charlie Pulliam wanted to serve as a Medical Missions Intern while he waited for acceptance into medical school. John Wright was still working with Clinica Cristiana at that time, so he enlisted Charlie's aid in expanding the fuel-efficient stove ministry into the Chocolá area. The stoves had two specific benefits: They routed the smoke from inside family homes to the outside plus used very little wood. The family desiring one of these stoves had to buy the materials (about $50) and Charlie would provide the expertise and labor. Despite the cost, Charlie was invited into many homes to build these stoves during his year in Guatemala. The community understood the benefits because smoky houses caused a great deal of asthma and upper respiratory illness and contributed to deforestation. His gentle nature, quick wit and dedication made us both grow to love him and sorry to see him leave.

While he was in Guatemala working as an intern, Charlie met Amy Reed, one the MET students that year. When he returned home, he married her.

Chocolá family's old stove…and family standing proudly by their new stove

Jeff Colvin: Jeff was from Birmingham, Alabama, and his mother actually recruited him. She and I met at the Nashville Jubilee as she gathered some HTI brochures to take to her son. She said, *"I think he would like this."* Jeff had been out of college for a year and was feeling restless, she told me. He was realizing the importance of following your dreams, and he was ready to do that but he did not have a clear focus.

Jeff's mother was right. He *was* interested and arrived in Santo Tomás in the summer of 1997. Jeff picked up where Charlie had left off and fell into step easily with the Rectors, Sergio, and Terri and James. His blond good looks, outgoing nature and ready smile paved the way for his acceptance by the local people. He was so well liked that he told me once that he felt like he was on "gringo TV" because everywhere he went, people watched him! Jeff was a definite asset to the ministry. He was such a great asset that when he returned home in 1998 the Board asked him to lead the new capital campaign. He agreed to do so and led the campaign to fruition. More about that later.

September 1997 Surgical Clinic

Throughout all these transitions, the ministry was running smoothly. Our relationships with area churches were growing stronger all the time. We continued to treat thousands of patients each year at Clinica Promesa, Xejuyup, and the mobile medical clinics both physically and spiritually, and for the most part our hundreds of surgical patients had done well. That all changed in September 1997.

It was a GYN/plastic surgery clinic. We had never done plastic surgery before. This team boasted two plastic surgeons that had been college roommates at Abilene Christian then had gone to medical school together. Both ended up specializing in plastic surgery. And they each specialized in burn stricture release. They lived in widely separated states, but when they heard about our clinic, they wanted to come and serve together. We were excited at the prospect of adding this surgical option for our patients.

We scheduled only a few patients for the plastic surgeons. The two youngest were Dorcas and Reuben Maximillian, whose mother called him "Ru-been." We called him Baby Max. We had only one crib so the babies shared it, with their parents ever present. Both babies had cleft palates and each was only a few weeks old, very weak, and severely malnourished. They were literally starving to death because they could not suckle. Plastic surgeons typically want babies to be at least a year old and weigh ten pounds before they attempt a repair. These babies were in such bad shape, however, that the doctors reasoned they would surely die without intervention, so they decided to try.

Another patient was Juana, a pretty, dark-haired Mayan woman of about 20 years of age who was a new bride. Sergio met her when she had recently come to his clinic for a minor medical problem. He noticed that her neck on down to her shoulder on her right side was badly scarred. He asked about it, and she explained that she had epilepsy and during a seizure as a small child she had fallen into the family "stove" (which was nothing more than a hole dug in the ground filled with stones that grew hot from the flames). She landed in the fire on her right side, so her right arm and shoulder were badly burned. As it healed, scar tissue grew between her upper arm and her right side, completely immobilizing her upper right arm.

Knowing plastic surgeons were coming on the next surgical clinic that specialized in burn stricture release, Sergio asked Juana if she would like to see if they could do something about her arm. She enthusiastically agreed. She seemed an ideal candidate.

The doctors operated on the babies first. Initially, both seemed to do well. One nurse was assigned to monitor the babies carefully. All day everything seemed fine. Very early the next morning the nurse observed that Dorcas was in distress. Despite all efforts to help her, she was clearly failing and soon began to exhibit signs of neurological weakness. Dr. Sergio made the decision to transport her to the hospital in Mazatenango for more intensive care.

This was going on with Dorcas as Baby Max laid just a couple of feet away. You can imagine the fear Max's parents were experiencing. Baby Max's Mayan mother seemed especially traumatized, even though her baby was doing well. She rarely made eye contact with any of us, and when she did her eyes were filled with fear.

After Dr. Sergio left with Dorcas, the surgeries continued. It came Juana's turn in the operating room.

It was a long, tedious surgery. The surgeons had to first cut through the scar tissue that was binding her upper arm and remove as much of it as possible. Next they took skin grafts from her thigh to replace the skin they had removed. The anesthesiologist monitored her carefully throughout the day as the surgery continued. They worked patiently over a period of six or seven hours, and were finally satisfied that they had done all they could do. They moved Juana to the patient ward and waited for her to wake up. All of her vital signs were good, so her condition was considered stable.

The nurses carefully monitored her progress, but Juana did not wake up. With every passing hour, the surgeons were more concerned. Everyone prayed for her to wake up, but she did not. A day later with still no sign of awakening, they observed that she was beginning to pull her body into a fetal position. That was not good.

Soon afterward the surgeons decided that she, too, needed to be moved to a place with better monitoring equipment, so Sergio took her to Mazatenango as well. That was a bleak night at the clinic, knowing that we had had to transport not just one but two patients to the hospital. It was even worse the next day when we received word that Dorcas had died.

A palpable grief settled over the team that night. We discussed over and over what might have caused the problems, but there was no way to know, especially with Juana. Dorcas was so tiny that many things could have tipped the balance for her. With Juana, though, except for her epilepsy she seemed healthy. We speculated that because of her epilepsy she might have endured some type of neurological event, but without the proper equipment there was no way to know. All we knew for certain was that in our entire four years of performing surgery in Chocolá, we had never experienced anything even remotely like this.

Jim Middleton, minister of the Northwest Church of Christ in Houston, was team chaplain that week. From the very first visiting mobile medical team, the HTI Board had insisted that we designate a chaplain for each team. His job was to bring us back daily to the spiritual center of our work. Through the years we have had many wonderful devotional thoughts that helped team members understand better the importance of what they were doing. We never expected to need grief counseling.

Jim Middleton, however, stepped up without hesitation and provided that for us. He did an amazing job of helping the team work through the blanket of pain that lay heavy on them. Dr. Ken Mitchell was the medical director for the week, and he helped the non-medical team members understand that occasional bad outcomes are inevitable whenever you perform surgery.

Enmeshed with the pain we felt for Dorcas' death was real fear of how the community would react. Only five years earlier we had endured the period when everyone was suspicious of gringos who might kidnap their babies. We spent much time in concentrated prayer that night.

The week of surgery was nearly over when we learned that Juana, too, had died. Her husband and her parents came back to Chocolá to tell us. My fear of possible retribution returned momentarily, but as soon as we spoke with the family we saw we had no cause for concern. Their primary emotion was sorrow. We shared their sorrow and they seemed to appreciate it and were grateful.

Because there had been not just one but two deaths that week, Dr. Sergio was required to appear before the medical ethics board in Guatemala City. He had to submit the patients' files to the committee as part of the investigation.

Prior to that meeting, the committee had sent an investigator to the Chocolá clinic to evaluate the facility. Sergio was there when the investigator arrived and showed him around. As old and well used as our equipment was, throughout the visit the investigator repeatedly kept saying things like, *"Wow! You have one of those? I've heard about them but I've never seen one."* Sergio was satisfied we had passed that hurdle.

After reviewing all the files, the committee ruled the deaths accidental. The chairman of the committee turned out to be one of Sergio's favorite medical school professors. He pulled Sergio aside after the meeting and offered him some words of wisdom. Quite simply, he cautioned Sergio to be extremely careful because these incidents had shined the light on what appeared to be jealousy of HTI's work among some Guatemalan surgeons. They would likely be quick to file complaints in the future. We found this to be ironic since the vast majority of our caseload was Mayan Indians, and the average surgeon in Guatemala did not operate on Mayans.

Though we have had some close calls since, nothing like that has ever happened again. The difference that it caused in my life is that I no longer take successful surgical clinics for granted. I had theoretically known all along that bad outcomes were possible, but up until the September 1997 clinic I had never consciously considered it to be an even remote possibility for us. I had naively possessed a basic assumption that things would go well. This dark week in time changed that for me. I still pray the same prayer I've always prayed before clinics, but I pray it more passionately now. *"Lord, be with us. Keep both us and our patients safe."* Now I add this phrase: *"If that isn't your will, give us strength."*

I carried the pain of that week with me forward. In time I felt God's mercy shine on me and He gave me comfort. The first sign of His awareness of my personal pain was about three months later. One morning I noticed a very small article in my morning paper about a 9-year-old boy from South America who had been taken by another mission organization to Vanderbilt Hospital in Nashville for facial-cranial surgery. The article stated that despite the successful surgery, the young boy never woke up.

As sad as that was, that tiny 2" article gave me such comfort. If such a thing could happen at Vanderbilt University with all the latest technology that we didn't have, it wasn't surprising that something similar could happen in our little clinic in Chocolá, Guatemala.

I had to wait three years to receive the final piece of comfort God provided me. Carolyn Freeman and I were walking down a street in Santo Tomás one day when Carolyn suddenly pointed to our left and said, *"Look! Isn't that Baby Max?"*

I turned and look in the direction she was pointing, and sure enough, it was Baby Max! He was now three years old. He was sitting on a stoop with his sister, and when we walked over to them he looked up and smiled a big beautiful smile at me! He was such a picture of health that I kept saying, *"Look at him! Just look at him! He is beautiful!"*

We then noticed his mother and father standing nearby. We were wearing our HTI scrub tops, so they knew who we were. When we waved, Max's mother waved and smiled broadly. It was the first time I had ever seen her smile. My heart was now at peace.

CHAPTER 12:
ROAD TO CLINICA EZELL

1997-2002

The year 1997 was a year of transitions. Halfway through the year Steve and Magda Sherman made the decision to separate from Health Talents and pursue other interests in Guatemala. Steve, Magda, Lisa, Sarah and Amy had been central to HTI's work for such a long time it was difficult to imagine how we could move forward without them. Their capable handprints were on everything we did from the Las Cruces clinic to Belize, Clinica Promesa, the ABC program, and the surgical ministry. Magda had been especially valuable in navigating the Guatemalan governmental waters. Their daughters had even translated in our clinics from a very young age. We knew we would miss them terribly, and we did.

John Wright, James and Terri Wheeler, and Jeff Colvin all concluded their service in Guatemala in either late 1997 or early 1998. John returned home to Texas after devoting four years to HTI; James and Terri completed their year-long commitment and went home to Nashville; and after his year-and-a-half in Guatemala, Jeff returned to Birmingham in the spring of 1998 to pursue grad school. Losing all these folks in such a short time left us short-handed, but we still had a ministry to run, so we got back to work.

The first task was to find someone to replace Steve in the Guatemala office. HTI values partnering with Guatemalan Christian nationals, so rather than try to recruit another North American missionary, we searched within Guatemala. Evangelist Roberto Alvarez seemed an ideal choice. He was the dynamic minister of the Zone 18 Iglesia de Cristo, educated at Baxter Institute in Honduras, plus he spoke excellent English. He and his lovely, talented wife Marta Elena had three young children.

Roberto's main concern in accepting the invitation to work with HTI was his love of sharing the Lord with others. Though one of HTI's charges to him was to expand HTI's evangelistic outreach through local churches, he was concerned that his administrative responsibilities would limit his time to be *personally* involved. Roberto served excellently with HTI for a year and gave it all he had. But his initial instincts proved to be correct. He missed terribly not being involved in day-to-day evangelism, so we reluctantly accepted his resignation and he returned to the Zone 18 church.

During Roberto's tenure in 1998 he hired Dr. Walter Sierra to be the physician at Clinica Promesa. Dr. Walter and his psychologist wife had two young daughters. This was a good move, as Dr. Walter is still a vital part of this ministry 15 years later.

We were fortunate to gain a new medical missions intern in Allen Smith, who arrived in Guatemala in the summer of 1998. Allen had made several trips to Guatemala as a youngster and teenager with his parents, and he was also a former MET student. His interest was more in the direction of evangelism than Appropriate Technology, so when he finished language school Roberto took him under his wing and found him a room in the basement of the Zone 18 Iglesia de Cristo. During an average week Allen worked with the staff at the Promesa Clinic in various ways, but during surgery clinics his life was quite different. He became the key person in coordinating the team's arrival and clinic readiness. Allen and his wife Sandy, also a former MET student, have since become full-time missionaries in Peru. They are the proud parents of four beautiful, blond-haired little girls.

We searched for Roberto's successor among the churches in Guatemala City. Ultimately, Nery Castillo recommended that we consider Hugo Fuentes of the Zone 11 Iglesia de Cristo. The Board knew Hugo's business background would be beneficial, so they hired him. He spoke no English, however, so I was challenged to beef up my Spanish studies.

Meanwhile, back in the States the Board became more determined than ever to build its own surgical facility. The

Chocolá facility had never been ideal, but it was becoming more and more of a liability and with each passing year as its electrical system grew worse and worse. On many occasions we did surgery by flashlight for the few moments it took to get the generator started. We urged all team members to bring flashlights and fresh batteries.

(You never knew when you might need a flashlight. On one trip I was standing in baggage claim in the Guatemala City airport along with hundreds of others when the lights went out. It was pitch black! We all stood perfectly still for a few seconds until I remembered I had a tiny flashlight hooked to my backpack. I turned it on, and as its little light lit up the darkness everyone around me took an audible breath!)

The water supply at the clinic was also grossly inadequate. We had been caught without warning (and without water) a time or two when we first began doing surgery, so we learned to fill tubs with water when the water pressure was strong. When it was low we resorted to the *dipper scrub* method. I have many photographs of one surgeon dipping water from a bucket and pouring it over another surgeon's hands as he scrubbed for the next case. Clearly something had to be done.

Though we had raised a sizable amount of money for construction, it never seemed enough. This was a continuing frustration to the Board. We had used some of the donations to purchase the land, remodel the Chocolá facility, and buy furniture and equipment that we could not otherwise get donated. We still had a substantial balance in the bank. However, each time we periodically requested an estimate from a Guatemalan construction firm, it was always for an estimated cost well above the amount we had accumulated. The Board continued steadfast in its resolve to go forward on a cash basis, so we kept on operating at Chocolá.

Finally, the Board decided that it was time to initiate another capital campaign that would, hopefully, provide enough money to begin construction. Not long after Jeff Colvin returned to the States in early 1998 the Board asked him to lead the new *Great Physician Campaign*. He agreed to defer grad school in order to accept this opportunity/challenge. Ed Welch, an elder at the GracePoint Church of Christ in Montgomery, Alabama, volunteered to serve as Campaign Chair. Ed had substantial experience with capital campaigns. We moved forward with confidence that the clinic was about to become a reality.

The new campaign began in mid-1998 with a base goal of $1,000,000 and a challenge goal of $2,000,000. As should happen with any good capital campaign, the Board members showed their belief in the campaign by being the first to contribute. The Board had 100% participation before it asked anyone else to contribute.

The HTI Board has always taken its financial responsibility seriously. For many years, as a matter of principle, the Board members personally covered my salary. That allowed me the privilege of telling everyone that 100% of their contributions would go directly to the ministry.

Jeff and Ed set out raising money and experienced a good deal of success. Their crowning achievement came in the fall of 1999 when they met with representatives from the Ezell Foundation in Nashville. The now deceased Miles Ezell Sr. had been the patriarch of the Ezell clan in Nashville. He and his wife Estelle had started Ezell's Dairy in 1925 with 14 rented cows. Despite the Great Depression and World War II, their dairy survived and grew. In 1945 they merged that dairy with another, and Purity Dairies was born. They began to prosper, and in 1964 created a philanthropic family foundation that his children and grandchildren now administer.

In late August 1999 Jeff, Ed Welch and Roger McCown traveled to Nashville to meet with Miles Jr. and his brother Bill Ezell. Ed, Jeff and Roger outlined the scope of the Health Talents ministry, its philosophy and goals. They then laid out the vision for the new surgical clinic. The Ezell brothers were intrigued. As the meeting drew to a close, Jeff, Ed and Roger felt good about the reception they had received, but they were thrilled when Miles committed to a grant from the Ezell Foundation in the amount of $250,000 to help make it happen!

Their incredibly generous gift put us over the top, both literally and figuratively. Health Talents had never received such a sizable gift and the Ezell Foundation had never given one that large, so everyone was excited. In gratitude for this blessing, the HTI Board voted at its next meeting to name the new clinic in honor of the family: Clinica Ezell. We were on our way.

Bates Medical Evangelism Scholarship Begins

Charles Bates was president of Health Talents for its first 15 years (1973-1988). Knowing it to be illogical to assume anyone could follow Charles' example of serving for 15 years straight, the Board established two-year rotating terms of service for the office of the president with a limit of two terms. Dr. Quinton Dickerson agreed to be the first to serve.

Faced with the gargantuan task of working full time and managing Health Talents part time, Quinton quickly felt the burden and responsibility that Charles had carried for so long.

When Charles resigned from the Board in 1998 due to increasing work pressures, Quinton began looking for a way to honor Charles. He and the Board designed the perfect way. In the fall of 2000, the Board announced the Bates Medical Evangelism Scholarship program. It was designed to "grow our own" medical professionals in Guatemala. Licensing of foreign-born medical professionals had become increasingly difficult, so this seemed a perfect solution. Not only would it provide an endless supply of medical professionals, it would help ensure the future of the work Charles loved. He was very pleased.

Darling Ayerdis of Managua, Nicaragua, and Alex Gonzales were the first two Bates Scholars. Darling wanted to study nursing, and Alex had applied to dental school. After only one year, however, Alex realized that dentistry was not for him. Marcos Lux was selected in his stead the next year. Bates Scholars are aware that they are obligated to work with HTI for the same number of years for which they received a scholarship.

When she finished school, Darling came to work as a resident nurse at Clinica Ezell. When Marcos completed dental school, he went to work with the Chichi team. Each of them has since completed their obligation but choose to continue working with HTI. We have since had three other Bates Scholars come to work. Dr. Jessica Romano completed dental school then worked with Silvia for a time, then her brother Dr. Ruben Romano worked in the highlands. Dr. Nehemias Lopez has just begun his tenure in the spring of 2013. Nidian Patricia Poz is expected to join the HTI team next year when she graduates from medical school. All are terrific assets to the work. Board member Harriette Shivers has chaired the Scholarship Committee for years, placing continued emphasis on attracting quality candidates. Her efforts have clearly paid off.

Movin' Them Rocks!

Because the estimates from the construction firm in Guatemala City continued to be unduly high, we decided to take a different approach. Nery Castillo volunteered and the HTI Board agreed for him to be construction project manager. He would organize and direct the construction himself.

One of the first things Nery did was to suggest that we hire Baldemar Ruiz. Baldemar was about 40 years old and a leader in the Chicacao Iglesia de Cristo, right down the road from the property. Preaching and construction were his vocations.

Baldemar was the son of Luis Ruiz. Luis had been a member of the Pentecostal church in Chicacao when in the early 1960's he stumbled upon a brochure inviting him to study the Bible. The brochure had been distributed by Church of Christ missionaries to Guatemala. Luis became convinced that he needed to be baptized the "New Testament" way, so he asked his Pentecostal pastor to rebaptize him. The pastor did so reluctantly, and Luiz became the leader of his Pentecostal church, preaching and baptizing regularly. He eventually took down the Pentecostal sign and put up an Iglesia de Cristo sign in its place. Jerry Hill, one of those early Church of Christ missionaries, made many trips to Chicacao to teach training classes in that church. Luis became one of the best, most ardent followers of Jesus in the area and planted many churches. He was enthusiastic about evangelism and taught his sons to be the same, Baldemar among them.

The Board asked Dr. Ken Mitchell and me to check out Baldemar's credentials when we next went to Guatemala. After dinner one evening during the subsequent clinic, Ken and I went to Baldemar's house. Whenever I think about that evening, I have to smile remembering how patient Baldemar was with us. We didn't have a resume to refer to, so we had to ask questions directly then probe indirectly for answers to questions that might be considered an insult. We quizzed him about his construction experience, then asked about the size of the largest job he had ever worked on. He told us that it was a 14-story building in Mexico. *"Well, that will do well enough,"* I thought.

We needed to know if he could read blueprints, so Ken spread the surgical facility blueprints across Baldemar's kitchen table and began pointing out various items. I would point at something and ask, *"What does this mean? What is this?"* Baldemar would glance down and tell me. After playing that little charade two or three times, I could sense his impatience. It was clear he could read blueprints. We left, satisfied he could do the job.

Steve Sherman and Baldimar Ruiz

Thankfully, Baldemar was willing to accept HTI's offer to serve as onsite supervisor for the project. He promptly began hiring able-bodied men from the surrounding area to help. We were pleased to learn how enthusiastic they had all been about being a part of something quite extraordinary in their community.

Once Baldemar was onboard and workers hired, we knew we could begin. Nery organized a groundbreaking ceremony to be held on the property on May 16, 2000. Representing the HTI Board, Roger McCown, Dr. Quinton Dickerson, Dr. John Peden and John Land traveled to Guatemala to attend, and they excitedly reported that 300 people from area churches and the community attended as well. Roger later reported...

"That was a grand occasion. Believers came from near and far to see the dirt turned on a dream they have shared for a long time. Our faith in them is confirmed when we hear them challenge each other, as recipients of God's grace in this visible form, to be a part of those who make it possible for their unbelieving neighbors to share in this grace and thereby be led to faith. It is reassuring to see those who will benefit from this wonderful facility already committing to helping make it a reality. They intend to have 'sweat equity' in this wonderful work. It will be all we can do to keep up with them."

The first and most difficult challenge was to clear the land of not merely trees but rocks. There were lots of rocks. Some of them were gigantic, often eight feet in diameter! Baldemar and his crew spent the summer of 2000 digging rocks out of the ground—with the help of a bulldozer. We have pictures to prove it. Once the rocks were out of the ground, however, they had to be moved from the construction site down to the far end of the property. It was back-breaking, arduous work, but Baldemar and his crew stayed with it until the site was cleared.

Rocks moved from building site

Construction itself could begin only after the rainy season passed, so it was November 2000 before Baldemar could begin digging the foundation. He anticipated that construction would take the better part of a year.

Roger McCown was president of HTI at this time, and it was a great advantage. Because Roger was a Spanish-speaker, he was able to communicate directly with Nery on what often seemed like thousands of details involved in erecting the surgical facility and dormitory.

Dr. Jeff Bennie had personally participated in many Chocolá surgical clinics, so he assumed the responsibility for clinic design. It was a tedious process. Jeff and his committee would present a draft and the Board would make its revisions. They would then send the blueprints to Guatemala to Dr. Sergio, who would make his revisions. This roundabout occurred three or four times before everyone agreed on a final plan. Nery hired an architectural firm in Guatemala City to work with HTI to ensure that the plans were drawn to Guatemala's construction regulations as well as its earthquake code.

The final plan called for the surgical building to contain three operating rooms, a patient ward for about 50, a nurses' station, sterilization room, and storage. There were also to be several exam rooms for use on mobile clinic days. The ward was divided into two parts with a half wall between the women's side and the men's side. The dormitory had 20 rooms; 18 were doubles and 2 were designed as family rooms, housing up to 6 people. The kitchen/dining area included sleeping quarters for the cooks, a lounge area inside, and two outdoor porches for relaxing and catching a cool breeze in the evening.

And the Work Goes On

Despite the swelling excitement about building a new surgical facility, life went on. In March 2000 a new dentist came onboard for Clinica Promesa. Dr. Silvia Albizures was a tall, strikingly beautiful young woman with an engaging smile and sensitive heart. She seemed especially attracted to the compassionate ministry of HTI and fit in well with the team immediately. She and Dr. Walter treated patients three days a week at the base clinic and traveled to mobile clinics twice a week.

It was about this time that we began noticing the demographics of the area were shifting. Initially, the majority of patients had been seen at Promesa, but now the team was treating many more patients on mobile clinic days than they did on Promesa days. They suspected the cause to be that Clinica Promesa was no longer the only medical clinic in the area. Several other clinics had sprung up in the blocks surrounding it. Hugo and the clinic staff were discussing ways to deal with that change. Clearly, they needed to modify the plan because something was changing.

The visiting U.S. mobile medical teams continued to have great impact. Dr. Sergio held clinics at our regular mobile sites of

Chocolá, Montellano (the name of the tiny community where Clinica Ezell would eventually be built), and Xejuyup and occasionally at more remote places, such as the pure Mayan communities of Pazité and Pasaquiyup. I loved going to these places and meeting the gentle people living in these isolated valleys or mountaintops. Pasaquiyup, for instance, lingers in my mind as one of the most beautiful places I have visited in Guatemala. Its location on a mountaintop beyond Xejuyup offers beautiful views. Its elevation is so high that each afternoon puffy clouds nestle down over the community and give everything a soft, fuzzy feeling, unlike anything I had ever experienced.

Dr. Sergio Castillo presenting a devo before clinic at Pasaquiyup

I have talked earlier about how vital mobile clinics are to the ministry. This is where church volunteers are likely to meet people from their community that they may never have met otherwise. The role of the local church members was to pray with incoming clinic patients. This presented the ideal opportunity to reveal the church's caring nature and crack open the door to a new relationship. HTI was determined to *help* local churches evangelize rather than do it for them. Roger McCown stressed that we remember HTI's role: It is to raise the *local church's visibility level* in the community, not get in between local churches and the people they are commanded to serve.

Additionally, we identified patients with surgical needs in mobile clinics. Time and again the medical team would discover people who had lived for long periods with medical conditions that not only could be *treated*, but could sometimes be *remedied* by surgery, such as men suffering from huge hernias and the women living with prolapsed uteri.

Each clinic's secret weapon, however, was love, kindness and respect. Patients always responded positively to that. Carlos Francisco Alvarado was a great example. Young Carlos was from a very poor family that lived in one of the most dangerous sections of Guatemala City. Until the day his older sister accidentally spilled hot water all over his little body, he had been an active five-year-old boy with dancing eyes. His family took him to the local church clinic for help…and received much more than they bargained for. The medical staff at the church addressed the physical crisis, and church members ministered to the family from a spiritual perspective. As the church members wrapped the entire family in loving compassion, they were drawn into a closer relationship with God and the Christian community.

In mid-2000 Dr. Jim Gill arrived as our new medical missions intern. Jim had just graduated from medical school, but he wanted to spend a year in a Spanish-speaking mission effort before beginning his residency in Emergency Medicine. Jim provided a great medical service as he worked alongside Dr. Sergio that year. He also assisted in surgery and served as the 2001 MET supervisor as well. In his free time he could often be found studying the Bible with others. We were sorry to see him leave!

Aubry Burr, daughter of HTI Board member Steve Burr, began a six-month internship in August 2000. Her primary responsibility was assisting Violeta Campos with many facets of the ABC program, from translating letters to delivering food. She also spent many weeks at Chocolá translating for visiting medical professionals during team weeks.

In Chocolá the surgeries continued as normal, except no day was ever *normal* on a surgery clinic. In February 2000 we were working away when late in the day a man showed up asking for help for his daughter. She had been in labor for 24 hours, he said, and didn't seem to be able to deliver the baby. It was our good fortune to have OB/GYN Dr. Ana Maria Gordon (now Gray) on that team. As a native Spanish-speaker, she would be able to easily communicate with the young woman. Several of us went to check on her. We drove as far as we could, parked, and then trudged down a steep rocky path to the *Three Little Pigs* bamboo house where the young woman lived. We found her lying on a bed in a dark corner of a room illuminated only by the light that found its way between the bamboo poles. Her mother stood anxiously nearby.

After examining her, Dr. Ana Maria judged that it would be safe to transport her to the clinic. The next question was *how?* The young woman was clearly in no condition to walk up that steep hill. Yankee ingenuity prevailed, and Jerry Ervin and three other men carefully picked up the four corners of the blanket on which she lay and carried her up that hill! The guys were careful not to let her body drag on the rocks, though there was often no more than two inches of clearance. Once at the truck, they laid her gently down on the mattress we had the forethought to bring. It was a bumpy, uncomfortable ride for her back to the clinic, but she made it.

Within an hour Dr. Ana Maria delivered a healthy baby girl. The Harding nursing students on the team were so excited to have witnessed a birth that they all huddled around the new infant on the other side of the room. I stood alongside the mother, sponging her forehead as Dr. Ana Maria busily finished up her work. I leaned down and asked what she was going to name her new baby. Her reply was immediate: *"Ana Maria,"* she said. *"Like her,"* nodding towards Dr. Ana Maria, who looked up and smiled broadly.

It was also on that February 2000 clinic that we ventured back into the plastic surgery ministry. After our disastrous first attempt in 1997, we were all a bit gun shy. Dr. Philip Strawther had agreed to come along and try it again. He had substantial experience in Third World settings because of his volunteer work with Operation Smile during the previous 10 years.

Along the way to the clinic, we stopped and picked up our ABC coordinator, Violeta Campos. She was accompanied by a woman holding a small boy who appeared to be about two years old. The child's head and neck were badly scarred, as if from a fire. Most of his hair was gone. Violeta explained that he had been severely scalded when he pulled a pot of boiling water off the stove onto his head.

I rode the rest of the way to Chocolá with my heart in my stomach. This child's injuries seemed far more serious than anything we could handle at our little clinic. I had only met Dr. Philip the day before and thus did not have any knowledge of how he would respond to a case like this. Because I had previously explained to him in detail about the 1997 clinic, I was confident he was aware of our need for caution. HTI could not afford another incident like the last one. I deeply hoped that he would not try to play *cowboy* and operate on this little boy. I was absolutely not going to allow it, but it would be so much better if he came to that conclusion on his own. So, I prayed...hard.

As soon as we arrived at Chocolá, Dr. Philip, the mother and her child, and a translator went off together into an exam room. I sat outside feeling almost physically ill. After what seemed like forever, they exited the room and Philip came over to me. He knelt down and almost apologetically told me that he believed that we should not operate on the little boy.

What a relief! The burden I'd felt only moments before evaporated in direct proportion to my rising respect for Philip! He went on to detail for me the challenges the child's case presented that he instinctively knew were beyond our capability in Chocolá. I was so grateful and reassured that I could trust him. Philip has since participated in plastic surgery clinics every year and has carefully molded our plastic surgery ministry into a viable and stable ministry. Several other plastic surgeons have participated in the ensuing years, but Dr. Philip Strawther has been our rudder in plastic surgery waters. We appreciate him, not only for his professional expertise and judgment but also because he started bringing his parents along.

Bill and Marjorie Strawther were always a joy when they came! Bill passed away a couple of years ago, but Marjorie still comes each February with Philip...and still leads the patients in a Conga line dance around the ward!

A key factor in operating on babies and small children is having adequately trained anesthesia personnel who are experienced with children. Dr. Jeff Bennie's brother, Jon, is a Pediatric Anesthesiologist who is at the top of his profession. He is excellent with babies. He has also developed for us a pool of experienced pediatric anesthesia providers that we have come to rely on. We never do plastic surgery on babies unless one of them is on the team.

Ever seen a mammoth-sized ovarian cyst? We did. In September 2000 a young and small (except for her belly) Mayan woman from Patzité was scheduled for surgery. Dr. Ken Mitchell operated on her and "delivered" an ovarian cyst the size of a watermelon! We weighed it, and it registered 21 pounds. Upon closer examination, Ken identified it as a dermoid cyst, complete with teeth and hair. The woman said she had been carrying that cyst for eight months. She was so relieved to be rid of it that she sobbed.

Two days later it became apparent that she was in trouble. She had lost a lot of blood during the surgical procedure and was just not bouncing back. She was in serious need of a blood transfusion. Dr. T. C. Krueger, a general surgeon on the team, told us he had O-negative blood and immediately volunteered to donate. This was the first time we ever transfused anyone. It was a dramatic moment when we carried the packet containing Dr. Krueger's still-warm blood across the room and began to transfuse the woman, who was growing weaker by the minute.

Her body's immediate reaction to the restorative power of fresh blood was amazing! Her cheeks suddenly regained some of their color, and within minutes she was markedly better. When she arrived, we guessed her "with cyst" weight to be 80 pounds. After the surgery, she was down to about 60 pounds. We prayed that now that she no longer had to carry that cyst comprising 25% of her body weight, she would gain both weight and strength back soon.

Clinica Ezell Construction Begins

By November 2000 Baldemar and his crew had completed the site preparation. The rainy season had ended, so construction could begin. That was critical to the successful digging of the foundation. Nery and Baldemar had calculated that construction would take a year, so that meant a tentative completion date of November 2001. Baldemar was eager to get started as there was much to be done structurally before the rains returned in May.

I remember visiting the site shortly after the foundation was poured and standing there thinking, *"Man, it is so big! I had no idea it was going to be so big!"* I was experiencing the shock of seeing for real what I had previously seen only in my imagination or on paper.

With each walk-through we made during the construction period, I was impressed with the quality of workmanship. Occasionally, some of us suggested design modifications. I made one upon seeing the completed wall that divided the patient ward into separate sections for men and women patients. Though the wall did not go all the way to the ceiling, it was high enough to restrict what limited air flow there was in the room. It also blocked line-of-sight access from across the room. At my suggestion, Baldemar removed three rows of concrete block to remedy the situation.

Bit by bit, the buildings grew. By the start of the rainy season, all the outside walls and roofs were up. The finishing work could continue regardless of the rain. As with any construction project, there were complications and delays along the way, but Baldemar and his men persevered. Knowing that the end of construction was in sight, the HTI Board declared that the September 2001 clinic be the final one held in Chocolá.

Final Clinic in Chocolá: Experiencing 9/11 in Guatemala

The surgical clinics in Chocolá had begun quite dramatically, so it seems somehow appropriate that the last clinic held there would end dramatically as well. But it wasn't by design.

It was September 11, 2001, a bright, beautiful Tuesday morning in Chocolá, and the clinic was in full swing. Both operating rooms had developed a rhythm and were humming right along. The post-op nurses had everything under control in the ward, and all seemed very peaceful. Then mid-morning Sergio's cell phone rang.

Dr. Sergio immediately called me aside and quietly spoke these words: *"Hugo just called from the City and told me to tell you that the United States is under attack."*

What do you do with those words when you are thousands of miles away from home and family, in a foreign country, and responsible for 30 people? I remember not being able to breathe for a few seconds. I then barked questions and demanded answers! *"What are you saying? When did it happen? Who did it? Is anyone hurt?"* Sergio told me what little he knew about the planes, the buildings and the fires. I listened with unbelief but knew it had to be true. And I knew I had to tell the others.

Rather than make a huge announcement that would interrupt the critical work underway, I went around to small groups of people and shared the terrible news. Everyone had the same shocked reaction. Sergio's wife, Veronica, sent someone to tell me that we could watch the news on their television to get more information. MTV had turned its station over to CNN so news of the attack could be broadcast in English around the world. The ones who could turn loose of their tasks ran to watch. I needed to call HTI President Roger McCown, so I went outside to search for a cell phone signal.

When Roger answered, I again asked for details and he told me what he knew. By then President Bush had closed all the borders and grounded all the planes. We had no way of knowing how long that hold would be in place. The one thing I did know was that we were safe in Chocolá, but I needed to call the American Embassy in Guatemala City to see what they thought we should do. I promised to call Roger back after I did so he could notify our families of our plans.

The American Embassy representative assured me that they had no reason to believe we were in danger. He suggested we maintain our schedule while keeping an eye on the news, knowing that our return flights might be delayed. That sounded logical to me, but I also knew we needed an alternate plan in case we weren't able to leave on Saturday. Since it was only Tuesday, we had a few days to formulate one.

I joined the others in front of the television and did what most Americans did that day—watch the planes crash into the Twin Towers over and over and over again. Our ABC coordinator Violeta Campos's teenage daughter Alejandra was with us, and she was the most upset of all because her father lived and worked in Manhattan. They had not been able to reach him, so they did not know yet if he was okay. Happily, Alejandra was able to speak with her father later that day and he reassured her that he was fine.

Because of what had happened in New York, we felt especially blessed that week because all our patients did well. We certainly did not need any more stress than we already had. Not only was there chaos at home, but we were sad because this was our last clinic in Chocolá. Most of the team members had been coming to Chocolá for many years, so leaving was hard. We had become part of the community.

We knew all the children: little sweet-natured Rosa, bright-eyed Derrick who had taught himself English by listening to gringos, and the little girl who from the age of five or six had always been looking after an increasing number of younger siblings. She carried one in a sling around her shoulders, and held hands with at least two others all the time. We had watched them grow up for the past eight years. Many of us had spent hours teaching Bible and hygiene classes to them in the courtyard. We taught them how to brush their teeth, and when we passed out toothbrushes, we taught them how to stand in line. We would miss them.

We knew our neighbors. We had enjoyed the bananas, papaya, and coconuts they offered as expressions of thankfulness for our presence. I've often laughed and said that Chocolá, Guatemala, was the only place where I believe I could have been elected mayor. Everyone seemed to know me there. From the moment we arrived and wherever I went in Chocolá, people would call out, *"Maria! Maria! Hola! Como estas?"*

On Thursday evening after dinner the community expressed its appreciation for the years of HTI presence among them by sending a marimba band over to entertain us! In yet another tender act to mark the solemnity and specialness of the occasion, the cooks had made tamales for dinner. Tamales are a very special food in the Mayan tradition and are served on special occasions. In light of what had happened at home and the anxiety of not knowing what perils our country might face in its aftermath, it was such solace to relax and let their kindness soak into our souls.

The words of my husband's deceased mother kept running through my head throughout the week. She had always been concerned about my going back and forth to Guatemala. She also worried about my sister Betty who lived in Venezuela with her Venezuelan-born husband. Having lived through World War II, my dear mother-in-law more than once expressed her concern saying, *"I just wouldn't do that. What if war broke out and you couldn't get back home?"* Now, all I could think was, *"War has broken out, and I can't get back home!"* Somewhere in heaven Granny was smiling. I had finally understood.

Tuesday soon became Friday, the day we were scheduled to drive to Antigua. We were encouraged because we had heard the night before that the planes were flying again. As we traveled down the highway on Friday morning, however, our travel agent Tami Pruitt called to say that our flight to Houston the next morning had been cancelled. Plan B would definitely need to be put into action. One option we jokingly discussed as we rode along was asking Wilmer the bus driver to drive north to the Texas border where we could just walk across like so many others did!

Hotel Antigua, our usual hotel in Antigua, is expensive. I reasoned that since we had no idea how long we would be in Antigua, we should switch to bed and breakfast housing in order to stretch our team money. Aubry Burr was again in Guatemala and had been with us all week. When we arrived in Antigua, she said she knew of some bed and breakfast establishments and was able to arrange accommodations for us at two adjoining ones. The cost was $10 per person per day. That would stretch out our trip money for several days.

The people in Antigua were so kind. Saturday was Guatemala's Independence Day, and we were deeply touched when we saw the Guatemalan flag flying at half-staff out of sympathy for what happened in our country. People stopped us in the market and on the street, clasping our hands in theirs as they told us how sorry they were. Many even offered prayers for our country as we stood there. When your heart is aching, kindness is a soothing balm.

It took three days to get everyone home. On Tuesday morning when the last of us were at the airport ready to go, a small plane crashed on the runway, causing several fatalities. It took five hours to get the runway open again. We would have been impatient and frustrated had it not been for the others in the waiting area. There was a large contingent of Guatemala women headed to Houston for an International Prayer Conference. Each and every one of them, even their children, wore a red, white and blue ribbon in solidarity with us. One beautiful young mother took the ribbon from her baby's blanket, pinned it to my shirt and prayed God's blessings on me and our country. I was so touched. I still have that ribbon today.

Eventually we boarded our plane and flew toward Houston. The moment the wheels touched down on U.S. soil the pilot came over the intercom and said, *"Welcome home. God bless America."* We all cried. As our plane approached the terminal building, we saw the biggest, most gigantic American flag any of us had ever seen hanging on the side of the building! With tears in my eyes, I mouthed a word of thanks to God above for bringing us home safely. I know I wasn't the only one to do so.

In our haste to get home, we deplaned quickly. I turned on my U.S. cell phone on as I walked hurriedly toward baggage claim. Just as I arrived it beeped, indicating I had a message. It was from my son David and was time stamped on Tuesday morning, September 11, at 10:30 a.m. He said, *"Mom, I have no idea if you will even get this message, but I wanted to let you know that Dad and I are okay. We've talked with Joanna (in Portland, OR), and she is okay. And we know YOU are okay because no one can find Chocolá, Guatemala!"* As I listened to his message, tears began streaming down my cheeks. The stranger next to me looked over and compassionately asked what was wrong, so I let him listen to it. He kept saying, *"Aw, that's nice. That's really nice."* I saved that message for a long time.

The Guatemala Grunt Group

Ever since Health Talents came into existence, we've stressed that everyone has God-given talents they can use in service to Him. Those talents don't have to be medical. We have urged people to go to Guatemala with the promise that there will be meaningful work for them to do, no matter what their skill level. That was never more accurate than with the Guatemala Grunt Group.

It was January 2002 and moving time was here. The construction of Clinica Ezell was nearly complete, and Dedication Day was only a month away. The biggest task remaining was to move everything over from the clinic at Chocolá. It was a mammoth, dirty and thankless task that would require many hands. I sent out a request for volunteers, and the Lord sent me just exactly who we needed. Veteran surgical RN Cathy Love became affectionately known as the *Chief Medical Officer*. Her expertise was vital to preparing the operating rooms for the first surgical clinic in Clinica Ezell. Two other RNs were on the team as well: Nancy Carlisle and HTI Board member Elaine Griffin were to organize the patient ward. These three were the "brains" of the group. Everyone else provided the enthusiastic brawn.

Gary Tabor acted as supervisor; and he and Nancy's husband Tommy, Elaine's husband Dennis, Darryl George, John Taylor, JoLee Thayer, and Valari Wedel formed a capable team. Aubry Burr volunteered to work with them. Of course, Baldemar, Sergio and Veronica shouldered much of the load, too.

My husband Carl and I had planned to be there, but the week before we were to leave on January 12, 2002, Carl had what is commonly known in the medical field as a Triple A: Abdominal Aortic Aneurysm. It required immediate surgery and lots of prayer. Both were effective; and three surgeries and two weeks of hospitalization later, he began to recover. But clearly, we would not be going to Guatemala. Nancy Carlisle later designed souvenir Guatemala Grunts t-shirts, and she graciously *photoshopped* us into the picture.

It was incredibly hard work. All week. It didn't help that the temperature at the new site felt at least 20 degrees hotter than Chocolá. When the team arrived in Chocolá, they were excited to see that Sergio, Veronica and some of the health promoters had already packed a great many of the supplies. They were momentarily heartened…until they realized just how many more there were. Board member Elaine Griffin remembers looking at a stack of very old supplies slated to be moved and noticing how dirty and dusty they were. She made an executive decision to burn them and a good many other items that had outlived their usefulness. She wondered if we had smelled the smoke all the way to Birmingham.

The only vehicles they had at their disposal were the van they had arrived in and a pickup truck, so they took the seats out of the van and began loading both vehicles and began shuttling back and forth to Clinica Ezell. The 45-minute travel time between the two clinics limited the number of loads they could take in a day, but like little beavers, they kept working. At some point, however, someone asked how they were going to move the hospital beds. Sergio replied that a big truck was coming on Tuesday.

Tuesday came and went with no big truck. Sergio said it would come on Wednesday. Wednesday came and went with no truck. Sergio then said, *"It will be here for sure on Thursday."*

The big truck finally arrived late Wednesday night. The problem was that it turned out to be only a *mid-sized pickup*! Not to be discouraged, the Guatemalan men helping them stacked the hospital beds, one on top of another, onto that not-so-big truck until they had loaded ten of them. They tied them down, stationed one of the workers on top of the stack and took off for Clinica Ezell. They moved all twenty hospital beds in only two loads! John Taylor said later that *"We may not have been impressed with the size of the truck, but we sure were impressed with the resourcefulness of the Guatemalan people!"*

On Monday evening the group was so tired they were "punch drunk." After dinner Nancy Carlisle and a couple of others penned a hilarious satirical report of their activity, dubbing it the **Grunt Group Report**. She included tongue-in-cheek notes about having had filet mignon for dinner after spending an afternoon sunbathing by the pool as they waited for the supplies to arrive. There was also something about planning a Willie Nelson concert. It's a good thing she did this on Monday while everyone still had enough energy to enjoy a good laugh. Tuesday night's report was very short. She said they were all too tired to be creative. Wednesday's report was never written.

One night after dinner Cathy Love asked for help getting some light in the back storeroom in Chocolá so she could continue to work. Tommy Carlisle and John Taylor, both graduate electrical engineers, grabbed a voltage meter and flashlights and ran to help. They traced out many electrical cords and finally found one that would work in the light fixture in the storeroom. John said, *"Just for fun...**before** we plugged in the cord we had so diligently sought, we put a new light bulb into the existing socket, and PRESTO! There was light!"* John added that *"This answered the age old question of 'how many engineers does it take to screw in a light bulb?' The answer, of course, is two."*

The Grunt Group was the last group to sleep at Chocolá. Clinica Ezell would have new beds with actual mattresses, shiny new furniture and freshly painted walls. That would strip us of any romanticized remembrances of the Chocolá dorm. Elaine summed up well the feelings many of us had about the inconveniences at Chocolá. She said, *"I was thinking how glad I would be when we didn't have to sleep there anymore. Those black things that fell out of the ceiling in the night were scary. And who can forget the COLD hot water shower bags? Makes you want to just run right down there and do it again!"*

I tell the *Guatemala Grunts* story because few people have any idea how challenging the transition from Chocolá to Clinica Ezell was. The fact that it took place as smoothly as it did was due in large part to the *Guatemala Grunts,* who had been willing to do whatever it took to make it happen. Despite the dust and dirt, overwhelming heat, and huge amounts of energy and stamina necessary to get the job done, these people felt *privileged* to do it. Because they were so dedicated, Clinica Ezell was ready when that first surgical team arrived. If that wasn't powered by the Love of God, I don't know what is.

Chapter 13:
Dedication of Clinica Ezell

2002 - Present

Clinica Ezell Dedication Day

Clinic construction was complete. All was ready for Dedication Day on February 3, 2002, and the first surgical clinic that would immediately follow. Nery had planned a dedication ceremony worthy of the occasion, and the invitations had gone out.

A large number of Board members traveled to Guatemala to attend. When we arrived at the compound, even those of us who had periodically witnessed the construction progress caught our breaths. It was absolutely beautiful! Nery had surprised us all by using his artistic design skills throughout the clinic. The entire facility was adorned with beautifully tiled floors, textured walls, and concrete blocks that weren't ordinary concrete blocks. They were a lovely textured pink with dark beige trim. The overall scene was stunning!

Clinica Ezell

Outside, the driveway was covered in intricately laid pavers and there were even streetlights. I kept saying, *"Street lights! I didn't know we were going to have street lights!"* The surrounding grounds were a veritable Garden of Eden. There were flowers of every hue, mandarin orange trees, breadfruit trees, coconut palms, cashew trees, and almost anything else you could imagine! We were incredibly excited and impressed with the fruit of many years' labor. We had done all this on such a limited budget that we did not expect such luxurious details. What a blessing.

The most exciting thing of all, however, was what we saw when we walked to the front door of the clinic. Board member Charles Campbell spotted it first and pointed it out to the rest of us. The bright Guatemalan sun had cast a shadow on the wall just left of the front entrance. It was in the perfect shape of a cross. We took it as one more sign of God's approval.

The ceremony was lovely. Local civic dignitaries and leaders from area churches gathered with us and seemed thrilled to be there. HTI Board member Dr. Meredith Ezell brought her mother, Marian Ezell, to represent the Ezell family. She shared our joy and pride in the new building as we dedicated it to the Glory of God.

At the start of the ceremony Violeta Campos and I carried our respective countries' flags to symbolize HTI's partnership with Guatemalan Christians. There were bi-lingual prayers of thanksgiving, lovely speeches, singing of national anthems and the awarding of appreciation plaques; but all too soon it was over.

The unveiling of the new Clinica Ezell sign

Everyone gathered outside at the new Clinica Ezell sign to witness its unveiling. After clapping, cheers, and photo taking, we adjourned to the food tent. We listened to a marimba band and visited with each other as we ate. All spent time reflecting on what a marvelous privilege it was to be a part of this ministry.

As an added bonus, we learned this day that in the course of the year-long construction, Baldemar had taught voluntary Bible studies every Friday for the 60 or so laborers. By the time the construction was complete, 12 of the workers had accepted Christ and had been baptized!

First Surgical Clinic at Clinica Ezell

The first clinic was to begin the day after the dedication, and we had specially selected the team. The main requirement was that prospective team members had to have served at Chocolá at some point during the last eight years. That meant we had quite a large team, but with three operatories, we could use one for eye surgery, one for general/plastic surgery, and the third for gynecological surgery.

We felt so much appreciation for the new clinic. We enjoyed good nights of restful sleep in the comfortable beds that came with the wonderful new dorm.

We were exceedingly grateful for the built-in generator and would no longer feel compelled to bring flashlights and lots of batteries. We rejoiced because everything was so clean. But, mostly we kept walking around saying we couldn't believe how gorgeous it was! Someone proposed enacting a rule that only those who had toiled at least once in Chocolá be allowed to participate. The theory was that no one could possibly appreciate the luxury of Clinica Ezell without having the Chocolá perspective! As right as that statement might have been, it didn't take us long to realize how self-defeating that would be. We veterans just resolved to hold our memories of Chocolá in our hearts...and go forward rejoicing!

All the preparation paid off in spades. The clinic week went well. The most memorable patient from that week was an eight-year-old Mayan girl named Clara, who had been born with a badly disfiguring cleft lip. Nurse Martha Oyston noted that Clara was very shy and guarded, then learned she had never been to school because she was so self-conscious of her appearance. Dr. Philip

Strawther's expertise in the operating room made a world of difference in Clara's appearance. Even with the swelling common after such surgery, Martha said she looked like a new person! She would now be able to face the world *head on*. Clara has always been a symbol to me of what the Health Talents ministry offers: a rebirth of sorts. HTI's ministry of offering compassionate care in the name of Jesus opens the door of hope for new life, both here and in the hereafter.

Closing Clinica Promesa

There is an old saying that "statistics don't lie." As the patient numbers continued to decline at Clinica Promesa, the Board discussed options. There was great logic on the side of consolidating the two efforts. They knew the potential for success would be greater if we focused on one area rather than dividing our efforts. After much discussion and prayer, the Board decided to discontinue clinic activities in Guatemala City and asked both Dr. Walter Sierra and Dr. Silvia Albizures to move to the coast where Clinica Ezell was located. They both agreed to do so, and in April 2002 they became part of the Clinica Ezell ministry team.

Fleshing Out the Ministry

Once Clinica Ezell was completed, the ministry seemed to take on new life, with one effort spawning another. Dr. Walter and Dr. Silvia moved to the coast and established many more mobile clinics in the area that only added to the church contacts and surgical patient load. Things were churning; we could feel it. There was an encouraging surge of energy as we moved into the future. The next couple of years brought a flurry of changes both to staff and scope of the ministry.

Rick Harper, Executive Director

As the HTI ministry expanded, it became even more apparent that I could no longer handle it alone. Though I had wonderfully capable and dedicated part-time help in the persons of my trusted bookkeeper Vanessa Mayfield, CPA Sandy Brown, who had performed all our accounting/reporting needs since 1989, and Mary Stephenson, my in-house Stateside ABC Coordinator, the load was often overwhelming. Recruiting for the increasing number of surgical trips took more and more time and managing a quickly growing budget required greater financial expertise and experience than I had. Most importantly, we needed someone to focus more deliberately on fundraising. As Dr. Quinton Dickerson put it in one of the Board meetings, "We were moving from a "Mom and Pop industry" into a much larger arena. We had previously hired a couple of different Directors of Development, but none had lasted much more than a year. The Board decided to search for an Executive Director.

In early 2003 long-time HTI Board member Rick Harper left his vice-president job in industry to follow his dream of a life in ministry. He requested to be considered for the HTI position. The Board agreed that he came with skills HTI needed, so they officially hired him at the April 11-12, 2003, Board of Directors meeting. Thus, Rick Harper became HTI's first Executive Director. His mandate was twofold and clear: provide direct oversight of the Guatemala effort and raise funds. I was to continue doing everything I had already been doing for the past 28 years.

Dr. Sergio Castillo and HTI Separate

Dr. Sergio Castillo had been a part of the HTI ministry from its earliest days in Guatemala City. It had become increasing clear that though we shared the same vision we no longer agreed on how to accomplish it. After a period of reflection on both sides, Dr. Sergio and HTI mutually agreed to part ways in August 2003. We continue to be grateful for Sergio and Veronica for their loving and dedicated contributions through so many long years. Interestingly, they moved to Chocolá, the site of our former surgical clinic, and Sergio began a family practice with occasional surgical clinics staffed by visiting medical professionals. They continue in that successful work today.

Carlos Baltodano Joins HTI

In an amazing *coincidence* my telephone rang in late summer 2003. It was Mamie Shuttlesworth, a young woman I had met in Guatemala a couple of years earlier. She had later married Roberto Batres, son of the Nicaraguan evangelist Pedro Batres, who had been a part of the team at Clinica Cristiana for a number of years. Sometime after Mamie and Roberto married, the entire family had moved back to Nicaragua. Mamie called me that day because she and Roberto wanted to move to the States and she had heard that I helped people find jobs.

I was excited about her call, however, because I already had a job in mind for her. It was in Guatemala. I thought she and Roberto would be perfect as administrators for Clinica Ezell. I knew Mamie and Roberto to be outstanding people. Each was spiritually minded, bi-lingual, intelligent and personable. When I discussed the HTI option with her, she seemed interested and said she would discuss it with Roberto and get back to me.

Mamie called back a few days later. Apologetically, she told me that she and Roberto had discussed the Clinica Ezell option but decided they were definitely ready to return to the States. She offered a recommendation for her friend, however. Before she told me his name, she described him. Despite his humble childhood where he had experienced many hardships, he did well in school, was very responsible and was respected by all who knew him. He had been selected to be a Walton Scholar at Harding University in Searcy, Arkansas, where he had learned to speak English. He was serious about his faith and determined to serve God in every way possible. Although he was only working in a convenience store at the time because of the scarcity of good jobs in Nicaragua, she knew he was capable of much greater things. His name, she told me, was Carlos Baltodano.

Rick Harper called him with the phone number Mamie provided and briefly discussed the position with him. Carlos was interested. He traveled to Guatemala to discuss it with Rick and me during the September 2003 surgical clinic. Vicky Ratts was on the Board (and on the clinic team) at that time, so she met him as well. We were impressed with Carlos and felt that he could do the job if he was willing to move to Guatemala. He affirmed he was willing. Rick made a formal recommendation to the Board, and Carlos officially became our Country Coordinator during HTI's 30th Anniversary Celebration in Birmingham in October 2003. Carlos moved to Guatemala in November 2003.

In early 2004 Hugo Fuentes announced that he was ready to leave his position with HTI and return to the business world. At that point Carlos assumed full administrative responsibility for the entire Guatemala ministry under Rick's supervision.

Carlos would live in Chicacao to be nearer the center of the activity, but the office in Guatemala City would continue to operate as the ABC office and center for governmental interactions. Things were stabilizing.

Sherman Scholarship Fund

At the same 30th anniversary celebration in 2003 the Board announced the creation of a tribute to Magda and Steve Sherman: *The Sherman Scholarship Fund for ABC Students*. Magda Sherman had conceived the idea for ABC and ran it very capably for many years. Steve had dedicated his life to the HTI ministry since the Las Cruces days. This new scholarship fund would acknowledge their long-term contribution to the HTI ministry and bestow upon them the honor they deserved.

The need for a program like this arose because ABC students were now graduating from high school and many had ambitions that reached beyond the outskirts of their villages. They wanted to become teachers, engineers and accountants. We had no way to help them because the Bates Scholarship was solely for training in the medical profession. The Sherman Scholarship would provide the means for capable ABC students to further their education without any payback obligation. It was a win/win. Local communities and churches would both benefit from having people who were more educated, better off economically and in possession of a broader world outlook.

Leadership Evangelism Training Seminars

Guatemala was heavily evangelized in the 1960s. After the civil war broke out, most foreign missionaries returned to the States. Guatemalan preachers knew that it would be up to them to spread the Word, and they did. The exciting result was a veritable maze of churches all over Guatemala. Because of the general lack of education in the country, however, most of the preachers had little formal Bible training. The HTI Board felt it could contribute to their evangelistic efforts by hosting weekend training seminars with Spanish-speaking lecturers and inviting preachers and church leaders to come for a weekend of study. The lecturers initially focused on a single book of the Bible so the listeners could learn in context what the text had to say. They have since branched out into topical studies such as forgiveness and marriage/family counseling. The first seminar was held in the spring of 2003.

These seminars continue to be well received with approximately 40 to 50 men attending each time. They were so well received that we began hosting similar seminars for women, with equally good reception. HTI now hosts seminars several times a year, conducting two or three classes a year for both men and women. The expense incurred in hosting these seminars is underwritten by interested congregations in the States.

Surgical and Mobile Medical Clinics Continue

Things were beginning to stabilize in the medical and dental areas. Dentist Dr. Silvia worked through the initial resistance she felt when she first arrived. By 2004 she felt more accepted and had begun utilizing various means to change the way people viewed dentistry. Dr. Silvia practices *holistically* and never hesitates to counsel with anyone she perceives as needing encouragement or advice. Nothing is off limits with her. She goes into classrooms to make dental presentations in an attempt to change attitudes about dental health. She provides teenage girls with valuable counsel on sexuality. When appropriate, she refers dental patients for surgical screening.

Because of safety concerns, the Board had asked her to work at Clinica Ezell, so she worked there most days but traveled to villages a couple of days a month for mobile clinics. Hugo reported that Christian Children's Fund operating in Chicacao had begun sending all of their sponsored children to Silvia for treatment. Her practice eventually grew so large that we built a dental building. Her personal life grew as well. She and Carlos were married in

2009. They now have two little ones, Dante and Dánika.

Dr. Walter settled into his routine of working on the coast from Monday through Friday then driving back to his family in Guatemala City for the weekend, only to make the drive again on Monday morning and do it all again. He has proven to be an able physician who cares deeply for his patients, with whom he often prays. He has two special interests: child nutrition and ophthalmology. For a long time Dr. Walter carried the portable refractory device and a box of eyeglasses with him to clinic, and he could often be seen examining a patient's eyes then searching to find just the right eyeglasses for them.

Likewise, seriously ill babies tear at his heartstrings. He knows that any childhood illness is exacerbated by serious malnutrition, so he developed a program to directly care for children at risk. At any given time he treats at least a dozen babies and young children, and sometimes as many as two dozen. He has identified the most common causes of malnutrition: chronic sickness, lack of food, lack of nutrition knowledge, congenital digestive sickness and discrimination by parents about which child to feed (or not feed). As children become well enough to *graduate* from his program, he adds others from the seemingly never-ending supply. He does all this while continuing to treat common illnesses, identify surgical patients and train health promoters. When Sergio departed, he assumed the responsibility for screening surgical patients, preparing the surgical schedule and providing follow-up care for the patients. All visiting physicians would now work under his Guatemalan licensure.

Community Development Program at Clinica Ezell

About five years ago Carlos began revitalizing Clinica Ezell's community development work to include agriculture. Former Clinica Ezell gardener Oscar Mejia heads this project. He works closely with the University of Tennessee's Agriculture Department to enhance nutrition through teaching better methods of growing basic foods. As a first step in the agriculture initiative, they built a garden "lab" on the Clinica Ezell grounds. It is now a veritable "Garden of Eden" with its wide variety of vegetables growing, like squash, melons, beets, many kinds of peppers, beans, and corn.

The tiny community of La Florida prompted a sense of urgency for such a project. Most of the people in that community are former migrant workers who had never actually farmed. HTI's first effort to help the people in La Florida was to provide them a means for having fresh water. Once that need was met, the focus shifted to food.

Another recent effort has been to place new water filters in the homes of ABC students, both in the Clinica Ezell area and in the highlands. Oscar and his team go into schools to teach the importance of clean drinking water. They also continue to place smokeless wood-burning stoves in the homes of families that request them. Basic stuff...but so important.

More Medical Missions Interns

Aaron Towler and Zach Self were interns for a few months in 2004. Because of their excellent Spanish skills, they participated in every way possible during that time. They were especially valuable with the MET students. Sadly for us, both left in late summer 2004 to continue their education. Zach was headed to medical school and Aaron had his sights set on becoming a nurse anesthetist. We knew we would miss them, and we did. Zach has now completed his medical training and has returned to Guatemala with Josefina, his Mayan wife, to set up a private practice in Santo Tomás. Josefina had been Dr. Silvia's dental assistant when they first met.

One More 2004 Mobile Medical Clinic Story

During the week of the October 2004 mobile medical clinic civilian demonstrations were taking place around Guatemala. We knew of the potential for such even before arriving, but we had no problem at all in reaching the clinic. Demonstrations are fairly frequent occurrences since Guatemala's civil war ended in 1996. Toward the end of the war the government had urged Mayan men to serve in the Civil Patrol to maintain order in the villages and promised to pay them. That payment never materialized, so Mayans demonstrate from time to time to remind the government they are still waiting. Though the demonstrations are usually peaceful, the potential for violence is always a concern.

On Thursday we were scheduled to go to both La Ceiba and Xejuyup. During breakfast, however, someone called to me saying there were policemen just outside the dining hall. I hurried out to see what was going on.

"*Buenos dias, señores,*" I said. "*¿Hay algún problema?*" (In English: "*Good morning, sirs. Is there a problem?*" They said they had come to tell us that there was a demonstration down the road at the intersection of the main highway and Nahualate, and they did not want us to leave the compound until they were convinced we would be safe.

Think about that for a minute. The community had enough respect for what we were doing that it had sent policeman to protect us, even though we had no idea we needed protecting. It made my heart sing!

We agreed to wait for the demonstration to clear. We waited around for an hour or so until someone remembered there was a shortcut we could take without going all the way to Nahualate. The road was unpaved and rough, but it would do in a pinch. I discussed it with the policemen; and not only did they agree for us to go, they insisted on giving us a police escort. Part of the way down the road we learned that the road to La Ceiba was also blocked, so we decided the entire group would go to Xejuyup. When we arrived, the policemen turned to go back to Chicacao but made me promise we would not leave Xejuyup without calling them first so they could escort us back to Clinica Ezell.

The day at Xejuyup was event filled, to say the least. A woman had an epileptic seizure in the middle of the clinic yard, then a laborer walked in with his right foot all bandaged up asking for help. Seems he'd accidentally whacked his big toe half in two with his machete. Later in the day Dr. Walter was asked to make a house call to the home of one of the church members, an 86-year-old man. He had fallen into a bed of hot ashes two weeks before, blistering his right thigh. It was now badly infected and needed care.

As we were winding down that afternoon, word came that the road was now totally blocked between us and Clinica Ezell. Carlos, the Board members present, and I discussed it and decided that we should try to get at least as far as Santo Tomás. If worse came to worse we could spend the night in the Church of Christ building there, with assurance that church members would feed us. Someone suddenly remembered that the protesters usually quit in late afternoon to go home for supper, so we decided to wait until 5:00 to leave so we would have the chance of making it all the way back to the clinic. I tried to call the policemen as they had requested, but I was not able to get a cell signal, so with a prayer on our lips we struck out toward Clinica Ezell.

All went well until we arrived in Chocolá, where we found the road completely blocked by rocks and tree branches. Four cars had already lined up and were waiting to get through. Carlos pulled up behind them and we sat there for a moment before we decided to get out and plead for mercy. The oldest man in the crowd appeared to be in charge. He eyed us suspiciously as we walked up wearing our HTI scrub tops. Carlos politely asked permission that our caravan be allowed to pass since we were North Americans and had nothing to do with any of the issues they were protesting.

The man was still staring at us when a waving hand in the back of the crowd caught my eye. It was Rigoberto, waving and smiling broadly. I enthusiastically waved back. Rigo had worked with us for a number of years at the Chocolá clinic. The old man witnessed that exchange and visibly softened. With a nod of his head, several men scurried out into the road to remove the barricades they had placed there earlier. As our caravan of several vehicles drove past the other still-waiting cars, several others in the crowd waved. They remembered us. God is good.

Rosario Poncio Comes Home

One of the best decisions the HTI Board ever made was to hire Rosario. We had known her for years before she became a nurse. In fact, while still a teenager she helped out at Chocolá and even at that young age her maturity and organizational skills were impressive. Quiche is her native tongue, but she also speaks Spanish. She was able to become a nurse because Dr. Tony and Dana Rector and John Wright personally made it possible.

When she completed her studies, she found employment at the children's cancer hospital in Guatemala City and worked there for six years. I mentioned her name from time to time, saying we should contact her to see if she was ready to return home and work with us. In 2005 her father sent word to me that she was indeed ready. She began work with HTI during the summer of 2005, and we have been blessed by her presence ever since.

Rosario serves at Clinica Ezell, and she and former Bates Scholar Darling Ayerdis run a tight ship. When North American teams arrive, they find everything in place. There is always an abundance of health promoters lined up to assist the nurses, and the pharmacy is well organized. Rarely does anyone ask who makes it happen. Just so you know...it is the Rosario/Darling team.

2013 Clinica Ezell Team

Chapter 14:
The Highlands Ministry

2005 - Present

From the earliest days of the MET program, HTI's goal was to inspire young people to serve in the mission field. We have had some degree of success. Teck Waters and Melissa Redding went on to work in Belize, John Wright served four years in Guatemala, and Dr. Mark Hall and Dr. Ellen Little moved to Uganda when they finished their medical training. It was not a total surprise then that Dr. Lisa and Kemmel Dunham called one day to say they were ready.

Lisa and Kemmel first met during the 1990 MET program. Kemmel had been a MET student the year before, and because he was such a good Spanish-speaker we invited him back to help with MET 1990. That month-long acquaintance was enough to let them know they wanted to spend the rest of their lives together, so three years later they married. Lisa finished medical school and ultimately became an internist while Kemmel worked as an executive with a national medical coding firm.

Twelve years after they were married, they made that call to me. They were ready to move to Guatemala, the country where Kemmel spent part of his childhood, and become a part of the HTI ministry team. They said they could move in 2005 and promised to stay for at least five years…perhaps longer. Needless to say, we were ecstatic! The Meadowbrook Church of Christ in Jackson,

Mississippi, agreed to serve as their sponsoring congregation. In June 2005 they settled in at Clinica Ezell for six months of orientation with plans to move to the highlands in early 2006. They were ideal for the next growth step in HTI's ministry...moving deeper into Mayan country.

Expanding the boundaries of the HTI ministry in Guatemala was a natural progression. Although HTI's patients back in the Las Cruces days had been primarily ladino, the ensuing years found us ministering to more and more Maya. This personal involvement created in all of us a greater awareness of their plight. We saw it from the first days of working with Dr. Mike Kelly, whose ministry was to the Maya. In fact, discrimination against the Maya was at the core of his pleading for HTI to begin a surgical ministry.

Our knowledge of widespread discrimination had grown during the Chocolá years. Dr. Sergio Castillo told of personal insults he had received because of his medical work with the Maya. Once, upon meeting a physician who was vaguely aware of Sergio's work, Sergio put out his hand to greet him. The surgeon glared at him and said, "*I don't shake hands with doctors who treat Indians.*" Patients sometimes told us chilling stories, such as the pregnant woman who had gone to the hospital for help with the delivery of her baby. She ended up giving birth on the floor of the waiting room because those in charge would not acknowledge her presence. Incidents like this motivated the HTI Board to tighten its focus. Roger McCown captured the sentiment well:

"We are called to those whom the world has forgotten and who live at the margins of society—the abandoned ones. We are sent to persevere in service to those who will remain unserved if we do not serve them, to those to whom the usual and customary avenues to social justice and physical well-being are summarily denied. In Guatemala, those are mostly the indigenous people. They are not persecuted; rather, they have been rendered invisible. We are sent to 'see' them and having seen them, to serve them."

Dr. Lisa and Kemmel possessed the maturity and professional skills needed to be at the helm of this expansion. On top of that, they were warm and friendly, too. We knew we had the beginnings of a great team. Dr. Josefina Lux and her brother Dr. David Lux joined the HTI ministry shortly afterward in 2006. We met them through Dr. Mike and Julie Kelly. (In fact, Josefina had learned English by living with the Kellys for three months when she was a teenager.)

Theirs was a well-known, highly respected Christian family. They had attended medical school in Cuba on scholarships awarded by Fidel Castro, graduated in 2005 then proceeded to complete their year of government service in Guatemala. HTI helped them from time to time by providing basic items such as stethoscopes and ophthalmoscopes. Upon completion of their government service, both Josefina and David went to work with Health Talents, Dr. David on the coast with Dr. Walter, and Dr. Josefina home to the highlands to work with Dr. Lisa.

Registered nurse Sheri Kretzschmar and Bates Scholar Marcos Lux, younger brother of Drs. David and Josefina, joined them in 2007 to round out the team. Sheri, with her winning smile and engaging personality, came to us by way of Dr. Jim and Mary Rackley. She is sponsored by her home congregation, the South Fork Church of Christ in Winston-Salem, North Carolina. She and Josefina formed one team; Kemmel and Lisa another.

Marcos Lux had just completed dental school on the Bates Scholarship and joined the highlands ministry team to fulfill his scholarship commitment.

Once in place, the first priority for Lisa and Kemmel was to hire a health promoter/translator to assist them. Following is Kemmel and Lisa's account of how they met Gaspar Chan, their loyal and trusted health promoter:

"Before we moved to the highlands, we had been to the area only a few times to work with clinic teams and once for a men's seminar in the local churches. We didn't really know many people when we arrived. Our greatest priority was to find someone to hire as a health promoter/translator for our mobile clinic work, and we had been praying for God to help us specifically with this task. We put out the word in a few area churches that we were looking to hire and 'accepting applications,' but we never heard back from anyone. One time during a scout trip to look for housing and a central office to rent in Chichicastenango, we were walking around in the plaza one evening after market day. There were still a lot of

folks in town and we enjoyed just doing some people watching. As we were walking down the street, Kemmel looked up and saw a guy he had met at the men's seminar in the area, named Gaspar Chan. Gaspar recognized Kemmel as well, and they stopped to talk. This brother was so friendly and encouraging and asked about our move and plans for clinic ministry. We told him that we were looking for someone with medical background to work with us. He asked if he could apply for the job, and we said that would be fine.

"He turned in his application the next day, and we were a little worried that he had only finished 6th grade and had taken only a nurse's aide course. But he had worked for another non-profit group in the past and had lots of experience in community development projects. We told him we would let him know soon, after reviewing 'all of the other applications.' Well, we didn't get any other applications. So we prayed some more and decided to hire Brother Gaspar. When we called him, he was ecstatic and told us that he really needed the work and had been considering going to Guatemala City or even the States if he hadn't found this job. He had asked God to provide work so he wouldn't have to leave his family.

"Gaspar Chan has been with us from the beginning and has been such a good friend and advisor, patient with our questions and cross-cultural quirks and missteps, and has taught us the importance of being involved in people's lives in order to be effective witnesses of the Gospel. We know God helped us find him and has obviously led us throughout the years as we added other team members."

They later invited Juan Quino from the village of Paxot II to work with them as well. Gaspar and Juan are both spiritual men, and Gaspar is an elder at his church in Xepocol. They later also hired Manuel Sut Gonzales from Paxot II and Tomas Garcia from Mactzul V to work with Sheri and Josefina. Tomas has seven children! We now had a solid gold team that has only improved with later additions of capable, God-loving team members.

Medical evangelism is so much more than giving a shot and saying a prayer. It is integrated compassionate care that involves the local church, so partnership with local churches is vital. The second priority for Lisa and Kemmel then was to confer with church leaders about hosting a clinic. This required more commitment than merely agreeing for HTI to hold a clinic in their church. They had to agree to *partner* with HTI, to be personally involved. It meant committing to three things: church members would be present to welcome patients from the community at each clinic; church members would pray with patients; and later they would provide follow-up in patient homes. The response from the churches was heartening, and it wasn't long before Lisa and Kemmel had developed a full schedule of clinics that would be held in church buildings. We were off to a good start.

Having a team without a central workplace was cumbersome to say the least, so the Board began an effort to build one. Through the generosity of the Caris Foundation in Irving, Texas, they were able to do just that. Clinica Caris is located on the border of the tiny Mayan villages of Sepela and Lemoa, in the shadow of Chichicastenango, and serves as both a clinic and administrative center for the Highlands effort.

During the dedication service on April 22, 2007, we took communion from tiny plastic medicine cups. The symbolism of Clinica Caris' mission came into sharp focus at this visual representation of the integration of the physical and spiritual. As stated earlier, medical evangelism is particularly effective in

Guatemala because both the physical and spiritual elements of the lives of the Maya are deeply entwined in their culture. When something goes wrong physically, they look for a spiritual cause. Conversely, when things go right, they give God the glory! We could learn so much from them.

Since 2007 the team and its Clinica Caris ministry have grown considerably. They now serve more than 22 communities. One of their clinical focuses is Women's Health. The overall health of women in Guatemala can be negatively affected by numerous factors: chronic malnutrition, illiteracy, young age of first sexual activity, high childbirth rates, high maternal mortality rates and high cervical cancer rates. Their list of services is remarkable and expanding all the time.

The medical consults include general medical, GYN consults, pap smears, and prenatal care. Dental offerings now include general exams, teeth cleaning, fillings and dental prosthetics. The community education program has expanded to include discussions on Bible study, menopause, mental/emotional health, nutrition, diabetes, sex education and abuse prevention (n*ever offered in this area before)*, prenatal education (nutrition, warning signs/ emergency planning, breast feeding), family planning and dental hygiene.

Nurse Sheri Kretzschmar has taken the lead in many of the community education courses. Her diabetes classes have been well received and helped many understand what diabetes is and just how dangerous it can be. She has helped them understand the importance of being diligent in the care of their diabetes. Likewise, when the ladies of the communities began asking questions about menopause, Sheri responded. She was amazed at the widespread ignorance of menopause and delighted at their interest in learning more.

The sex education classes are a first for the area because this topic is rarely addressed openly among the Mayan population. The classes have been well received because Dr. Lisa and Kemmel took care to lay careful groundwork in the local churches.

They are also alert to possible surgical needs of their patients and escort them to Clinica Ezell if necessary. Sheri, particularly, gathers up babies in need of cleft palate repair and takes them to the surgical clinic.

The team sees spiritual needs continually. A woman who always brings her children for sick (and even well-checks) recently came to the clinic. She is not a Christian, but took time that day to say how much she appreciated the clinic and the church for opening its doors to the community. She said she had often wanted to come to worship services, but her in-laws (who are traditional Mayan worshipers) made it clear that she could pack her bags and leave (without her children) if she dared to do so. She said she prays to God every day and knows that He hears her. Lisa prayed with her that she would one day be free to follow Christ.

One of their most satisfying achievements was the conversion of the Mayan priest shown seated in the picture below.

The priest's daughter began visiting the local church clinic when her daughter became ill. This opened the door to the team and members of the local church to build a relationship with her, and she was eventually baptized. Her father was not happy, and he made it known widely. The men of the church kept talking with him about the Lord at every opportunity, and the day came when he told them he wanted to accept Jesus as his Lord and Savior. His was quite a witness to the community!

Evangelistically, churches seem to appreciate the Clinica Caris team more every day and frequently ask them for help. At the beginning of March Lisa and Kemmel received a call from Santos Lares, a church leader from a small ABC community called Las Cuevas. Santos called asking for help because leaders in his community had asked him if his church would organize a thanksgiving service for the entire village! They wanted their small community to gather and thank God for their 23 years as a community, their schools, and for the current project to ensure that each home has potable water. Lisa, Kemmel, Gaspar and several other church leaders helped extensively to plan the service. (Then Lisa and Kemmel thoughtfully stayed away so as to prevent it from being considered a gringo service.) Afterward, the community leaders expressed warm gratitude for the spirit of cooperation that exists in the church there.

This is just one illustration about how well the Clinica Caris ministry has been accepted by area churches. The HTI ministry is markedly more effective through these relationships, and churches are empowered in ways they may not have even considered. The opportunities that arise through Health Talents allow them to connect with members of their communities in valuable ways.

Clinica Caris Medical Team (Dr. Sandra Aldana, RN Sheri Kretzschmar, Kemmel & Dr. Lisa Dunham, Dr. Sara Castellanos...absent Dr. Marcos Lux)

Chapter 15:
Looking to the Future

2013 –

Changing of the Guard Stateside...Again

I have been at this work on some level since 1975. In 2005 I began to feel it and began to think about backing down. Enter Julie Wheetley. As a recent graduate of Lipscomb University, she went to Antigua, Guatemala, to study Spanish, prompted by her experience on an earlier trip to Guatemala with Lipscomb. Rick and I became acquainted with her when she translated for some of our teams. When it came time to hire a replacement for me, Rick called her. Despite her young age, she had a maturity about her that we knew would serve her well. She also smiled all the time and spoke Spanish like a pro! The Board made her an offer she couldn't refuse, and she didn't.

In 2007 Julie signed on to learn all there was to know about recruiting and leading mission teams. When I retreated to part time work in June 2009, she assumed responsibility for many of my tasks, with the exception of writing newsletters. At the close of 2012 when I completely retired, she took over that task as well. There wasn't even a ripple to mark the transition. We had clearly made a good choice.

The Vision Continues...into El Salvador

There is an old saying that *"if you aren't moving forward, you are falling back."* The model HTI established in Guatemala is a good one that can be replicated almost anywhere. As things stabilized, the Board began asking the inevitable question of *"What do we do next?"*

El Salvador seemed the logical answer. It first came into view because of Deborah Rivas, the deceased wife of Mario Rivas of Austin, Texas. When she passed away, Mario wanted to honor her life in some way. Deborah had a great love for missions, and whenever they traveled internationally for Mario's work Deborah sought out a local Church of Christ to attend. Mario was originally from El Salvador, so he decided to both honor his wife and his homeland by establishing an educational scholarship in her name for Salvadoran students. He did just that through Health Talents and called the new scholarship the *Deborah G. Rivas Medical Scholarship*. In 2009 Norma Tisset Romero was selected to be the first Rivas Scholar. She is currently in her fourth year of medical school. Two other recipients have been added since.

Interviewing scholarship applicants gave HTI the opportunity to connect with Churches of Christ in El Salvador. As a result of that, two years ago we began hosting one or two mobile medical clinics a year there. The Board is moving slowly to allow the ministry to develop as it should, but it anticipates growing a stable, effective ministry there that will again be a tool for local churches to use in their effort to bring people to the Lord.

In Conclusion

The Health Talents ministry in Guatemala has matured over these past 40 years. Its mobile medical and surgical clinics are running well, with a patient load of currently 35,000 a year. Since HTI's surgery clinics began in 1993 more than 7,000 people have received compassionate surgical care. Working relationships with local churches are continually strengthening. And, most importantly, people have experienced God more fully in both physical and spiritual ways because of HTI's presence in Guatemala.

It seems clear that one of the keys to maturity, tranquility and success is having quality people on the team. Throughout HTI's history we have been blessed with dedicated U.S. Christians who have been willing to serve God in often difficult circumstances. We are sincerely thankful for them and their deep motivating faith that have impacted the lives of so many. We have been equally blessed by Guatemalan, Nicaraguan and Salvadoran Christians who serve side-by-side with us as they minister to their own people.

Local ministers sometimes traveled with our mobile medical teams to meet with villagers during clinic. They ministered unceasingly, from preaching in the courtyards to discussing the Bible to praying with anyone who had a need. Javier Leon and Marcos Dias are two special ones that I specifically remember for their gentleness of nature and sincerity of heart. Their very lives were an example to us as they live lives of deep gratitude for every blessing from the Father.

Creating a new ministry and managing the details of it have at times felt to me like raising children. In the beginning, there were moments we felt the pangs of giving birth, then we rejoiced when the effort of the moment developed into something beneficial. As the ministry developed in fits and starts and we seemed to move from one crisis to another, it felt as though we were raising teenagers. Finally, after 40 years we have come to a place where we can look back and say it was all worth it. These years of effort by so many good people have produced a maturity in the ministry that is awesome. God has been faithful and led us through what sometimes felt like a wilderness to where we are today.

Every step of this journey has been important, from the drama of Las Cruces until today. The good times taught us to be thankful; the tough times increased our reliance on God. In the beginning the Board knew where it wanted to go. The journey clarified our focus and made us even more determined to succeed.

Who knows where God will lead us after El Salvador? No one. The task that falls to each and every one of us who has ever been a part of HTI is to simply trust...and continue to follow His lead, walking through doors that He opens. If we go forward with resolve to continue using the considerable talents He has given us to serve compassionately in His name, our lives will have been worth living. The world needs Christ's compassionate touch. Many will come to know Him as Savior because you offered it.

If you are reading this and have never participated in a true ministry of the heart, I urge you to step out. If you have ever desired a closer, more intimate relationship with Jesus, you can count on it happening if you follow His example of a mission-filled life. It isn't necessary to live in a grass hut in a faraway land to make a meaningful difference *in the name of Jesus* in the world. You can start today. We invite you to join hands with Health Talents as we step into the future.

Ask God to give you the courage to get *mud on your own boots.* Trust me...you will never be able to shake it loose.

HTI Board of Directors
1973 – 2013

HTI Presidents
Charles Bates, PhD
  1973-1988
Quinton Dickerson, MD
  1989-1992
John Peden, DDS
  1993-1996
Roger McCown
  1997-2000
Robert Lamb, DDS
  2001-2002
Jeff Bennie, MD
  2003-2006
Charles Campbell, JD
  2007-2010
Harriette Shivers, JD
  2011-2012
John Land
  2013-

Directors
Marie B. Agee
Cynthia Allen
Alfred Anderson
Philip Bates, MD
J. Claude Bennett, MD
Paula Betz, LPN
Alan Boyd, MD
Grady Bruce, MD
Homer Burke
Steve Burr
Alice Sorrells Bush, RN
Rick Carlton, MD
Nery Castillo

Robert Clark Jr MD
Newton Collinson III
Michael Duncan, CMA
Pat Dwyer
Robert Elder, MD
J. David Ellis, RPh
Dale Entrekin, DMD
Meredith Ezell, MD
Joe Glenn
Irene Gordon, MD
Elaine Griffin, RN PhD
James Grigsby, DDS
Lesca Hadley, MD
James Haller, DDS
Randall Harley
Rick Harper
Stephen Harvey, MD
Pancho Hobbes
Arthur Hume, MD
Jon Jernigan, MT
John Johnson, JD
Roy Kellum, MD
Michael Kelly, MD
Theo Kirkland, MD
Carl Lancaster
Gene Luna
Jimmie Lawson
Billy W. Long, MD
Carolyn Maddux
Frank Maddux
Lee Maier
James Miller
Danny Minor, MD
Kenneth P. Mitchell, MD

Melissa R. Myrick, RN
Robert Netherton
Timothy North, MD
Larry Owens, RPh
Willis Owens, PhD
Larry Patterson, MD
Sidney Ragland
Dennis Randall
Vicki Ratts, RN
Max Reibolt, CPA
Brian Smith, MD
Scott Smith, MD
Van Smith, OD
Fran Sutton, RN
Gary Tabor
John Taylor
Alan Towler
Valari Wedel
Mark Whitefield, DDS
Richard Whitley
Dan Wilson, MD
Marilyn Worsham, RN
David E. Young Jr.

MET Alumni

Class of 1981
Lisa Cregeen/HU
Meg French/HU
Lelia Jones
Melissa Redding/HU*
Lori Schloffman/HU
Teck Waters

Class of 1989
Kevin Bryant/ACU*
Selma Cardenas/ACU
Janet Davis/ACU
Kemmel Dunham/ACU
James Gerardon/Purdue
Mark Hall/LCU*
Gina Hammons/ACU
Bill Shumate, Jr/ACU
Dietlinde Spears/DLU*
Tony Tabora/HU
Pedro Velasquez/HU
Tracy Weldy/HU
Mark Whitefield/DLU
Nathan Wight/ACU
John Wright/ACU

Class of 1990
Tommy Copley/ETSU
Gina DeCarlo/U-Illinois*
Theresa Gartman/HU
Nellie Gomez/ACU
Travis Hughes/ACU
Janice Johnson/ICS*
Keri Merritt/ACU
Lisa Paschall/U Texas
David Turner/ACU
Helen Vu/ACU

Class of 1991
Kelly Bennett/ACU
Jamie Goodman/DLU
Jeff Lancaster/DLU
Ellen Little/ACU
David Meredith/ACU
Kristi Morris/DLU
Tammy North/DLU
Ann Parker/ACU
Luke Shouse/DLU
Scott Womble/MTSU*

Class of 1992
Angela Abair/DLU
Tammy Callahan/HU
James Elmore/UN Chapel Hill
Julie Falkner/Univ of South FL
Imre Golden/Univ of Calif Davis
Lesca Hadley/ACU
Darren Jones/OCU*
Kenn Norris/Angelo State, Texas
Norman Poorman/ACU
Richard Rasberry/HU
Dwight Sutton/MTSU
Yvonne Warf/Virginia Tech

Class of 1993
Bernie Bledsoe/Milligan College
Melanie Copelin/ACU
Hilary Dalton/ACU
Jon Moultrie/DLU
David Osborne/ACU
David Sellers/Tenn Tech
Douglas Thacker/Univ of Texas Austin
Sarah Thompson/OCU
Janet Todd/HU

Jennie Walker/ACU
Jeff Williams/DLU
Brian Woods/ACU

Class of 1994
Colleen Cahill/Notre Dame
Scott Guthrie/DLU
Craig Harr/ACU
Kim Hendershot/DLU
Ronnie Holdaway/DLU
Janelle Jones/Southwest Missouri State
Jennifer Mayben/U Texas Austin
Doug McDonald/OCU
Jon Moultrie/DLU
Andrea Parke/Univ of Kentucky
Matt Richardson/ACU
Nathan White/ACU

Class of 1995
Amy Crittenden/ACU
David Brown/OCU
Christopher Collie/UTenn
Ben Doke/ACU
Jason Funderburk/LA Tech*
Mark Levi/HU
Jeff McKissick/ACU
Ashley Smith/LA Tech
James Vincent/ACU
Rick Warpula/HU
Jami Young/Southwestern Okla State
Beth Henderson/DLU
Rachel Newsome/FHU
Eric Newsome/FHU
Don Zeigler/HU

Class of 1996
Cheryl Berry/ACU
Courtney Collinson/Pepperdine
Jason Harlan/ACU

Diana Harlan/ACU
Justin Hauser/U North Carolina
Sara Holthouser/Freed
Matthew Miller/ACU
Jason Paltjon/ACU
Amy Reed/Wellsley College
Hunter Reynolds/ACU
Justin White/Univ of Arkansas
Kathryn Wood/ACU

Class of 1997
Richard Dennis/Lubbock Univ
Tim Hinton/HU
Jennifer Hook/St Louis Univ
Christian Heuer/DLU
Jama Kendall/OCU
Erick Mida/ACU
John Middlebrook/ACU
Casey Riley/OCU
Jennifer Rodgers/OCU
Kerry Rodgers/OCU
Allen Smith/LA Tech
Alicia Welch/HU

Class of 1998
Sandi Beasley/LA Tech
Amy Dozier/HU
Andrea Eden/ACU
Lisa Gearhart/HU
Caron Hill/ACU
Barry Jordan/HU
Brian Mansur/OCU
Nathan Sneed/ACU
Scott Staton/Cornell Univ
Andrea Taylor/HU
Jonathan Wilson/ACU
Rachel Wilson/HU

Class of 1999
Aubry Burr/ACU
Kathy Keller/HU
Lane Lanier/ACU

Andrew Page/Pepperdine
Angela Snell/DLU
LeeAnn Stephenson/Johnson Bible College
Rebecca Long/OCU

Class of 2000
Brad Buck/Auburn Univ
Kelli Cole/out of school/teaching
Shea Freeland/ACU
Stephany Hawk/ACU
Kim Hooten/York College
Kara Lipsmeyer/HU
Jason Oliphant/DLU
Marcus Wagner/HU

Class of 2001
Jared Berryman/ACU
Angelina Brummett/LCU
Ruth East/DLU
Jennifer France/ACU
Lauren Gilbert/HU
Brent Hawkins/LCU
Kristen MacKenzie/ACU
Kay Reitz/OCU

Class of 2002
Bryan Fischer/Boston College
Adam Harrell/HU
Kimberly Hatchett/Univ LA Monroe
Rachel Henderson/LCU
Maurice Miller/DLU
Ellen Shinnick/Samford Univ
William Tarrant/HU
Melissa Weaver/ACU

Class of 2003
Jason Brewington/Tenn Tech
Catherine Brumfield/Samford Univ

Joshua Dunham/Univ of MO
Danae Evans/Pepperdine
Nathan Gray/ACU
Brittany Hayes/OCU
Dustin Hyatt/OCU
Katie Kelly/OSU
Janet Ma/Cornell Univ
Rachel McGee/Univ of Missouri
Tamara Stuart/Applachian State
Jewelie Rombach/ACU

Class of 2004
Hossain Ashraf/HU
Autumn Banister/Pepperdine
Jason Barnhart/HU
Leslie Branch/Pepperdine
Adrienne Childers/DLU
Michele Gourley/ETSU, Johnson City
Sarah Gregg/HU
Rosser Powitzky/UTexas, Lubbock
Holly Russell/HU
Michelle Storck/OCU
Dee Ann Stults/Ind. School of Medicine

Class of 2005
Jared Brockington/ACU
Nathan Dewitt/UTenn, Memphis
Megan Gentry/ACU
Ryan Head/Univ of Memphis
Ashley Jamison/HU
Jennifer Oakley/ETSU, Johnson City
Rachel Smith/ACU
Tara Studer/ACU
Joe Thurman/OCU
Katrina Weatherly/ACU
Dustin Woods/OCU
Kate Zeigler/Ohio Valley

Class of 2006
Collin Bills/HU
Jason Booton/DLU
Curtis Copeland /Texas A&M
Marlaina Frunk/OCU
Jennifer Henderson /DLU
Joshua Hendrickson/OCU
Nate Hill/DLU
Katie Hitzing/DLU
Courtney Hobson/ACU
Lindsey Pierce/Univ of Texas
Liz Redican/DLU
Melissa Young/Grove City College

Class of 2007
Dylan Carey/ACU
Blake Dozier/ACU
Megan Kite/Univ of TX
Alicia Lay/Texas A&M
Sarah Manley/OCU
Tara McComas/OCU
Jeff Muszynski/ACU
Michael Patterson/FHU
Theo Rogers/HU
Amanda Royse/HU
Daniel Townsend/ACU
Abby Trejo/ACU

Class of 2008
Colin Carroll/OCU
Michael Daniel/HU
Aaron Hall/DLU
Taylor Hendrixson/HU
Brett Hicks/ACU
Jordan Stanley/HU
Melina Calderon/HU
Kassi Larkins/UTenn, Chattanooga
Allison Smith/HU
Kelsey Young/ACU

Class of 2009
Ashleigh Banda/ACU
Nichelle Barbari/Colorado State
Anna Carlson/OCU
Holly Delassandro/OCU
Philip Handley/ACU
Katherine Kramer/OCU
Thomas Marshall/Univ of Ga.
Jennifer Savage/FU
Nathan Schandavel/HU
Amy Scott/ACU
Lisa Warren/OCU
Stephanie Wicks/Wisc-Parkside

Class of 2010
Amy Archer/ACU
Amanda Bowers/DLU
Carrie Gentry/Auburn Univ
Jay Green/TX A&M
Caleb Hancock/HU
Michelle Heasley/HU
Kate Huggins/ACU
Nate Hurley/ACU
Amanda Jernigan/HU
Sarah Jones/Texas A&M
Amanda Kelly/Faulkner Univ
Garrett Rampon/DLU

Class of 2011
Molly Alexander/HU
Amber Ashley/Auburn Univ
Merideth Bush/Asbury College
Marah Casey/FHU
Abbey Greer/Univ of Alabama
Becca Lynn/DLU
Haleigh Maudsley/HU
Michaela Mengel/HU
Zach Moore/ACU
Elizabeth Rhoden/Univ of Ala.
Phillip Scheid/Blinn Jr. College (Texas A&M)
Lindsey Willburn/ACU

Class of 2012
Jeremy Archer/Univ of Alabama
Gabby Brown/ACU
Anna Cobb/DLU
Rachel DePrimo/DLU
Audrey Palmer/DLU
James Gleaton/TX Christian
Kyle Jordan/HU
Ruth McCoy/HU
Whitney Pirtle/FHU
Meredith Thornton/ACU
Easton Valentine/HU
Kelsey Foy/FHU

Class of 2013
Landon Belcher/HU
Karli Blickenstaff/HU
Ryan Brown/HU
Maggie Bumpus/HU
Brette Dollins/HU
Weston Gentry/HU
Brianne Hillier/HU
Brittney Mullen/HU
Amanda Norris/HU
Stephanie Santa Ana/DLU
Jonathan Stites/ACU
Carlissa Shaw/DLU

Abbreviations Decoded
ACU – Abilene Christian University
DLU – David Lipscomb University
ETSU – East Tennessee State University
FHU – Freedman Hardemon University
HU – Harding University
ICS – Institute for Christian Studies
LA Tech – Louisiana Tech
LCU – Lubbock Christian University
MTSU – Middle Tennessee State University
OCU – Oklahoma Christian University
U-Illinois – University of Illinois at Champaign/Urbana

Made in the USA
San Bernardino, CA
29 May 2014